The Complete Guide to Torque X

The Complete Guide to Torque X

A GarageGames Book

John Kanalakis

A K Peters, Ltd.
Wellesley, Massachusetts

Editorial, Sales, and Customer Service Office

A K Peters, Ltd.
888 Worcester Street, Suite 230
Wellesley, MA 02482
www.akpeters.com

Library of Congress Cataloging-in-Publication Data

Kanalakis, John.
  The complete guide to Torque X / John Kanalakis.
     p. cm.
  "A GarageGames Book."
  Includes index.
  ISBN 978-1-56881-421-6 (alk. paper)
  1. Computer games--Programming. 2. Microsoft XNA (Computer file) I. Title.
  QA76.76.C672K35 2008
  794.8'1526--dc22
                                        2008022176

Printed in the United States of America

12 11 10 09 08   10 9 8 7 6 5 4 3 2 1

Contents

Foreword   ix

1   Introduction to Torque X   1

I   Torque X Game Design Tools   11
2   Creating Scenes with Torque X Builder 2D   13
3   Constructing New Tilemap Levels   43
4   Creating Scenes with Torque X Builder 3D   65

II   Programming with Torque X   77
5   A C# Primer   79
6   Exploring the Torque X Framework   101

III 2D Game Programming   123
7   Programming with Tilemaps   125
8   Creating a Robust Player Object   145
9   Adding Game Functionality   173
10   Adding 2D Artificial Intelligence   197

IV   3D Game Programming   219
11   3D Programming with Torque X   221
12   3D Player Object   245
13   3D Game Objects   269
14   Adding 3D Artificial Intelligence   297

V   Finishing the Game   311
15   Working with Audio   313
16   Adding the Game GUI   325

17   Lighting, Shaders, and Materials   349
18   Torque X Game Distribution   367

     Index   379

Foreword

Physics, collision, animation, rendering, artificial intelligence. These are the concepts that excite the imagination when thinking about what it takes to make a game. But it is often the things that tie these systems together, the "plumbing," if you will, that determine how easy it is to use a game engine and how easy it is to do new exciting things with it. Torque X provides solutions for the aforementioned systems, to be sure, many of them adapted from systems originally written in C++ for GarageGames' other highly successful game engines: Torque Game Engine, Torque Game Engine Advanced, and Torque Game Builder. But I am most proud of the "plumbing" in Torque X: the object model, the component framework, the XML integration, and editor support. It is these things that allow the game developer to select parts in the editor, put them together in a unique way, and immediately start playing with this new creation. Torque X, in my opinion, opens up a new frontier of editor-driven game development that is exciting for hobbyists, educators, students, and even experienced game developers.

In the spring of 2006, GarageGames was poised to begin development of our next C++ game engine. But after learning about XNA and Microsoft's plans for it, we decided to redirect that effort into writing a new game engine in C#. At the time, conventional wisdom was that writing a game engine in a managed language like C# was a fool's errand. The belief was that managed code would not run fast enough, and that intermittent garbage collection calls would result in choppy frame rates. We ourselves had such concerns, too. But it did not take long for us to put those concerns aside once we started to see the performance we could get out of C# (with a little care). What C# allowed us to do really well, though, was to quickly prototype a lot of the concepts we had planned to put into our next C++ engine and quickly select the ones that were winners and put aside the ones that were not. So in a very short time, we were able to produce a game engine that runs on the PC and the Xbox 360, that supports 2D and 3D games using the same underlying concepts, and that has bulit-in support for all those systems I mentioned above.

When I learned that John Kanalakis was going to write a book on Torque X, I was thrilled. John understood what we were doing with Torque X long before we had enough documentation for him to rightly "get it." He thinks clearly and explains things clearly. This book covers all the key Torque X concepts and more. After reading this book and playing with Torque, the reader should be well on the way to becoming an experienced game developer.

Clark Fagot
Technical Director, Torque X

Introduction to Torque X

1

For the first time in history, a major game console manufacturer has opened up its exclusive gaming platform to anyone who is interested in creating console games. Now, anyone can create a game for the Xbox 360 console without a publishing contract or expensive and hard-to-get developer versions of the console. Microsoft's XNA Framework is a free library and set of tools for creating games for Windows and the Xbox 360 game console. Anyone can download the tools to create games and then join the Xbox Creators Club to push their games to the Xbox 360. The Torque X Framework makes game development even easier, with a rich game engine framework and a robust set of design tools. This book unravels the Torque X Framework and tool-set to provide you with a clear and comprehensive guide to creating games.

XNA Game Studio 2.0

XNA is not an acronym but a brand name for the game development framework that Microsoft developed. It was first mentioned at the Game Developers Conference in 2004. Two years later, Microsoft released a community technology preview of a solution, named XNA Build. It was a build-and-release solution for building large game projects. At the same time, Microsoft also released the entire source code for the *MechCommander 2* game as a Shared Source Release.

In August 2006, Microsoft announced further details of the XNA Framework and XNA Game Studio Express at their annual Gamefest conference. At the same event, GarageGames introduced Torque X and demonstrated a version of *Marble Blast* that was built with the XNA Framework (see Figure 1.1). *Marble Blast* was ported to the XNA Framework within a few short weeks and was demonstrated on a retail Xbox 360.

Figure 1.1. Technology demo of *Marble Blast* on XNA. © 2006, GarageGames.

When finally released, XNA Game Studio Express was greeted with much acclaim and excitement. Many developers were drawn to the XNA Framework to try their hand at coding games for the Xbox 360 game console, an opportunity previously reserved for large-budget game studios. The final release of Game Studio Express was in December 2006.

Microsoft continued the XNA push and released version 2.0 at the end of 2007. This more mature version of XNA now featured improved performance, networking services, consistent rendering behavior between Windows and the Xbox 360, and even easier game deployment to the console. The word "Express" was also dropped from the title as the XNA Framework added support for all flavors of Visual Studio. Finally, at GDC 2008, Microsoft announced the year's roadmap for XNA, which includes upcoming support for games on the Zune consumer device as well as a Community LIVE Marketplace in an effort to "democratize game distribution."

XNA Game Studio 2.0 is an evolved game-development framework that is bolted on to any version of Microsoft's Visual Studio. It includes framework libraries, project templates, and the option to select an Xbox 360 device to which to deploy a build. You can use XNA Game Studio to build games and simulations that take advantage of the powerful shader-based hardware of the Xbox 360.

Torque X

Torque X is a game engine created by GarageGames that is that is built on top of the XNA Framework. Although the XNA Framework does an amazing job of working with 3D shapes, textures, audio, and shaders, it is not quite enough to build a game. For example, the XNA Framework does not include services for level loading, scene graphs, GUI, spawning, physics, triggers, tile mapping, input management, and so on. That's where the Torque X game engine comes in, leveraging GarageGames' many years of game engine development. Torque X is a full-featured game engine that provides these game creation tools so that you can spend less time creating your own game's infrastructure and start building the actual game mechanic. Torque X offers many clear advantages over writing games in straight XNA, such as a strong component framework, clear level management, efficient memory management, and a solid game creation framework.

The ultimate goal of this book is to teach you how to think about coding game functionality as smaller, more reusable components. You will quickly find that the time you put into well-thought-out and well-designed components will help you get the most out of Torque X.

Component Aggregation

Torque X also promotes a new approach to game programming: the aggregation model (also known as the composition model). Unlike the classic inheritance model, objects share common components that provide reusable functionality instead of sharing a common base class. For example, when an object needs to process collisions, you simply add a collision component. The aggregation methodology results in more code reuse and less copy-and-paste code sharing.

Level Management

Torque X also adds a consistent method for creating and managing game levels by deserializing objects from XML. The XML file format is a great way to represent game levels because it is nonproprietary and allows for easy integration of custom editors. The XML deserialization built into the Torque X Framework allows game objects to reference other game objects, so complex links between objects can be supported.

Memory Management

Torque X has built-in methods for memory management and garbage collection within the managed .NET environment. If your game is allocating too much memory, you may get frequent garbage collections, which can cause lagging behavior or pauses in game play. When you create an object template, you can mark it as a pooling object. When a pooling object is removed from the game, it is added to an object pool for that type of

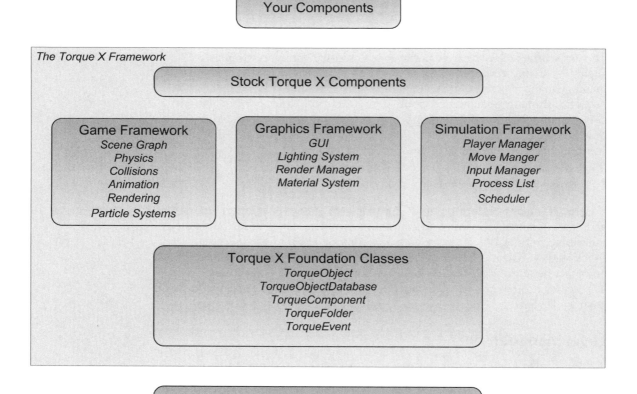

Figure 1.2. The Torque X Framework diagram.

object so the next time the game needs one of those objects, it won't have to allocate a new one. You can turn this feature on and off for individual objects, giving you a great deal of control over how memory is allocated for your game. Typically, you will want to turn on object pooling for projectiles and explosions and other features that are created often and then turn it off for game objects with longer lifetimes. With Torque X, you'll have this level of control when it comes time to fine-tune your game for best performance.

The Torque X Framework

The Torque X Framework is a rich collection of classes, data types, and interfaces. Everything rests between your custom game code and the XNA Framework. As Figure 1.2 illustrates, the Torque X Framework can be organized into five blocks.

- **Torque X Foundation Classes**: These classes provide the basic data types used in any Torque X game and include game-object registration, object management, and event-based communication.

- **Torque Game Framework**: This supports all the necessary elements to create 2D and 3D games, including scene-graph management, physics, collision handling, animation, rendering, and particles.

- **Graphics Framework**: This supports key functions, such as GUI management, lighting, render management, and materials. Everything related to drawing the scene is managed within this block.

- **Simulation Framework**: This supports core services, such as player management, move management, device input, tick processing, and event scheduling. Just about anything you need to keep the game state updated will be managed within this block.

- **Torque X Components**: These demonstrate the powerful code aggregation methodology built into the framework. These stock components provide services such as physics, collision, basic movement, lighting, and world limits to help get your game off the ground.

So, as you can see, the Torque X Framework adds real game-building functionality to the basic XNA Framework. Once you have a solid grasp of the core Torque X Framework classes, you will be quickly on your way to creating your own games for the Xbox 360 game console.

Figure 1.3. Types of games created with the Torque X Framework.

Types of Games You Can Create

Torque X is perfect for making all sorts of game types and genres. The Torque X Framework includes full support for both 2D and 3D scene graphs. You can make a wide range of games, including tilemap-based platformer games, arcade side-scroller games, popular puzzle games, map-based strategy games, multiplayer racing games, and even a first-person shooter game. Figure 1.3 shows some games that have already been made with Torque X.

You will also find that creating games with XNA and the Torque X Framework is highly productive. The robust framework classes provide a rich set of functions that make traditionally difficult problems, such as vector and matrix mathematics, much easier. Also, the C# programming language balances the ease of a scripting language with the performance of compiled code. Altogether, you will find that programming a Torque X game will be relatively fast, shifting most of the burden to art creation. With such high productivity, Torque X quickly becomes a great solution for taking new game ideas, building out quick prototypes, and then testing them on a game console.

About this Book

The purpose of this book is to introduce you to the Torque X Framework and tools and provide you with a solid foundation to create your own games for Windows or the Xbox 360 game console. This book will explain important framework classes and describe best practices for using them.

What You Should Already Know

This book does not require any prior knowledge of Torque X, XNA, or C#. These technologies will be uncovered throughout the course of this book, but you should already have some familiarity with the game-creation process. This includes taking a game idea to a design by breaking down that idea into smaller elements, such as player input, animated characters, artificial intelligence, and user interface. In other words, you should be able to take your game vision and break it down into smaller, easier-to-handle segments.

Your knowledge of mathematics will also determine the types of game programming problems you can solve. Exposure to trigonometry and algebra will be helpful for solving 2D vector problems, while exposure to linear algebra and matrices will be helpful for solving 3D transform problems.

You should also be able to produce or obtain the art assets you need for your game, which will most likely include 3D models, graphics, animations, and sounds. This book does not provide the details of creating art assets, only how to bring them into your game project.

Topics in this Book

The remaining chapters are organized to present you with the fundamentals of game programming with Torque X. They are ordered by increasing complexity and build on each other.

Part I: Torque X Game Design Tools

In Chapter 2, you will dive right into game development by becoming familiar with the Torque X Builder 2D game-design tool. You will begin by creating a new game project in XNA Game Studio and then use

Torque X Builder 2D to pull together game art assets and organize them into game levels. At the end of the chapter, you will build a simple game using only the stock Torque X components applied to different scene objects.

In Chapter 3, you will work with two more important Torque X Builder 2D editors: the Tilemap Editor and the Particle Editor. Both are important tools to understand when building games with Torque X. In Chapter 4, you will become familiar with the Torque X Builder 3D game-design tool, which you will use to create material definitions, create and position game objects, assign components, and then save your resulting 3D scenes.

Part II: Programming with Torque X

In Chapter 5, you will begin shifting game development work from the designer to code. This chapter presents an introductory overview to the C# programming language and outlines the fundamental aspects of the C# language that will be used most often throughout the remainder of the book. Concepts, such as classes, objects, interfaces, and delegates, will all be spelled out.

Chapter 6 introduces the key classes that make up the powerful Torque X Framework. With a solid understanding of these core classes, you will be able to use them to create new functionality that is specific to your game. This is where you will become familiar with the power of components and how to use them.

Part III: 2D Game Programming

In Chapter 7, you will begin working with the Torque X Framework code by manipulating tilemaps. You will become more familiar with the Torque X class library as you select and use classes to build out a simple game. In Chapter 8, you will learn about onscreen representation of the player and related responsibilities, such as responding to player input by positioning the player on screen, animating the character, and interacting with other game elements. This chapter presents the inner workings of components and best practices for creating them. Chapter 9 presents more common game functionality, using components. In doing so, we'll uncover more useful Torque X Framework classes and reveal best practices for designing and creating your own game components. In Chapter 10, you will continue to create additional component that enhance game-play features. We will create three new components that implement some basic artificial intelligence for our game enemies. In addition to adding some interesting game functionality, these components demonstrate some important lessons.

Part IV: 3D Game Programming

Chapter 11 introduces the fundamentals of 3D game programming and discusses the concepts of 3D coordinates, vectors, scene graphs, models, and animations. In Chapter 12, you will apply your new knowledge of the Torque X 3D Framework to create a series of player-centric objects. You will apply the same techniques of modular design to create reusable game components that will move and animate a player. In Chapter 13, you will create additional 3D game objects that will work together for a basic first-person shooter game. Chapter 14 reviews some of the AI concepts discussed earlier and translates them into 3D space. (You will find that creating AI components quickly gets complicated when it applies to 3D space.)

Part V: Finishing the Game

In Chapter 15, you will explore the audio tools for XNA and create an audio emitter component for a game. Adding audio to a game using XNA is much more restrictive than a game for the PC, since the game must run within a managed code environment. There are restrictions on audio formats and compression that must be met. In Chapter 16, you will learn the fundamentals of GUI building with Torque X. Then, you will apply those fundamentals to create some game set-up screens and HUD controls. The Graphical User Interface, or GUI for short, encapsulates all controls that are used to interact with a game. In Chapter 17, you will learn about creating visual effects using materials and shaders. Shader effects can significantly enhance the visual appeal of a game by adding more to the screen-rendering process. This chapter dives into the Framework code, tools, and effect files that put shaders to work. In Chapter 18, you will focus on what's involved with moving your game to the Xbox 360 game console. First, you will find out what it really takes to create a game for the console and television. Then, you'll walk through the specific steps involved in moving your game code onto the Xbox 360, using the Xbox project converter, XNA Game Studio Connect, and a Creators Club membership.

Getting Started

You can download everything you need to get started with XNA and Torque X at no charge. All of the technology frameworks and tools can be downloaded from the web. You can also find all of the sample programs and artwork in this book online at http://www.TorqueXBook.com.

Downloading a Development Environment

The first component you will need is a development environment for your Windows operating system. The development environment is where you will type your game code, compile it, and then deploy it to your Xbox 360. Presently, XNA Game Studio 2.0 supports most versions of Visual Studio 2005:

- Visual C# 2005 Express Edition,

- Visual Studio 2005 Standard Edition,

- Visual Studio 2005 Professional Edition,

- Visual Studio 2005 Team Edition.

If you do not currently own a version of Visual Studio 2005, you can download Visual C# 2005 Express Edition for free from http://www. microsoft.com/express.

The Visual Studio 2005 Standard Edition, and higher, is still available for professional development tasks. Once you have installed a development environment, you will need to install a Service Pack 1 to support XNA Game Studio 2.0.

Downloading XNA Game Studio

After you have downloaded and installed Visual Studio, you need to install the XNA Game Studio 2.0 extensions. Game Studio adds the necessary XNA library files and project templates needed to create new games. You can download this at http://creators.xna.com/.

Starting Visual C# 2005 Express Edition

Now that your development environment is set up, you're all set to start running Visual C# Express. Begin from the Windows desktop by clicking Start ➤ All Programs ➤ Microsoft XNA Game Studio 2.0 ➤ Microsoft Visual C# 2005 Express Edition. You are now ready to start creating games! In the next chapter, we'll create a new game project and add some basic game functionality with Torque X Builder.

Torque X Game Design Tools

Creating 2D Scenes with Torque X Builder

2

In this chapter, you will dive right into game development by becoming familiar with the Torque X Builder game design tool. Your will start by creating a new game project in XNA Game Studio. Next, you will use Torque X Builder to pull together game art assets and organize them into game levels. Last, you will build a basic game by attaching some basic components to different scene objects.

When working with the Torque X Framework, it's important to keep a couple of abstract concepts in mind: (1) the *scene* is the virtual world where the game simulation or level exists and is loaded or unloaded by the game code, and (2) *scene objects* are the entities, such as players, walls, bullets, and so on, that decorate a scene. The purpose of Torque X Builder is to decorate a scene with multiple scene objects.

Creating a 2D Project with XNA Game Studio

Creating a Torque X game begins with XNA Game Studio. As mentioned earlier, XNA Game Studio is the development environment used to create XNA games for Windows and Xbox 360. When you install Torque X, it adds several project templates to XNA Game Studio. These project templates offer different starting points for creating a new game. When you start a new project from a template, it sets up, in order,

1. the directory structure for your game that Torque X expects,

2. the References in your project for Torque X and XNA,

3. the source code as a starting point for your game, and

4. all the necessary files to use with Torque X Builder.

Torque X installs the following templates:

- **StarterGame 2D:** This provides a basic starting point for a 2D game with a moveable sprite.

- **StarterGame 3D:** This provides a basic starting point for a 3D game with a terrain, sky box, and floating camera.

As you become more familiar with Torque X, you will likely select the starting template that best matches your game. For now, we will start with the StarterGame 2D template.

Choosing a New Project Template

Creating a new Torque X game is boiled down to a simple three-step process with the help of project templates:

1. Start XNA Game Studio, and select File ➢ New Project from the main menu.

2. Select the StarterGame 2D template.

3. Set the name of the project to XnaBreakout, as shown in Figure 2.1.

This will start the code generation process as XNA Game Studio takes the template and builds out a new solution containing your starter game code. The project file, with the default name Game, appears at the top of the Solution Explorer. We instructed XNA Game Studio to create the project in the C:\XnaBreakout folder.

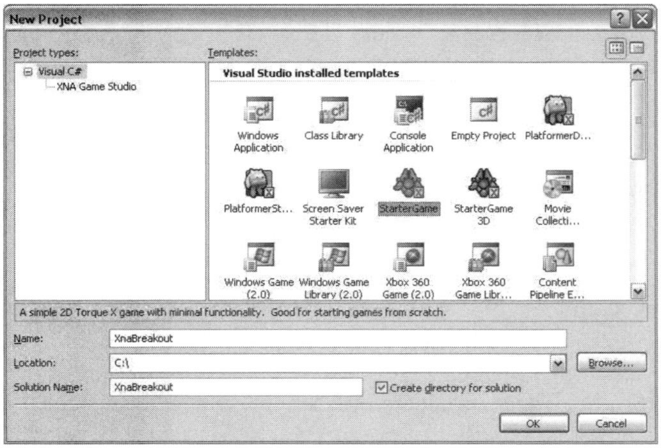

Figure 2.1. New Project template selection dialog box.

Compiling and Running Your 2D Game

After XNA Game Studio creates the Torque X game project, compile and run the game by selecting Debug ➢ Start Debugging from the main menu or by pressing F5. This build step creates a running game as well as a file named myschema.txschema that helps Torque X Builder understand your project. This file is created and updated automatically each time you rebuild the game code.

As for your new game, it may not seem like much because it only displays the GarageGames logo and lets you move it around the screen using the keyboard or gamepad. But in reality, you have the beginnings of a game, complete with a canvas and camera, a player sprite rendered to the screen, input captured from devices, and a framework for adding much more.

Starting Torque X Builder 2D

Now that you have an XNA Game Studio code project created, you can start Torque X Builder 2D. There are three ways to get started, as shown in Figure 2.2:

1. Create a new Torque X Builder 2D project.

2. Import an existing Torque Game Builder project.

3. Open an existing Torque X Builder project.

Since XNA Game Studio has already created the Torque X project file, we can open it by clicking the large Open button. Use the Open File dialog box to select the Game.txproj file. Once Torque X Builder is started, select File ➤ Open Scene and browse to the existing levelData.txscene file. This is the starter level file that was created with the project from within XNA Game Studio.

Figure 2.2. Beginning a Torque X project.

Torque X Project Files

Torque X organizes your game into two different files. The first is the project file. The new project template selected from within XNA Game Studio has created a new project file named Game.txproj. The project file keeps track of all the art assets you have imported into Torque X Builder, including definitions for materials, animations, scrollers, and so on.

The next organizational file is the scene file. The new project template also created a file named levelData.txscene. The scene file defines the positions and properties of all the scene objects within a level. A project can have multiple scene files.

Navigating Torque X Builder 2D

Torque X Builder is divided into three functional areas: panes, rollouts, and the viewport. The three panes on the right side include Edit, Project, and Create. Each pane is organized into rollouts, which can be expanded or collapsed to show or hide their contents. The viewport on the left side is a window into the scene, where game's scene objects are placed.

Figure 2.3. The Create pane.

The Create Pane

The Create pane appears at the far right of Torque X Builder, as shown in Figure 2.3. It contains several rollouts that group available scene objects. These rollouts include Materials, Animations, Scrollers, Particle Effects, Tilemaps, and Other.

Materials

Materials are all the images that are added to the game project. Scene objects, such as your player sprite, projectiles, translucent particle images, user interface elements, and more, can share materials. Materials are created by adding images into Torque X Builder. A material definition is also much more than just an image. It also contains additional information such as lighting, blending, and animation cells.

Animations

Animations are a series of individual images that are shown in sequence over time to present the illusion of motion. Animations are based on materials that are added to Torque X Builder.

Scrollers

Scrollers are images that vertically or horizontally slide across the viewport at a fixed speed. Scrollers are based on materials that are added to Torque X Builder.

Particle Effects

Particle Effects are scene objects that describe the complex motion of sprites within a scene. Images that Particle Effects will put into motion must first be imported into Torque X Builder as a material.

Tilemaps

Tilemaps are arrays of repeating images that can be efficiently used to create a game level. A scene can use multiple tilemaps together of different sizes and cell counts as needed.

Others

Other scene objects include a Spawner object and a Blank scene object. The Spawner object is useful for creating one or more instances of a template object across a period of time. The Blank scene object is useful for adding a collision polygon at an arbitrary point in the scene.

The Viewport

The viewport presents the scene in the state in which it will be loaded when the game starts. It is represented by grid lines, a center axis, and a safe-region box. The viewport's grid assists with the placement of scene objects and can optionally enable grid snapping for the placement of scene objects. The safe-region rectangle indicates the area in which the scene is expected to be fully visible. On computer displays or high-definition televisions, the entire scene is expected to be visible when the game is running. However, on older, standard definition televisions, there is no guarantee that the full scene will be visible. Therefore, you should ensure that the primary focus of your game and all

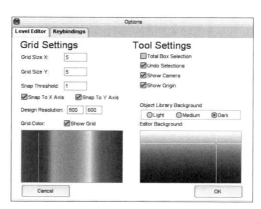

Figure 2.4. The Torque X Builder preferences window.

user interface elements remain within the safe-region box. Chapter 18 goes into deeper detail about safe regions and why they are important to game design.

Viewport Preferences

The preferences window shown in Figure 2.4 can be used to configure the look and behavior of the viewport. The size of the grid can be customized in the Torque X Builder preferences window. The grid lines and the background colors can also be modified within the same preferences window. Grid snapping can be enabled for the X-axis, Y-axis, both, or none. Also, the viewport can be configured such that objects can be selected by either a full bounding box or a partial bounding box.

Moving around the Viewport

You have a great deal of control over the appearance of the viewport with the mouse. This comes in handy as you create larger and more complex game levels and need to look over the entire landscape for a specific part of the scene.

To zoom in and out of a scene, you can either roll the mouse wheel or choose one of the zoom ranges from the View menu. You can also press the plus and minus keyboard keys to zoom in and out. The Show Selected menu command will help you to locate scene objects when your game level grows and becomes filled.

To pan around a scene, click an empty area within the viewport to ensure that no scene object is selected. Then, right-click the viewport background and drag the mouse to pan across the scene. You can use the keyboard arrows to pan around the scene as well.

Interacting with Scene Objects

You add scene objects to a game level by dragging them from the Create pane and dropping them into the viewport. You can easily add materials, animations, scrollers, particle effects, tilemaps, and spawners to your scene. When a scene object is selected within the viewport, it displays a bounding box with blue grab handles. You can use these grab handles to quickly resize the scene object. To move a scene object around the viewport, left-click within the bounding box, and drag the mouse to move the scene object into position. You can also rotate a scene object by holding the Alt key, left-clicking the grab-handle, and dragging the mouse around the selected scene object.

As you mouse over other scene objects within the viewport, a gray border appears around the scene object. This is a preselection border that indicates which object will be selected next if you click the mouse button. Since objects in the viewport can be organized into multiple layers, clicking in the same spot multiple times will cycle through selections across each layer.

You can also select one or more scene objects in the viewport by left-clicking an empty area of the viewport and dragging a bounding box. By default, any scene object that touches, or is contained within, this bounding box will be selected. In the viewport preferences, you can require the selectable bounding box to fully enclose an object in order to select it.

The Edit Pane

The Edit pane (Figure 2.5) is probably the most widely used pane of all. It contains several rollouts which group properties specific to an object selected in the viewport.

The Project Pane

Figure 2.5. The Edit pane.

The Project pane (Figure 2.6) is a great resource for working with busy scenes. The object tree is important for finding and selecting a specific scene object. As your scene grows more and more complex with multiple layers, the object tree may become the only way to find something specific. Therefore, it is important to properly name the objects you place into a scene so that their names appear in this list. Scene object names are entered into the Scripting rollout within the Edit pane.

The Undo History view is another important resource. It lets you back up and undo recent changes to the scene if you accidentally delete, move, or change a property. You can undo or redo actions by selecting the curved arrow toolbar buttons or by selecting Edit ➤ Undo or Edit ➤ Redo from the main menu.

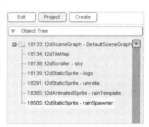

Figure 2.6. The Project pane.

Working with Torque X Builder

Torque X Builder integrates a few different image editors that manipulate how images appear and behave in your game. These include the Material Builder, the Animation Builder, and the Scroller Builder.

The Material Builder

The Material Builder (Figure 2.7) is responsible for bringing images into Torque X Builder and specifying unique visual properties. All images, whether they are static sprites, background images, animations, or scrollers, must first be opened through the Material Editor. You can add a new image into Torque X Builder in one of three ways.

<figure>**Figure 2.7.** The Material Builder.</figure>

1. Selecting Project ➢ Material Builder from the menu.

2. Clicking the Create New Material button at the top of the Create Pane.

3. Dragging an image file into Torque X Builder from File Explorer.

When the Material Builder is opened, it loads your selected image as shown in Figure 2.7. The Material Builder displays a preview of the image and allows some additional properties to be specified.

Additive

Additive blending adds the native color of the object to the color that is beneath it in the scene. A great example would be to create a green translucent forcefield image that is mounted to a player ship. When the forcefield material is set to additive blending, it will produce a myriad of colors as it passes over other objects within the scene.

Enable Lighting

The Enable Lighting property specifies that the selected material should render with lighting information applied. Lighting information is set by the LightRegister component, which maintains a light list. Each light in the light list has properties that define color, position, radius, and direction.

Specularity

The Specularity of a material specifies the shininess of an image to give it the illusion of three-dimensional depth. The power indicates how shiny a material is. The higher the number, the shinier it is, like a steel ball. The lower the number, the duller it is, like a rubber ball. The shininess of a material also can be shaped across a material, just as a cracked sphere shines differently from a smooth sphere. A normal map file indicates the pattern that the shininess should follow.

Refraction

The Refraction property specifies that the selected material will refract the scene behind the material. This property also includes an index value ranging from zero to one. It identifies the amount of refraction that is applied to the material. A small value, such as 0.1, results in a low index of refraction, whereas a large value, such as 0.8, results in a high index of refraction. The refraction shader requires a normal map to be attached to selected material.

Normal Mapping

Normal Mapping (Figure 2.8) is used to add shading details without using more polygons. Normal Mapping uses multiple channels (red, green, and blue) to represent the x, y, and z coordinates of the normal map at the point corresponding to that texel.

Figure 2.8. A normal sprite graphic with its normal map to the right.

    Normal Mapping is most commonly used to enhance the shading appearance of a low polygon model by applying a normal map that is generated from a high-polygon model. When a light is added to the scene, Torque X renders the normal mapped material with shadows based on the position of the light and the definition of the normal map. Chapter 17 goes into greater detail about normal maps and how they interact with scene lighting.

Image Mode

In Torque X, animations are performed by using animated sprite sheets. A sprite sheet contains a number of sprite images in various states of the animation. When the Image Mode is set to CELL, you can specify how many columns and rows a sprite sheet contains. Torque X reads a sprite sheet from left to right and from top to bottom. (See Figure 2.9.)

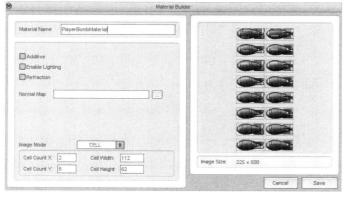

Figure 2.9. Identifying a material as an animation.

The Animation Builder

The Animation Builder (Figure 2.10) takes a material that has already been added to Torque X Builder and converts it into an animation.

Frame Selection

You can fine-tune your animation by choosing how you add the individual frames. To add all the frames from the animation sheet, click the green Add button at the top of the Animation Builder. To add frames individually, double-click the frames at the bottom of the Animation Builder.

Frame Rate

Torque X can also set the playback frame rate for each animation. Try varying the Frames per Second field while the animation preview is running. You can fine-tune the frame rate to achieve the best animation results.

Starting Frame

If you want an animation to begin at a frame other than zero, you can either specify a Start Frame or enable the random selection of a frame. This is a great way to add some variety when there are a lot of similar animations in a scene. For example, if you have a few tree sway animations in a scene, it might look odd to have all trees swaying in the same exact motion. Instead, you can start off each tree sway animation from a random point for a more natural result.

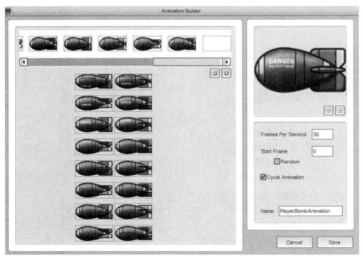

Figure 2.10. Selecting frames in the Animation Builder.

Cycle Animation

You can choose to cycle an animation endlessly. Some animations, such as a tree sway, are perfect to cycle. However, other animations, such as an explosion, should only play through once. When an animation cycles, it returns to the first frame of the animation.

The Scroller Builder

In Torque X, Scrollers (Figure 2.11) take an image and slide it across the screen. Images can scroll in either direction horizontally or vertically. They can be added to a scene at any layer and to fit any desired size. Scrollers are very common in classic platformer games as an easy way to present the illusion of player motion. Even non-platformer games can benefit from a Scroller and use it to slide translucent fog or haze across the screen to add more depth.

The Scroller Builder takes a material that has already been added to Torque X Builder and converts it into a Scroller scene object that can be placed into a level. It checks to see if the image is sized as a power of 2. Therefore, your image width and height should be sized as 2, 4, 8, 16, 32, 64, 128, 256, 512, or 1024 pixels.

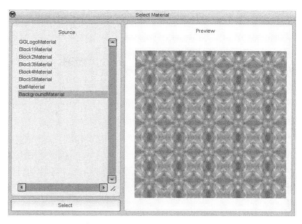

Figure 2.11. Selecting a Scroller material.

Using Object Toolbar Editors

When an object is placed into the viewport, it carries a mini toolbar with it that appears when the object is selected (see Figure 2.12).

Figure 2.12. The popup object toolbar.

Edit Collision Polygon

A scene object's collision polygon defines where a collision is resolved. Usually, a collision polygon resembles the image shape, though that is not a requirement. The only true requirement is that the shape of a collision polygon is convex and not concave.

As Figure 2.13 shows, a concave polygon has "inward" angles that are less than 90 degrees. These inward angles are difficult to resolve and for performance reasons are simply not permitted.

It is important to remember that the collision polygon does not need to perfectly match the image. Figure 2.14 shows a collision mesh that approximates the shape of our ball image. Because collisions occur so quickly, we will not even be able to notice that the collision polygon is not perfect.

It is also important to create a collision polygon with the minimum number of sides possible. Each side added to the polygon translates into exponentially more collision processing per tick. If we were to refine the shape of the ball's collision polygon to have 30 sides instead of 8 sides, then Torque X would need to spend even more time per tick, just to resolve the collision.

Figure 2.13. Concave (left) has inward-facing angles. Convex (right) does not.

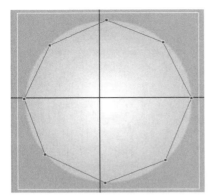

Figure 2.14. Defining a collision polygon for a material.

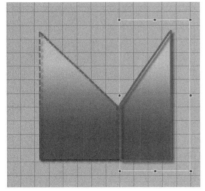

Figure 2.15. Enabling a concave collision by adding a blank scene object.

Figure 2.16. Adding link points to a sprite.

When you click on the edit collision polygon button, the selected scene object zooms to fill the viewport. You specify the edges of the collision polygon by left-clicking the mouse button. With each click, the polygon shape grows. To remove a polygon point, right-click the mouse button over an existing point. You can move an existing collision polygon point by left-clicking the point and dragging it to a new position.

Although each scene object can only have one collision polygon, which must be convex, there may be a case in which you specifically want a concave collision mesh for an image. One way to handle this situation is to use an additional scene object to help. The Blank Scene Object found in the Others rollout of the Create pane helps. First, mark the convex collision polygon for half of the image. Next, add the blank scene object and mark the other half of the collision polygon, as shown in Figure 2.15.

Edit Link Points

Link points (Figure 2.16) identify where on a sprite another object can mount. You can add multiple link points to an object by left-clicking different points on the scene object. You can also add a link point that is not directly over the sprite but still within the scene object's bounds. You can always remove a link point by right-clicking it.

Edit Sort Point

The sort point (Figure 2.17) determines where on a sprite the layer sorting method is resolved. This marker works in conjunction with the Layer Management properties to help determine which scene object within a same layer appears on top. By moving the sort point around, you can specify where the overlapping of sprites within a scene is tested.

For example, click an empty area of the scene and open the Edit pane. Expand the Layer Management properties rollout and change the Layer 0 sort method to X Axis. Next, add two sprites to the scene on Layer 0 so that they overlap. Figure 2.17 demonstrates this with a fuel sprite and a tank sprite. The sort point for the fuel sprite is represented by a square, and the sort point for the tank is represented by a circle. Since this layer's sort method is set to X Axis, the sprite with the highest X-position will appear on top. In the left image of Figure 2.17, the square sort point for the fuel sprite has a higher X-position value, so the fuel sprite appears on top. In the right image, the

Figure 2.17. Specifying a sort point for a sprite.

circle sort point for the tank sprite has a higher X-position, so the tank appears on top.

Remember that in the Torque X 2D Framework, the X-position increases from left to right and the Y-position increases from top to bottom. The origin, where the X and Y values are zero, is at the center of the screen.

Figure 2.18. Mounting one sprite to another.

Mounting to Another Object

Torque X also has the ability to mount one scene object to another. When a child object is mounted to a parent object, the child's position and rotation is set by the parent. A perfect example appears in Figure 2.18, where a tank turret is mounted to the tank. This allows us to move the tank around, knowing that the turret will also move. Although the child object's rotation will follow the parent object's rotation, you can still manually set the rotation of the child relative to the object to which it is mounted by disabling the Track Rotation mount property.

Setting the World Limits

The world limits of a scene object determine at which point a world limits collision should be resolved (see Figure 2.19). This is helpful for moving scene objects that need to take some sort of action when the world limits is encountered. This might include the removal of an object, such as a projectile, from the scene after it falls

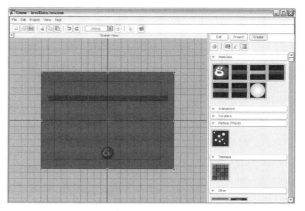

Figure 2.19. Setting the world limits for a sprite.

out of view. Or in the case of our *XnaBreakout* game, we will want the ball to bounce off the sides of the viewport.

Editing Scene Object Properties

Now that you have added a few scene objects into the viewport, it's time to start editing some properties. The following section describes the different properties available to you when designing a game level.

Types of Scene Object Properties

Camera

The Camera rollout (Figure 2.20) is only available when there are no scene objects selected within the viewport. The Camera properties specify how the scene is rendered. By setting the camera position, you can control which part of the scene is displayed on the screen. Setting the width and height

Figure 2.20. The Camera properties rollout.

controls how much of the scene appears on the screen. This effectively controls the scene's zoom level. If you set the camera's width and height to an aspect ratio that doesn't match the aspect ratio of the screen, the scene will appear squashed or stretched in the X or Y direction when it renders.

Name: The name used to reference the camera object in code.
Camera X, Y: The center position of the camera; where the camera is pointed within the scene. In our sample game, the camera position will be fixed in one place. However, other game types, such as platformers, constantly move the camera position to follow the player.
Camera Width, Height: The width and height of the area in the world that fit into the camera's field of view and show up on the screen
Fixed Width: Locks the width of the camera across all aspect ratios.
Fixed Height: Locks the width of the camera across all aspect ratios.
Use Camera View Limit: Enables view limits for the camera with a range of minimum and maximum width and height.

Scene Data

The Scene Data rollout (Figure 2.21) is only available when there are no scene objects selected within the viewport. Here, you can create different surface materials, each with unique physical characteristics, such as a slippery surface or a high-traction surface. You can also specify different object types. Scene objects can be associated with an object type to share a lot of common behaviors, such as collision, visibility, and so on.

Collision Material Name: The name of the new collision material. You can create several collision materials for your game, each with different reactions.

Collision Material Friction: The amount of friction in rigid body collisions.

Collision Material Restitution: The amount objects will bounce as a result of a collision. The lower this number gets, the less bounce objects will experience from collisions.

Collision Material Priority: The priority of the collision.

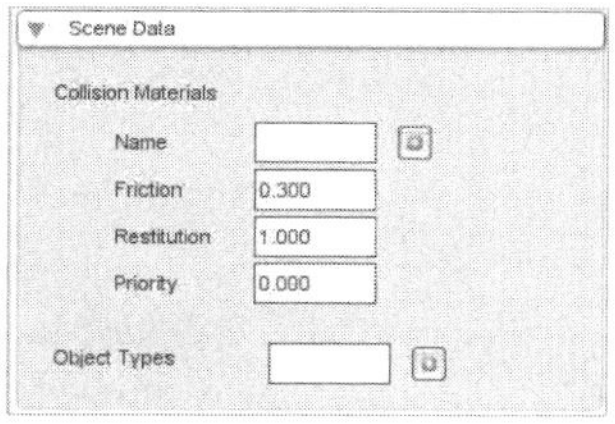

Figure 2.21. The Scene Data properties rollout.

Object Type: The name of a new object type. You can create several object types. Object types represent a way to group together similar scene objects. They are useful for performing actions against an entire collection of scene objects rather than having to test each scene object one at a time. In our sample game, we can create an object type for the ball and for the brick. Then, we can simply test for collisions between the ball object type and the brick object type. To create the new object type, type in the name and then click the green Add button.

Layer Management

The Layer Management rollout (Figure 2.22) is only available when there are no scene objects selected within the viewport. The Layer Management rollout is used to selectively show, hide, lock, unlock, and set the sort method for each layer within the scene. This is especially useful for working with large scenes with lots of objects organized into different layers.

Figure 2.22. The Layer Management properties rollout.

Show/Hide Layer: Hides or shows all scene objects that are within this layer.

Lock/Unlock Layer: Locks an entire scene layer. When locked, scene objects within this layer **cannot be selected or modified.**

Layer Sort Method: Specifies the rule for how scene objects within the same layer are ordered. When set to −Y Axis, a scene object with a lower Y axis position value (positioned above) will appear on top. When set to X Axis, a scene object with a greater X-axis position (positioned to the right) will appear on top. By default, resolving scene object position is based

It won't be too long before you are creating very complex scenes with hundreds of scene objects. By organizing your scene objects into layers, you can easily use the Layer Management rollout to hide entire layers that contain collections of objects to make it easier to edit large scenes.

on the center of the scene object. To change the point on the scene object where this resolution occurs, select the scene object and modify its sort point position.

Debug Rendering

Figure 2.23. The Debug Rendering properties rollout.

The Debug Rendering rollout (Figure 2.23) is only available when there are no scene objects selected within the viewport.

Bounding Boxes: Displays square bounding boxes around every scene object within the viewport. This is very helpful when working with scene objects, such as particle emitters, that have no visible bounds.

Link Points: Displays the link points for every scene object within the viewport. This is useful when you are mounting several objects to each other.

World Limits: Displays the world limits for every scene object within the viewport.

Collision Bounds: Displays the collision polygon and polygon points for every scene object within the viewport.

Sort Points: Displays the sort point for every scene object within the viewport.

Static Sprite

Figure 2.24. The Static Sprite properties rollout.

Static Sprite properties (Figure 2.24) apply to any scene object that is added into the scene.

Material: Sets the material for the selected scene object in the viewport. In many cases, you may want to have two scene objects that share similar object properties, components, a collision polygon, and so on. Instead of dragging another material to the scene and setting the same values, you can copy and paste the original scene object and simply change the material.

Animated Sprite

Figure 2.25. The Animated Sprite properties rollout.

Animated Sprite properties (Figure 2.25) only apply to animation materials

Animation: Chooses the animation that the selected scene object should play. This is similar to the selection of a material for a scene object. This property is most useful when accessed programmatically to trigger animations in response to user input. For example, different animations can be selected and played for a player character in response to user input, such as walking, running, and jumping.

Play On Load: Instructs the selected scene object to play back the selected animation once it is loaded into the scene. This is useful for objects, such as power-ups, that may always have a glow animation. It eliminates a line of code that instructs the scene object to begin the animation playback.

Remove On Finished: Instructs Torque X to remove the selected scene object immediately after its animation cycle is completed.

Scroller

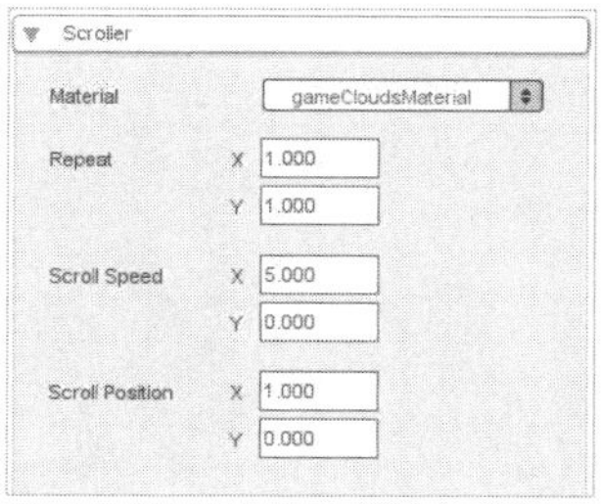

The Scroller rollout (Figure 2.26) contains properties relating to a Scroller scene object placed into the viewport. Its properties determine how the Scroller will behave as the game runs.

Material: This dynamic drop list contains materials that are available to be scrolled across the screen.

Repeat X, Y: The number of times an image will be repeated within Scroller at any given time. For example, if X is set to 2, then the Scroller will contain two instances of the image horizontally squeezed into the Scroller.

Scroll Speed X, Y: The speed at which the displayed image will slide the image. A higher number produces a faster scrolling speed. A negative number reverses the direction of the scroll. Setting an X and Y value results in a diagonal scroll.

Scroll Position X, Y: The offset position of the texture within the scroll.

Figure 2.26. The Scroller properties rollout.

Particle Effect

The Particle Effect properties (Figure 2.27) are only visible when a particle effect scene object is selected in the viewport. We will dive into the particle effect designer in the next chapter.

Load Effect: Opens a browse dialog box to locate and load an existing particle effect (*.eff) file.

Save Effect: Opens a save dialog box and accepts a new file name to save the selected particle effect.

Effect Mode: Selects the lifecycle mode for the particle effect. The Infinite mode plays the effect endlessly. The Cycle mode plays the effect over a fixed period of time and the resets automatically. The Kill mode plays the effect only once over a fixed period of time and then removes the effect from the scene. The Stop effect mode functions in the same manner as the Kill effect mode, but it does not remove the effect object from the scene.

Figure 2.27. The Particle Effect properties rollout.

Restart Effect: Restarts the particle effect's timeline, effectively taking it back to the point of the effect's initial creation.

Emitter: Groups together all of the emitters that make up the selected particle effect. For complex and visually stunning particle effects, you will often use more than one emitter.

Tilemap

The Tilemap properties (Figure 2.28) are displayed when a Tilemap scene object is selected in the viewport.

TileCount X, Y: Indicates the number or cells wide (x) and high (y) that make up the selected Tilemap.

Figure 2.28. The Tile Map properties rollout.

Tile Size X, Y: Indicates the width and height of each individual cell of the Tilemap.

Size Object to Layer: This useful function calculates the overall size of the Tilemap, based on the cell width and height and the number of cells in each direction. It then sets the scene object to a size that matches so there are no void spaces visible.

Edit Tile Layer: This function changes the viewport mode from Tilemap viewer to Tilemap designer and enables you to set the individual Tilemap tiles.

Scene Object

Everything that can be dragged into the viewport from the Create pane is a scene object. The Scene Object properties (Figure 2.29) are displayed for any object selected.

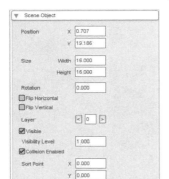

Figure 2.29. The Scene Object properties rollout.

Position X, Y: Indicates the selected scene object position within the scene.

Size Width, Height: Indicates the width and height of the selected scene object.

Rotation: Indicates the rotation of the scene object, measured in degrees. For example, a value of 45 rotates the scene object 45 degrees clockwise.

Flip Horizontal: Flips the scene object horizontally.

Flip Vertical: Flips the scene object vertically.

Layer: Indicates the layer for the selected scene objects, between 0 and 31. Scene objects with a lower layer value will be rendered on top of scene objects with higher layer values. Any number of scene objects can appear on a single layer.

Visible: Indicates if the scene object is currently visible or not.

Visibility Level: Sets the transparency level of the scene object. A value of 1 is completely solid, whereas a value of 0 is completely invisible. Anything in between makes the scene object translucent.

Collision Enabled: Indicates that collision processing should be performed for the selected scene object. A collision component is still required to process the collision, but this flag can quickly enable or disable processing.

Sort Point X, Y: Indicates the position of the layer sort point. By default, a sort point is located at the absolute center of the scene object, but you may wish to modify the location, especially in an isometric style game where characters can be partially blocked by other scene objects.

Scripting

The Scripting properties rollout (Figure 2.30) appears for every scene object in the level. It enables you to specify the properties that bind the scene objects to code.

Name: Specifies the reference name for the selected scene object. The C# source code can refer to this value to identify the scene object at runtime. For example, when the Name field is set to "player", the source code can access the scene object as follows:

T2DSceneObject myObject = TorqueObjectDatabase.

Instance.FindObject("player");

Figure 2.30. The Scripting properties rollout.

Object Type: Specifies a grouping for the selected scene object. A scene object can have multiple object types. To associate an object with a type, select a name from the drop-down list and then click the green Add button. As mentioned earlier, object types are defined in the Scene Data properties rollout, accessible when no scene objects are selected. One use for specifying an object type is in defining collisions; you can specify a particular collision behavior between object types instead of defining collisions against all of the scene objects individually.

Pool: Specifies that the selected scene object should be pooled with other objects.

Pool With Components: Specifies that the selected scene object should be pooled along with its selected components.

Template: Specifies that the selected scene object is a template. When a scene object is converted into a template object, it is not automatically created and rendered when the scene starts. Instead, C# source code or a Spawner object is required to create an instance of the template object.

Persistent: Specifies that the selected scene object is persistent and appears across all levels.

OnRegistered: Specifies a method that will be automatically called after the selected scene object is loaded and registered.

Align

The Align property rollout (Figure 2.31) contains buttons that can quickly set the position and size of a scene object.

Figure 2.31. The Align properties rollout.

Align: Horizontally or vertically aligns the selected scene object.
Match Size: Adjusts the width or height of the selected scene object.

Components

The Components rollout (Figure 2.32) is essentially a container for all of the code components that are attached to the selected scene object. Torque X Builder constantly scans the game project produced by XNA Game Studio for new Torque X Components. Each one that is discovered is immediately added to the list of available components to work with.

Figure 2.32. The Components properties rollout.

Components Selection: A list of all available components. To attach a component to the selected scene object, click the droplist, choosing a component to attach, and then click the green Add button.

Components List: Every component attached to the selected scene object has its own subrollout, which may include additional parameters specific to that component. To remove a component from the selected scene object, expand the component's rollout and click the red button labeled Remove This Component.

Template Reference and Spawning

The Template Reference and Spawning property rollouts (Figure 2.33) appear when a Spawner scene object is selected. Spawners are created when they are dragged from the Create pane into the viewport. Spawners can create multiple instances of any template object. To designate a scene object as a template object, click the Template checkbox, back in the Scripting properties rollout.

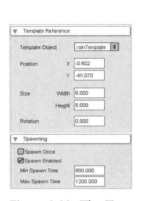

Figure 2.33. The Template Reference and Spawning properties rollouts.

Template Object: Specifies the template object that the selected Spawner will create. Once a template object is selected, the Spawner's default icon is replaced by the material of the template object.

Position X, Y: Specifies the horizontal and vertical start positions of the Spawner object.

Size Width, Height: Specifies the width and height of the Spawner object.

Rotation: Specifies the angle of rotation for the Spawner object, measured clockwise in degrees.

Spawn Once: Specifies that the selected Spawner object will only create one instance of the specified template object.

Spawn Enabled: Enables or disables the current Spawner's ability to create instances of a template object. In some cases, you might have a Spawner automatically create instances of a template object every few seconds. A player might be able to switch off the automatic spawning of objects by reaching a trigger that ultimately sets this property to disabled.

Min Spawn Time: Specifies the minimum amount of time that must elapse before a Spawner is permitted to create another instance.

Max Spawn Time: Specifies the maximum amount of time that may elapse before a Spawner must create another instance. To remove any variation in the time period between spawnings, set min and max spawn times to equal each other.

Working with Components

In the context of Torque X, Components are packaged units of code that add specific functionality to scene objects. Components are coded in C# and compiled with XNA Game Studio. You assign Components by first selecting the scene object in the viewport, then opening the Edit Pane, and then expanding the Components rollout.

Types of Components

Torque X comes packaged with a few stock components that come in handy. We will code additional Components that add more specialized game functionality in later chapters.

MovementComponent

The MovementComponent (Figure 2.34) binds the selected scene object to the player input control. It's a fast and easy way to connect a player object to a controller.

PlayerNumber: Specifies which controller is driving the selected scene object. In a two-player game, one scene object might leave the default value of zero and set another scene object's value to 1.

Figure 2.34. The MovementComponent properties rollout.

LightRegisterComponent

The LightRegisterComponent (Figure 2.35) defines the properties for lights that illuminate the selected scene object.

Enabled: Enables or disables the lighting for the scene object.
LightList: The complete list of lights that project onto the selected scene object.
ObjectLocalLightList: The complete list of local lights that project on to the selected scene object.
LightInfo: Specifies the type of light created, either Directional or Point.
AmbientColor X, Y, Z: The ambient color of the light projection.
DiffuseColor X, Y, Z: The diffuse color of the light projection.
Radius: The radial extent of the light projection.
LightModelName: The name of the lighting model that
Direction X, Y, Z: The direction of the light projection.

Figure 2.35. The LightRegisterComponent properties rollout.

T2DPhysicsComponent

The T2DPhysicsComponent (Figure 2.36) adds the ability to simulate physics for the scene object. This includes linear and angular velocity properties, as well as mass and rotational inertia. This component works with the T2DCollisionComponent, T2DForceComponent, and T2DWorldLimitComponent, but it can function without them.

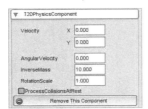

Figure 2.36. The T2D-PhysicsComponent properties rollout.

Velocity X, Y: The initial velocity of the scene object when created.

AngularVelocity: The initial Current rotational velocity of the scene object in degrees per second.

InverseMass: The inverse mass of a scene object. Setting this to 0 is the same as marking an object Immovable. InverseMass is used when responding to collisions and when forces are applied.

RotationScale: Scale of the inverse inertia.

ProcessCollisionsAtRest: Specifies if collisions will be processed even while the scene object is at rest. If false, an object with zero velocity and angular velocity will not process collisions. Setting to false can lead to better performance but in some situations can miss collisions.

T2DCollisionComponent

The T2DCollisionComponent (Figure 2.37) adds the ability for the selected scene object to collide with other scene objects. You can install any number of collision images on the component. Each collision image will be tested against the scene, making the effective collision the union of all collision images.

The T2DCollisionComponent works with the T2DPhysicsComponent to support physics simulation. However, the collision component can operate without the physics component. In this case, you must programmatically drive the movement yourself and call it into the collision component.

Figure 2.37. The T2DCollisionComponent properties rollout.

RenderCollisionBounds: Instructs Torque X to render the collision polygon around the specified scene object during the game's runtime.

CollidesWith: Specifies the object types with which the selected scene object will resolve a collision.

EarlyOutObjectType: Determines which object types to test for early out on collision processing. If one or more object types are added to this list, then collisions with those object types will result in only a single collision notification. If early out is not set, a continuous stream of collision notifications will be sent to the collided object until the collision stops.

OnCollision: Specifies a delegate that is called whenever a collision occurs, possibly multiple times per tick.

ResolveCollision: Specifies how collisions are resolved: Bounce, Clamp, Rigid, Sticky, or Kill.

- Bounce collision obeys the law: "The angle of incidence equals the angle of reflection." It doesn't take into account any other physics parameters, such as mass or momentum, only the velocity at which the objects are moving when they collide and the angle of impact.

- Clamp collision prevents objects from interpenetrating. When an object runs into another object, its velocity in the direction of the other object is clamped down to zero, while its velocity perpendicular to the other object is unaffected. Characters in platformer games often have Clamp-type collisions against walls and floors, which allows the character to slide along them, but not go through them.

- Rigid collision uses rigid body physics and Newton's laws of motion to determine what happens to the colliding object. It uses physics parameters like mass, velocity, and angular velocity to determine how the colliding object should move as a result of the collision, as well as the friction properties of the Physics materials of the colliding objects. A game with hovercraft that can ram into each other might implement a Rigid-type collision on the hovercraft.

- Sticky collision sets both the linear and angular velocity of an object to 0 when it collides with something. It simply *sticks* where it is when it hits. The pieces in a stacking game like Tetris might have a Sticky-type collision.

- Kill collision causes the object to be deleted when it collides with something. Projectiles will often be set up with a Kill collision response. Once they hit something, you don't want them to hang around in the game; you want to get rid of them.

SolveOverlap: Specifies whether or not overlaps are solved. An overlap between two objects can occur for a variety of reasons, the most common being that an error was introduced during the collision processing. Solving the overlap removes accumulated error, but in some cases you don't want the small displacements that can occur as a result. For example, projectiles that will be immediately destroyed do not need to solve the overlap, and setting this property to false can get rid of the slight push that projectiles otherwise might have.

CollisionMaterial: Collision material to be used in collisions of this object with other objects.

TestEarlyOut: Tests whether or not a given object should be collided against. Use this for objects that sometimes collide and sometimes don't. If true is returned, then collision processing does not continue against the object. This can be used to make certain objects have collisions only under certain conditions—for example, when going one way through a platform but not another. This only affects collision processing when this object moves into another. Objects that move into this object do not use the TestEarlyOut delegate.

T2DWorldLimitComponent

The T2DWorldLimitComponent (Figure 2.38) sends notifications when an object collides with the world limit specified. This is an easy way to specify

Figure 2.38. The T2D-WorldLimitComponent properties rollout.

the bounds of the world. You receive an OnWorldLimit callback when you hit the world boundary. This component is added automatically by Torque X Builder when you click on the Change the World Limits button.

Setting world limits can be very useful for keeping the number of objects within your scene under control. If you set up projectiles with the Kill response set on their world limit, they will effectively clean up after themselves when they miss. This is because the projectiles will delete themselves from the scene when they hit their world limit.

WorldLimitResolveCollision: Specifies how the selected component should resolve the collision with the world limits. Options include Bounce, Clamp, Rigid, Sticky, and Kill.

OnWorldLimit: Specifies an optional event delegate to receive the collision notification.

T2DForceComponent

The T2DForceComponent (Figure 2.39) adds arbitrary forces to your object. There are several types of forces that can be added, including Force, MasslessForce, DragForce, DragForceDirectional, and DragForceBidirectional. Any number of forces can be added and removed during the game. You can also control the strength of given forces, allowing the player to control, for example, the thrust of a spaceship or the acceleration of a car.

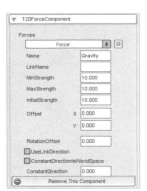

Figure 2.39. The T2D-ForceComponent properties rollout.

Forces List: Lists all directional forces acting upon this object. Since there can only be one component of any given type attached to an object, the T2DForceComponent can have multiple forces listed by name. Then, you can programmatically enable or disable each individual force. The remaining component properties are used to describe each individual force added to this list.

Name: A human-readable name for the force.

LinkName: The link node to which to attach the force. This can be left empty, in which case the object center will be used.

MinStrength: The minimum strength of the force.

MaxStrength: The maximum strength of the force.

Offset X, Y: The offset of force from the object center (or link node if there is one).

RotationOffset: The rotation offset of force from the object (or link node if there is one).

UseLinkDirection: If true, the direction of the link point is used to determine the force direction. If false, the constant direction is used.

ConstantDirectionIsWorldSpace: If true, then the supplied constant direction is in world space. If false, the constant direction is in object space.

Constant Direction: The constant direction of force.

Creating an XnaBreakout Game

Now that you have a solid overview of Torque X Builder, let's put some of that new knowledge to work by creating a very basic game that uses only the built-in components that come with Torque X. As we've just seen, there are only a handful of components that come with Torque X, and they are pretty limited in what they can do. In the coming chapters, you will be coding your own custom components that can perform more specialized game tasks.

As you might recall from the original game, *Breakout* features a ball that starts off falling toward the player's paddle at the bottom of the screen. The player moves the paddle around to knock the ball back to the top of the screen. When the ball strikes a brick, it disappears. When all of the bricks disappear, the player wins. If the ball lands at the bottom of the screen, the player loses. Let's try to implement as much of this game functionality as we can, using only the stock Torque X components.

The stock Torque X components might be limited in their functionality, but it's just enough functionality to create a simple game. We'll use these components to create a Torque X variation of the classic game of *Breakout*. Begin by creating and opening the *XnaBreakout* project described at the beginning of this chapter.

Import the Game Images

The first step in creating our simple *Breakout* game is to import the graphics that will make up the game into Torque X Builder and then turn them into materials. The graphics requirement for this game isn't very high. You can either download the sample images from TorqueXBook.com or create your own equivalents in just about any paint program. Essentially, the graphics package contains the following graphics:

- Background.png,
- Ball.png,
- Block1.png, Block2.png, Block3.png, Block4.png, Block5.png.

To add these images to your project, select them in Windows Explorer and then drag them into Torque X Builder. You can also add them individually from within Torque X Builder by Project ➢ Material Builder.

Once the materials have been added to your Torque X project, save the level. You can replace the existing "levelData.txscene" file. This way, we don't need to change the game code, which looks for this file by default.

Defining Some Object Types

Even a simple game like *XnaBreakout* needs some basic smarts about what types of objects are in the game. Different game elements will behave differently. The ball will move around and bounce off the walls. The bricks will disappear when the ball strikes them. And the player-controlled paddle moves around in response to the player input. Let's create these three different object types from within Torque X Builder.

With no scene objects selected, open the Edit tab. If something is selected, press the Escape key to deselect it. Expand the Scene Data rollout, and create three object types—objBall, objBrick, and objPlayer—by typing in each name and pressing the green Add button. Be sure not to confuse Collision Materials with Object Types.

Creating the Scrolling Background

The first element we will add to the scene is the background. Begin by turning the Background image into a Scroller object. This is accomplished by clicking the Create a New Scroller button at the top of the Create pane. In the Select Material dialog box, select BackgroundMaterial and click the Select button. Anytime you add a new graphic into Torque X Builder, it appends the word *Material* to the end of the filename. Now that the Scroller object has been created, drag an instance of that object into the scene and stretch out the image to fill the entire render area.

Next, let's edit some of the scene properties for the Scroller. With the Scroller object still selected within the scene, open the Edit pane. Let's get this Scroller moving by editing the Scroller rollout properties. Enter a value of 2 for X and Y components of the Scroll Speed property to start the scrolling.

Next, expand the Scene Object rollout. Since the Scroller should be placed in the background of our scene, set its Layer property to 31. (That's as far back as it can go.) Next, uncheck the Collision Enabled property, since nothing in the scene should be colliding with the background. That's it for the background.

Adding the Bricks

We can start decorating the scene with the traditional bricks along the top of the screen (see Figure 2.40). Return to Torque X Builder's Create pane. Drag an instance of the Block1Material to the scene. The brick may appear *really* big, so drag its selection border and bring it down to a more reasonable size. Remember, holding the Shift key while resizing will keep the scene object's proportions intact.

Next, let's edit some properties for this object. Open the Edit pane and expand the Scripting rollout. Set the brick's Object Type to objBrick and

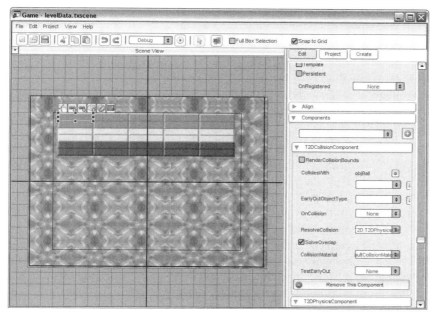

Figure 2.40. The brick layout for the *XnaBreakout* game.

click the green Add button. Next, expand the Components rollout and open the T2DCollisionComponent properties. Set the CollidesWith property to objBall, and then set the ResolveCollision property to KillCollision. This indicates that when the ball collides with the brick, the brick should be deleted from the scene.

This brick is now fully configured for the game. We just need several of them to fill up the scene. Select Edit ➢ Copy (or CTRL+C) from the menu and then Edit ➢ Paste (CTRL+V) to make a copy of this brick. Repeat the process until you have enough bricks to fill the scene. For the upper rows of bricks, you can easily change the color of the brick by selecting a different Material in the Static Sprite rollout.

Adding the Player

Instead of creating a paddle for the player to move around, let's just drop in the GarageGames logo and call it the paddle. Add the GGLogoMaterial to the bottom center of the scene and resize it to something more appropriate.

Next, let's set a collision polygon for the player object. With the player selected within the scene, click on its "Edit This Object's Collision Polygon" mini toolbar button. When Torque X Builder zooms into the player material, start clicking around the perimeter of the logo to create its collision polygon.

You should be able to create a good collision polygon with as few as 8 points. Press the Escape key when you're finished.

Next, let's set some boundaries for the player. Click on the ball's "Change the World Limits for This Object" mini toolbar button. Resize the gray World Limits box to match the width of the background Scroller and a height slightly larger than the size of the player logo. This will be the extent to which we allow the player to move around. Press the Escape key when finished.

When the player reaches the world limits, we want it to remain with the area we defined. Fortunately, Torque X already provides a component to handle this. Open the Components rollout on the Edit tab and expand the T2DWorldLimitComponent. Set the WorldLimitResolveCollision property to ClampCollision. This will restrict the freedom of the player.

Next, let's get this player to respond to some player input. Open the Components rollout on the Edit tab. At the top of the rollout, click on the drop-down list and select the MovementComponent, and then click the green Add button. This will automatically add the stock MovementComponent to our player. When the game runs, the player object will respond to the WASD and Arrow keys as movement input.

Last, set the object type for the player. Open the Scripting rollout within the Edit pane. Then set the Object Type to objPlayer and click the green Add button. This will come in handy later on.

Adding the Game Ball

Now that we have some bricks and a player, we can add the game ball. Return to Torque X Builder's Create pane. Drag an instance of the BallMaterial into the scene, near the middle. The ball graphic may need to be resized by dragging the corner drag-handles.

Setting a collision polygon for the ball is similar to the player. Again, you should be able to create a good collision polygon with as few as 8 points. Press the Escape key when you're finished.

Next, set some boundaries for the ball. Click on the ball's "Change the World Limits for This Object" mini toolbar button. Resize the gray world limits box to match the dimensions of the background Scroller. This will be the extent to which we allow the ball to move around. Press the Escape key when you are finished.

When the ball reaches the world limits, we want it to bounce back. Open the Components rollout on the Edit tab and expand the T2DWorldLimitComponent. Set the WorldLimitResolveCollision property to BounceCollision. Unlike the player's clamp collision, the bounce collision will keep the ball bouncing off the walls.

The ball should also bounce off the player and brick objects. Open the T2DCollisionComponent rollout and set the CollidesWith property to objPlayer and then objBrick. Also, set the ResolveCollision property to BounceCollision.

Finally, let's get this ball moving with a starting force. Expand the T2DPhysicsComponent and enter a value of 20 for the Y velocity and 8 for the X velocity. This will get the ball moving in a diagonal direction.

Running the Game

Now that the scene is complete with bricks, a player, and a ball, you can save the level file. You will need to recompile the game code from within XNA Game Studio. Anytime new graphics are added to the project, they need to be compiled into the project before the game can be run. After recompiling, you should be able to play *XnaBreakout*. It's not a very exciting game, but it also was accomplished without a single line of code.

Summary

In this chapter, you created a new game project with XNA Game Studio and became familiar with the basics of Torque X Builder, including navigation, how to create scene objects, and how to edit them. You successfully imported images, animations, and scrollers and then added them into a scene by dragging them to the viewport. Finally, you added basic game-play functionality to these objects by attaching Components and setting some basic reaction properties—all without writing any code! In the next chapter, we will learn more about Torque X Builder's ability to create game levels, with a close look at its Tilemap builder and particle effect designer.

Constructing New Tilemap Levels

3

In the last chapter, you became familiar with Torque X Builder by importing graphics and adding them to a scene. In this chapter, you will work with two more important game editors: the Tilemap Editor and the Particle Editor. It is important to understand how both tools work when building games with Torque X. We will also use the Tilemap Editor to create a simple tile-based game resembling the arcade classic *Frogger* by Konami.

Working with Tilemaps

A Tilemap is one of the most commonly used level-design frameworks in 2D games. The use of Tilemaps dates back to the early arcade platform games and is still found in commercial games today. In essence, a Tilemap is a two-dimensional grid filled with cells that each hold an individual tile. A tile is an individual image that is placed somewhere within the Tilemap to create a 2D scene, like a mosaic.

Figure 3.1 shows the classic game *Super Mario Bros.* by Nintendo. The image on the right shows the screen capture on the left with a grid overlaid on top of it. The grid makes it easy to see how a Tilemap is used for this game. In fact, Figure 3.2 further dissects the image to create an approximation of what the individual tiles probably look like. This collection of tiles is commonly referred to as a *tile set*.

Using a Tilemap to create repeating elements has many advantages. One of the most important of these is that memory is used more efficiently. Instead of having to load a large graphics file with your whole map in it, your game

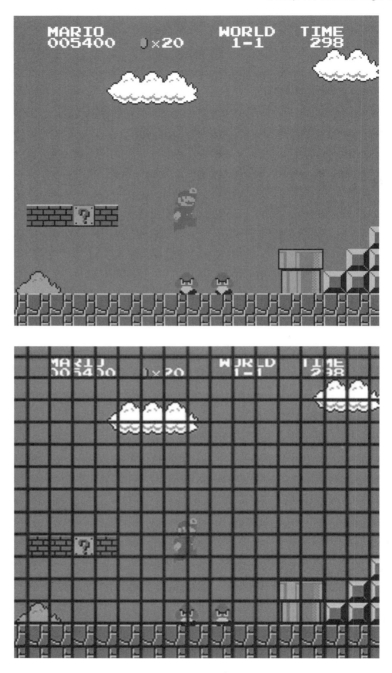

Figure 3.1. *Super Mario Bros.* © 1985, Nintendo.

refers to a few small files that are repeated. This
decreases overall file size for your game as well,
which means faster download times for online
games. Another advantage is the ease of level
construction. When you use a Tilemap system,

Figure 3.2. An approximation of the *Super Mario Bros.*
tile set.

you have a level construction set that makes changes and initial construction
very quick and simple.

Creating a Tilemap

A Tilemap is created in four steps: gathering the tile images, creating the
Tilemap scene object, and painting the tiles. This chapter concentrates only
on creating the Tilemap scene object and painting it.

Importing the Tilemap Materials

Tilemap tiles are no different from the material images that were imported
and used in Chapter 2. Torque X does not support tile sheets or images
composed of multiple tiles that form a single image. Torque X also does not
support animated materials as tiles. You can, however, place an animation
scene object in position over a Tilemap in a separate layer. Figure 3.3 shows
the Material tab filled with a few simple tile materials.

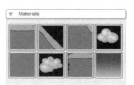

Figure 3.3. Collection
of tile materials.

If you have existing tileset images that you
would like to reuse with Torque X, consider
using an image-editing program, such as Adobe's
ImageReady, which can slice a source image and
produce a series of individual tile files.

When you create your own Tilemap
textures, be sure to identify a consistent naming
convention for the files. When you start painting
your Tilemap and have a long list of material
names to choose from, you're going to need a
fast and easy way to identify a tile. I normally
use the naming convention of *group_direction*.
png. The *group* refers to the texture family, such
as dirt, or a cave, or a metal platform. *Direction*
refers to the position of the tile, as shown in
Figure 3.4.

When you create new tiles, it is more efficient
to reuse as many tiles as possible. Torque X has
the ability to flip tiles vertically and horizontally.
So, if you design symmetrical platforms, you can
probably get away with fewer tiles textures.

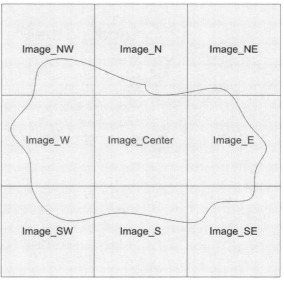

Figure 3.4. Directional naming convention for tile
graphics.

Adding a Tilemap to the Scene

To add a Tilemap to the scene, open the Create pane and drag a Tilemap object into the viewport. Within Torque X, a Tilemap scene object has two states: edit and render. By default, when a Tilemap scene object is added to the viewport, it appears in its *edit* state, ready to be painted. To exit the edit state, press the Escape key. In its *render* state, you can interact with the Tilemap as a scene object and modify its scene properties, such as its position in the viewport, its size, and its layering.

Loading and Saving a Tilemap

Tilemaps are saved to disk and can be loaded into different scene files. Tilemap files are saved with a .lyr file extension. You must select a Tilemap scene object and enter Edit Mode to load and save (Figure 3.5). Although you might be able to view all the layers at once, you can only select and save one Tilemap at a time.

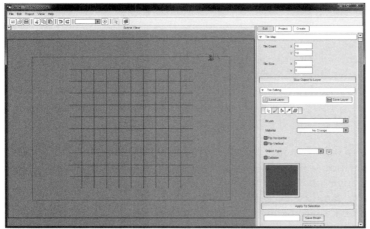

Figure 3.5. The Tilemap appears in the viewport in Edit Mode.

Choosing the Tile Sizes

When adding a Tilemap to a scene, something you first must consider the size and the number of tiles that make up the Tilemap. Different games will have very different needs when it comes to the size and number of tiles. Also, one game's scene may have multiple Tilemaps with very different sizes and counts. As a rule of thumb, you should try to create tiles that are one to two times your player's size.

Setting the Tilemap Size and Count

There are two different values that determine the Tilemap's overall size within a scene: Tile Count and Tile Size. The Tile Count specifies how many tiles, horizontally and vertically, make up the Tilemap. The Tile Size specifies the width and height of each individual tile. Figure 3.1 shows a dissection of *Super Mario Bros.* A 15 × 15 grid was superimposed over the screen capture. The actual Tilemap dimensions are probably much larger, closer to 400 tiles wide by 45 tiles high to construct an entire game level. Each individual tile size in that example is probably 64 × 64 pixels. *Super Mario Bros.* was also created for hardware with very limited memory space. Since your games will target Windows or Xbox 360, you can create much higher-resolution tiles that capture more detail.

Choosing a Tile Count and Tile Size for your game will largely be driven by your art and the scale at which it is to be presented. In our example, we'll start with a Tilemap that has a Tile Count 10 cells wide by 10 cells high and a Tile Size that is also 10 × 10. Also, your tiles are not required to be square-shaped. Anytime you adjust the Tile Size or the Tile Count of a Tilemap, you can click the Size Object to Layer button. This will resize the Tilemap scene object bounds to match the newly computed dimensions of your Tilemap.

Keeping Perspective

Remember that your game isn't confined to the size of your viewport. In the case of Super Mario Bros., the viewport could only render a small portion of the entire scene. Fortunately, you can pan the viewport around in all directions. To see more of your map, you can zoom out with the open bracket ([) key and zoom in with the close bracket (]) key, or you use the mouse wheel. You can also pan around in all directions, using the arrow keys or by right-clicking an empty area of the viewport and dragging the mouse around. To return to the default view, press the Home key.

Painting the Tilemap

Painting Tools

The Tilemap Editor also includes some very useful painting tools that are accessible from toolbar buttons (Figure 3.6). The Select tool allows you to select one or more tiles to work with. This is helpful for deleting or replacing a group of specific tiles. The Paint Brush tool paints the selected material into a Tilemap cell. The Flood Fill tool paints a group of connected Tilemap cells that share the same property as the cell selected. The Eye Dropper tool selects the chosen tool and displays its properties within the selection tab. The Eraser tool clears out the selected Tilemap cell entirely.

Painting Tiles

To paint a tile, select a material name from the Material drop-down list. Next, left-click any cell within the empty Tilemap to paint the tile. Shift-Left-Click and drag to create an area that will be filled with the selected tile. You can see how quick and easy it is to draw out a complete level. If you make a mistake while painting, you can select Edit ➢ Undo from the menu.

Figure 3.6. The Tilemap painting tools.

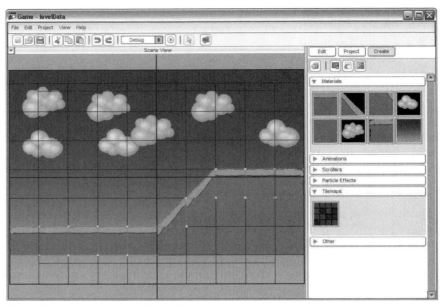

Figure 3.7. Painting a simple platformer scene.

Another way you can save the number of materials displayed on screen is by flipping a material vertically or horizontally. Try to design tiles in a way that left sides and right sides (or tops and bottoms) can be used interchangeably (Figure 3.7).

Creating a Brush

Figure 3.8. Creating a new tile brush.

The Tilemap Editor can also create reusable brushes. A *brush* is a combination of a selected material and properties for a specific tile that you can draw in multiple places. If you have to paint several tiles that have a custom collision polygon, object name, and flipping, it could require a lot of work to set up for each tile. When you create brushes, the selected tiles are copied, including any tile information defined (Figure 3.8).

To create a brush, select a material and edit its properties, such as collision, object type, and flip preferences. Next, enter a name for the brush, and then click the Save Brush button. To use a brush, choose one from the Brush drop-down list and paint. It's useful to choose brush names that have some meaning. Brushes cannot be modified after they are created, but you can delete a brush, redefine its properties, and then save it as a brush with the same name. Notice that deleting an existing brush will not delete tiles already painted within the Tilemap.

If you find that you're creating a lot of identical tiles, you can quickly turn one into a brush. Select the tile from the Tilemap, using the Eye Dropper tool, then add a brush name, and click the Save Brush button.

Setting Tile Collisions

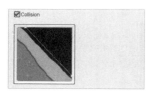

Figure 3.9. Creating a collision polygon for a tile.

Torque X offers a lot of flexibility with collisions within its tile system. The simplest way to set up a tile that will be the object of collisions is to select a material and click the Collision button. It should be outlined in a green square. By default, the entire tile is surrounded by a square collision polygon (Figure 3.9).

In most cases, a simple square collision polygon won't be enough. Fortunately, Torque X enables custom collision polygons for each tile. You can add polygon points by clicking within the collision polygon window, as shown in Figure 3.10. You can also move points around by left-clicking and dragging them. Remember, collision polygons must be convex, and you can delete points by right-clicking on them.

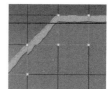

Figure 3.10. Adding collision polygons to a Tilemap.

Working with Layers

Torque X Builder supports multiple layers of Tilemaps. This way you can create backgrounds and other effects using layers. You can use this to create backgrounds with smaller versions of tiles, creating the illusion of distance, or to cover a greater area with fewer tiles.

In Figure 3.11, a second Tilemap is added and set to a layer above the main Tilemap. In this case, the Tile Count is set to 4 tiles wide and 1 tile high, and the Tile Size (both width and height) is set to 20. This makes tiles twice as big as the set of tiles we used in the first Tilemap. When you do this, you'll see that the grid has changed size. As you can see, we can use fewer tiles to cover a larger area.

Figure 3.11. Adding another Tilemap layer for the ground.

Working with Particle Effects

Torque X Builder includes a very powerful and very flexible particle effects editor. It can be used to create amazing commercial-quality visual effects, such as explosions, smoke, sparkles, and so on. So many variables can be set, however, that it can be a little intimidating.

Creating Particle Effects

A particle effect is a collection of graphics that move and change in a predefined manner to produce a particular visual effect. Particle effects are created by setting a series of parameters within Torque X Builder. These parameters combine to create almost any visual effect you can imagine.

Particle Sprites

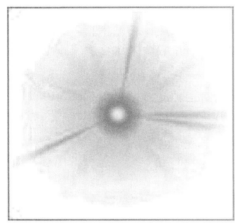

Figure 3.12. A simple particle sprite graphic.

Particle sprites are used to create specific visual effects, such as smoke or flames. They tend to appear as translucent with soft, faded edges, as shown in Figure 3.12. For the most part, particle sprites are the exact opposite of game sprites. Whereas game sprites can contain a high level of detail, it is really recommended that particle sprites have minimal detail with a small file size. This is because particle sprites tend to appear on the screen for a very short period and are displayed in large numbers to create an effect.

Particle Effects

Within the context of Torque X Builder, a *particle effect* is the finished product that is saved. (Think of it as a container for emitters.) An *emitter* is an object that creates the individual particle and directs its behavior. A *particle* is the most basic element of the effect: an image that is spawned and controlled by the particle emitter. You can easily create an effect such as an explosion, which contains separate emitters for smoke, fire, and debris, all of which are made up of one or more particles.

Adding Particle Effects to a Scene

Begin by dragging a new particle effect from the Create tab to the viewport. Initially, the only visible elements that appear are the grab handles that surround the effect. If you click away from the particle effect, remember to use the object tree in the Project tab to select it again. Next, click the Edit tab to begin editing. The particle effect object has a lot of the same editable characteristics as the sprite object. You can align it within the viewport, add components to it, and set its position and size.

Using the Particle Effect Editor

To add a particle effect to your scene, drag New Particle Effect from the Create pane into the viewport. The default particle effect already has a single emitter attached, but it doesn't have a material associated with it. You can select a material by clicking on the rollout labeled Emitter - UntitledEmitter and then selecting a material from the Material drop-down list. You can add additional emitters to this effect by typing an emitter name in the Create Emitter field and then clicking the green Add button

Setting the Effect Mode

Each particle effect has a property called Effect Mode that specifies how particles will be emitted. The default effect mode is Infinite, which creates particles constantly. The Cycle mode creates particles constantly but will reset itself, based on its lifetime. The Kill mode spews particles for the duration of its lifetime and then destroys itself. The Stop effect mode creates particles for the duration of its lifetime and then stops; the effects remain. If you select any effect mode other than Infinite, a text field will prompt you to enter the lifetime of the particle effect in seconds.

Setting the Effect Properties

In addition to the material selection, emitters have several properties that control its behavior. These properties work together to produce the final visual effect you want to create (Figure 3.13).

Type: Tells an emitter where to create the individual particles. When set to Point, particles will emit from the center of the particle effect object. When set to Line X, particles emit from a horizontal line through the center of the effect object. Similarly, when set to Line Y, particles will emit from a vertical line, and when Type is set to Area, particles are emitted from the entire area of the effect object. You can resize the particle effect object to increase the spawning area of each particle.

Orientation: Defines the angle at which particles are emitted. When set to Aligned, particles are emitted at the same angle as the emitter's rotation. When set to Fixed, particles are emitted at a constant angle, no matter what the emitter's rotation is. The constant angle is set in the Fixed Angle property. And when set to Random, particles emit at random angles.

Pivot: Defines the local point on the particles to rotate around. The X and Y values range between 0 and 1.

Fixed Aspect: When checked, any changes to the width of a particle will also change the height of the particle. If turned off, the X and Y dimensions must be sized separately.

Fixed Area Aspect: When checked, the *Area* emitters will use the X dimension of the emitter to determine both horizontal and vertical sizes. When unchecked, the horizontal and vertical emitter size can be changed separately.

Figure 3.13. The Particle Effect properties tab.

Single Particle: When checked, the emitter will release only a single particle. This is useful for several effects, as well as testing certain properties.

Attach Position: When checked, individual particles will follow the emitter as it moves. Otherwise, particles will function as dictated by the emitter graphs.

Attach Rotation: When checked, individual particles will rotate with the emitter. Otherwise, they will function as dictated by the emitter graphs.

Rotate Emission: When checked, the emitter is aligned with the effect object. This can be used to create jet trails and similar effects.

First in Front: When checked, the older particles will be rendered on top of the newer ones. Otherwise, new particles are rendered on top. For visual effects, such as smoke, enabling this option results in a much more natural look.

Working with Emitter Graphs

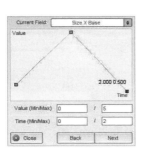

Figure 3.14. The Particle Life Emitter Graph.

As previously mentioned, the emitter is the actual object that produces particles and directs their behavior. Emitters direct the behavior of particles as defined by the Emitter Graph (Figure 3.14). Each emitter will produce one type of particle, and all particles from the same emitter will share similar behavior.

The Emitter Graph is the primary mechanism for defining the behavior of particles within Torque X Builder. It's a very powerful tool that lets you see the results of your adjustments in real time. However, with such power also comes some initial confusion about how to use it. In short, the Emitter Graph enables you to set different particle emitter characteristic values over a timeline.

Setting Keyframes Values

Keyframes are markers that are set along a timeline to define the value of a particle characteristic when that point in time is reached. The Emitter Graph lets you set keyframes along the timeline with associated values for each characteristic. For example, a particle may begin its life with a size of 1.0 at 0.0 seconds, then grow to size 5.0 at 1.0 seconds, and then shrink to size 0.5 at 2.0 seconds, the end of its lifetime. All you have to do is set the desired particle size at each point in time. Torque X performs the necessary scaling over time to result in a smooth animation.

Keyframing is important to making dynamic particle systems because of the amount of time it saves. In Torque X, keyframes are represented as percentages of particle lifespan and effects scale smoothly between keyframes. You can set as many keyframes as you need to achieve your desired effect.

Understanding the Life Base

The first emitter graph in the collection is Particle Life Base. This value is perhaps the most important setting throughout the particle system. All keyframes are based on the particle's lifetime to determine when each keyframe is reached.

All units of time in a keyframe timeline are measured as a percentage of the particle life. For example, a value of 1.0 equals 100% of the particle's lifespan, whereas 0.0 equals 0% of the lifespan. Keyframes with a value of 1 occur at the end of the particle's lifespan (Figure 3.15).

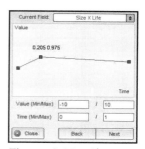

Figure 3.15. Changing the particle's size with keyframes.

The Differences between Base, Life, and Variance

Several different core parameters define a particle emitter: Particle Life, Quantity, Size X, Size Y, Emission Angle, Emission Arc, Visibility Life, Speed, Spin, Fixed Force, Random Motion, Emission Force, and Color Emitter. These core parameters define the behavior of the particle once it has been emitted. Several of these core parameters also have modifiers to make the resulting effect even more interesting. For example, you can use a Particle Life Base to set the lifespan of a particle, and you can set a Particle Life Variance, which adds some variety to the lifespan. By adding some variety, particles look less uniform and more random. Overall, the three types of core parameter modifiers are Base, Life, and Variance.

The Base modifier tells the emitter that you are setting the initial value of the parameter. For example, if you set a keyframe for Size X Base, you are adjusting the initial size at which the particle is created.

The Life modifier tells the emitter that you are changing the particle over time. For example, you may set a series of keyframes to increase and then decrease the object's size over time in the Size X Life graph.

The Variance graph introduces an element of randomness into the value of any graph. For example, if you set a series of keyframes in the Size X Variance graph, you will be telling the engine to modify the size of a particle up or down by a value equal to half of the number entered. If you enter a keyframe of 1.0 for size X variance, and the base value was also 1.0, you would create particles with a size X range of between 0.5 and 1.5.

Emitter Graph Parameters

The Particle Life parameter determines how long an individual particle will live, in seconds, before it dies. All other keyframes are based on a percentage of this value.

The Quantity parameter determines how many particles per second Torque X will create. Most effects look best in the 10 to 20 particles/sec range.

The Size X parameter determines the horizontal size of an individual particle. SizeXBase sets a particle's beginning size, and Size X Life is a keyframe modifier that allows you to change a particle's size over time. Aspect ratios are fixed by default, so changing the horizontal size will also change the vertical size.

The Size Y parameter determines the vertical size of an individual particle. If Fixed Aspect is unchecked, the vertical and horizontal sizes can be modified separately. Otherwise, these graphs are disabled.

The Emission Angle parameter determines the angle, in degrees, that an emitter faces by default. A default value of 0.0 faces to the right of the screen.

The Emission Arc parameter sets the angle, in degrees, at which an emitter will put out particles. This defaults to full 360-degree emission.

The Visibility Life parameter determines the opacity of a particle, expressed as a percentage. A setting of 1.0 is fully visible, while a setting of 0.0 is completely invisible.

The Speed parameter sets the speed of a particle, in world units per second. Speed Base allows you to set the default speed, and Speed Life allows you to change it over time.

The Spin Emitter parameter sets the rotation speed of a particle.

The Fixed Force parameter sets a constant force acting on the particles. You can use this to create wind or gravity effects. The value entered for Force Angle in the emitter bar determines the direction of the force.

The Random Motion parameter allows you to cause a particle to travel in a semi-random path after it is emitted from the graph. Effectively, once the particle's position is calculated by the engine, that location is adjusted by this value. This position change is omnidirectional.

The Emission Force parameter sets the force with which a particle is emitted. Speed adjustments can override this value. When in doubt, use speed for most adjustments.

The Color Emitter parameter determines the color component over the particle lifetime. Changing the Color Channel allows you to modify the color of your particles on the fly. This is a subtractive process, so a value of 1.0 will give you the full amount of your given color, whereas a value of 0.0 will eliminate it entirely.

Creating an Explosion Effect

Now that we have a better understanding of how to use the Emitter Graph, let's put that knowledge to work by creating a simple explosion effect, using only one simple graphic.

Begin by creating the particle and adding it to Torque X Builder. The graphic isn't very special—just a white fading circle in the center of a transparent square. Figure 3.16 illustrates the graphic with a black background added for some visible contrast. Many popular graphics applications, such as PhotoShop, PaintShop, Gimp, and Paint.Net, can paint on a transparent background. Be sure to save the file in the .PNG file format, such as MyParticle.png, to retain the translucent background.

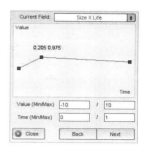

Figure 3.16. A simple white particle graphic.

After the particle graphic is imported into Torque X Builder, drag a new particle effect from the Create pane into the viewport. Switch to the Edit pane and expand the Particle Effect rollout. Set the Effect Mode to cycle and the Effect Lifetime to 3.0 seconds. Now the particle effect will play out for 3 seconds and restart the effect from the beginning. This helps you see the effects of our changes in real time as we are making them within the Emitter Graph.

Particle Effect objects can have multiple emitters attached to them, so lots of different particles and behaviors can be packaged into one easy-to-manage effect. By default, a newly created particle effect comes with one emitter attached to it, named UntitledEmitter. We'll update this emitter to create an explosion burst effect.

Creating the Burst Emitter

Start expanding the emitter rollout. Let's choose the one particle graphic for which this emitter will be responsible. Select the name of your newly added particle graphic—for example, MyParticleMaterial. Next, click the First in Front checkbox so that particles will be created on top of existing particles. This results in a more natural-looking effect. Finally, we're ready to jump into the Emitter Graph. Click the Edit Emitter Graph button.

Our goal with the Emitter Graph is to take this simple white circle and turn it into a glowing burst of red flame. The first task is to specify how long an instance of this particle will be around. Set the Particle Life Base from its default value of 2 to a value of 3, as shown in Figure 3.17(a).

Next, change the Emitter Graph field to Quantity Base. This determines how many particles will be created over time. Set the initial value to 40, and then, at 0.5 seconds into the effect, create another keyframe set to a value of 40, followed by a third keyframe set to zero. Figure 3.17(b) illustrates this more clearly. The result is that particles will be created at a rate of 40 per second until we reach the half-second mark. Then, particle creation drops to zero. The result you see from the emitter at this point should be a nice ring of smoke.

(a)

(b)

Figure 3.17. (a) The Particle Life Base settings. (b) The Quantity Base settings.

The Emitter Graph is a very powerful tool for editing particle effects. You can easily slide keyframes around to set values by dragging them with the mouse. At the same time, it is also difficult to set a specific value. You might end up setting a value of 3.104 instead of a desired 3. In this case, try setting the display range, at the bottom of the Emitter Graph, so that the maximum range equals the value you want to set. In Figure 3.17, the Max Value was set to 3 and 40, respectively. This way, the keyframe could be positioned at the top of the graph, setting it to exactly 3 and 40, respectively.

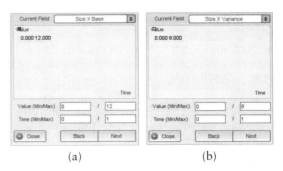

(a)   (b)

Figure 3.18. (a) The Size X Base settings. (b) The Size X Variance settings.

Next, let's adjust the size of the particles that are emitted (Figure 3.18). Move on the Size X Base properties and set a value of 12.0. Move on the Size X Variance and set its value to 8.0. This results in the creation of particles that are 12 units in size with a variation of 8 units.

You might notice that the particles are created at a specific size and hold that size for the life of the effect. Let's change that so that the particle actually grows. Switch to the Size X Life properties. Set the Size X Life to start at a value of 0 at 0 seconds and then grow to a value of 2.0 at 0.1 seconds, as shown in Figure 3.19. Now the particles will quickly grow as time progresses.

Figure 3.19. The Size X Life settings.

So far, the burst is looking pretty good, but it really doesn't seem to fit the description of a burst. So, let's add some speed to these particles. Switch to the Speed Base properties and set a value of 30. Add some randomness by switching to the Speed Variance properties and setting a value of 5, as shown in Figure 3.20.

Now the particles are moving along more quickly. But, their speed is still constant, so let's make some changes to how that speed is controlled. Switch to the Speed Life properties and set an initial value to 1 at 0 seconds. Next, drop the value down with another keyframe with a value of 0.06 at 0.04 seconds. Drop the value even further with a third keyframe with

(a)   (b)

Figure 3.20. (a) The Speed Base settings. (b) The Speed Variance settings.

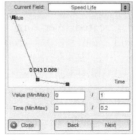

Figure 3.21. The Speed Life settings.

a value of 0 at 0.01 seconds. Just by looking at the curve in Figure 3.21, you can see that particle speed (set to 5.0 in the last property) quickly comes to a crawl at about 4% of that original speed.

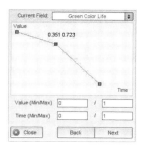

Now, that looks more like an explosion, or at least a white one. The best part about working with a white particle is that you can easily manipulate its color by adjusting its red, green, and blue color components. In Figure 3.22, we draw a curve for each color component over the timeline of the particle effect.

Let's take this white particle and make it first turn red and then a dark gray. Start by setting all three colors at full value at the beginning of the timeline. All three color components at full value should result in white. Next, drop the curve in the middle of the effect for the green and blue component so the particle turns redder. Finally,

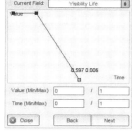

Figure 3.22. The Red, Green, and Blue Color Life settings.

have all color components join together with a value near zero, resulting in a dark gray color. The curves for each color component are shown in Figure 3.22.

Now that the colors are set for a nice reddish glow, let's give these particles a nice fade-out. Switch the Emitter Graph to the Visibility Life properties. Start by setting an initial keyframe with a value of 1 at 0 seconds. Next, add a second keyframe with a value of 1 at 0.2 seconds. This will keep the visibility level constant for that period. Add a third keyframe with a value of 0 at 0.6 seconds. This gradual slope in visibility, shown in Figure 3.23, translates into a gentle fade of all created particles.

Figure 3.23. The Visibility Life settings.

Creating a Score Particle Effect

Although particles are most commonly used for adding extra flare to a scene, there are other hidden benefits. Remember that the particle emitter simply creates one or more sprites and sets a lifetime, a motion, and some visibility characteristics. These features can come in handy for a number of other uses, such as indicating score increases.

In Figure 3.24, a particle emitter is used to display a number that represents a scoring increase in the game that gently slides upward and fades away. This is a common effect found in classic arcade games when an enemy is destroyed or a pickup item is collected.

Figure 3.24. Using a particle emitter to show bonus points.

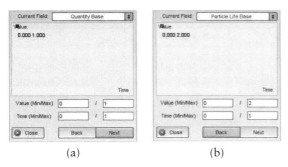

Figure 3.25. A sample collection of scoring images.

(a)   (b)

Figure 3.26. (a) The Quantity Base settings. (b) The Particle Life Base settings.

Achieving the effect is relatively easy. The first step is to create a few sprite graphics that represent the score increases. Each sprite should be in its own file with an easy-to-recognize filename, such as Add10Points.png. Figure 3.25 shows a collection of such images, placed side by side.

Simply add these images into Torque X Builder just like any other material. Next, drag a Particle Effect object from the Create pane into the viewport. Expand the Particle Effect rollout and then the Emitter rollout. Click the Edit Emitter Graph button and make the following changes.

First, set the Quantity Base to 1.0. This way, we have only one particle emitted during the course of the effect. Next, we need to set the length of the entire effect. Set the Particle Life Base to 2.0 seconds, as shown in Figure 3.26.

Next, we want to make the score value slowly drift upward. Set the Emission Arc Base to 0 degrees (Figure 3.27). This will cause the particle emitter to emit the particle at an angle of zero degrees, which happens to be upwards. You can experiment with different angles, entered as degrees, to emit the scoring particle in different directions.

That's all there is to it! You can create a different particle effect for each scoring value, or you can change the material used in the particle effect programmatically in C#. You can position each scoring particle effect next to an object, such as a collectible, and then begin the particle effect in response to a player collision.

Figure 3.27. The Emission Arc Base settings.

Creating an XnaFrogger Game

Now that we have gone through the steps of creating tilemaps, let's put some of that new knowledge to work by creating another basic game that only uses the built-in components that come with Torque X.

As you might recall from the original game, *Frogger* features a small frog that starts at the bottom of the screen and works his way to the top of the screen by avoiding dangerous objects and hitching a ride on safe objects. Let's try to implement as much of this game functionality as we can, using only the stock Torque X components.

Again, the stock Torque X components are limited in their functionality, but it's just enough functionality to create such a simple game. Begin by creating and opening a new project, called XnaFrogger, based on the StarterGame template.

Import the Game Images

The first step to creating our simple *Frogger* game is to import the graphics that will make up the game into Torque X Builder and then turn them into materials. The graphics requirement for this game requires a little more than the last game. You can either download the sample images from TorqueXBook.com or create your own equivalents in just about any paint program. Essentially, the graphics package contains the following graphics:

- Frog.png, Bug.png
- Car1.png, Car2.png, Car3.png, Car4.png
- Grass_back.png, Grass_corner.png, Grass_inner_corner.png
- Lillypad.png, Log.png, Turtles.png
- Road.png, Wall.png, Water.png

To add these images to your project, select them within Windows Explorer and then drag them into Torque X Builder. You can also add them individually from within Torque X Builder by Project ➤ Material Builder.

After the materials are added to your Torque X project, save the level file. You can replace the existing levelData.txscene file. This way, we don't need to change the game code, which looks for this file by default.

Defining Some Object Types

Even a simple game such as *XnaFrogger* needs some basic smarts about what types of objects are in the game. When the frog collides with a car, it dies. But when the frog collides with a log, it hitches a ride. Let's create these three different object types from within Torque X Builder.

Start Torque X Builder and, with no scene objects selected, open the Edit tab. If you have a scene object selected, just press the Escape key to deselect it. Next, expand the Scene Data rollout. Create five object types—objPlayer, objCar, objLog, objTurtle, and objPad—by typing in each name and pressing the green Add button. Be sure not to confuse Collision Materials with the object types.

Creating the Tilemap Background

The first scene object we will add to the scene is the tilemap background. In the Create pane, expand the Tilemaps rollout and drag an instance of that

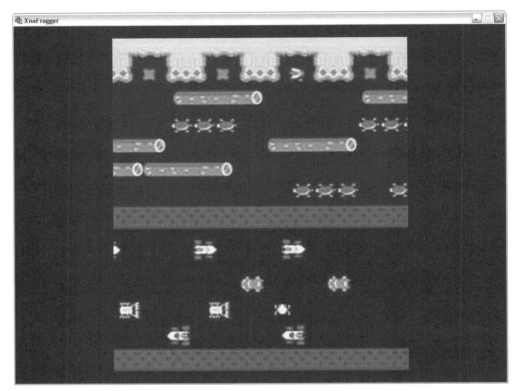

Figure 3.28. The brick layout for the *XnaFrogger* game.

object into the scene. Next, let's edit some of the properties for the tilemap. With the Tilemap scene object still selected, open the Edit pane. In the Tile Map rollout, set the Tile Count X property to 12 and Y property to 14. Then, set the Tile Size X and the Y properties to 5 and then click the Size Object to Layer button. Next, move the Tilemap scene object to the center of the screen by setting its Position X and Y properties to 0. Finally, click the Edit Tile Layer button to start painting the individual tiles.

Painting the Tiles

Painting the individual tiles is fairly quick and easy. As described earlier in this chapter, you only need to select the desired material and paint it to the screen. There's no need to set a collision polygon for any of these tiles, since this Tilemap is simply a background for the game. Remember to use the Flip Horizontal and Flip Vertical check boxes to properly set the tiles. Take a few moments to paint the Tilemap scene object to match Figure 3.28, excluding the cars, logs, and turtles.

Adding the Player Scene Object

Now that the background for the game is set, let's add the actual player scene object. Drag the frog material from the Create pane into the scene. In the Edit pane, open the Scene Object properties and set the frog's Width and Height properties to 5.

Next, let's set a collision polygon for the player object. With the player selected within the scene, click on its "Edit This Object's Collision Polygon" mini toolbar button. When Torque X Builder zooms into the player material, start clicking around the perimeter of the frog to create its collision polygon. You should be able to create a good collision polygon with as little as 4 or 5 points. Press the Escape key when you're finished.

Next, let's set some screen boundaries for the player. Click on the frog's "Change the World Limits for This Object" mini toolbar button. Resize the gray world limits box to match the width of the background Tilemap. This will be the extent to which we allow the player to move around. Press the Escape key when finished.

When the player reaches the world limits, we want it to remain within the area we defined. Fortunately, Torque X already provides a component to handle this. Open the Components rollout on the Edit tab and expand the T2DWorldLimitComponent. Set the WorldLimitResolveCollision property to KillCollision. This will remove the player from the game if he reaches the edges of the game.

Next, let's get this player to respond to some player input. Open the Components rollout in the Edit pane. At the top of the rollout, click on the drop-down list, select the MovementComponent, and then click the green Add button. This will automatically add the stock MovementComponent to our player. When the game runs, the player object will respond to the WASD and Arrow keys as movement input.

Last, let's set the object type for the player. Open the Scripting rollout within the Edit pane. Then set the Object Type to objPlayer, and click the green Add button. This will come in handy later on.

Creating Templates and Spawners

Several things are moving around in the game, including cars, turtles, and logs. The next step is to add these game elements. Let's start with the logs. There are a couple of different ways to make logs slide across the screen. The first way is to create a Scroller scene object that will move a picture containing a couple of logs across the screen. It would result in the right visual effect, but it can't process the collision between the frog and the log.

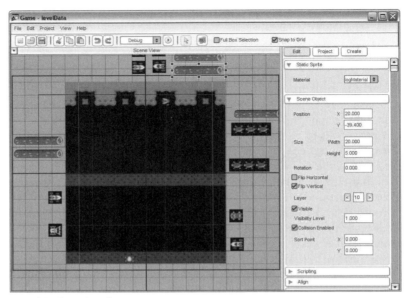

Figure 3.29. Creating the *XnaFrogger* game.

Another approach is to create a scene object that resembles the log and send it across the screen using a physics component. In fact, we want several logs to move across the screen. This sounds like a perfect case for a Template and Spawner. We can set the log scene object as a Template and use a Spawner scene object to create as many as we like.

To turn any scene object into a template, just open the Scripting rollout within the Edit pane and check the Template check box. Also, be sure to set the Name property to something like LogTemplate, so we can identify this template later. You should also set the appropriate Object Type, such as objLog, for each template. Next, position the log template outside of the view area. You can repeat this process to create turtles and cars, too.

Next, create a few Spawner scene objects to the left and right of the Tilemap. For each Spawner, go to the Edit pane and expand the Template Reference rollout. Find the appropriate template name, such as LogTemplate, within the Template Object drop-down list. Note that every time you specify a template, the Spawner takes the shape of the selected template. Next, expand the Spawning rollout. Uncheck the Spawn Once property to create an unlimited amount of scene objects. Then, set the Min Spawn Time to 3000 and the Max Spawn time to 4000. This means that the selected template will be cloned into a new scene object every 3000 to 4000 milliseconds, or 3 to 4 seconds. Position the Spawners as shown in Figure 3.29.

Setting the Physics Components

Next, let's get these logs, turtles, and cars moving. For each template, go to the Edit pane and expand the Components rollout. Next, expand the T2DPhysicsComponent rollout. Set the Velocity X and Y properties for the various templates to values ranging from positive 5 to 10 to −5 to −10. A negative X value will make an object move from right to left, so its Spawner should be located to the right of the background.

Setting the Collision Component

In the real *Frogger* game, the player's frog handles collisions with different objects uniquely. When the frog collides with a car, the frog dies. When the frog collides with a swimming turtle or a log, it hitches a ride. And when the frog collides with the landing lily pad, the player wins the game. To accomplish this original game play, we need to add some game code to handle these collisions differently. So, for now, we'll simply change the dynamics of the game such that all collisions simply push the frog along. But, to add some risk, the frog dies when the player is pushed off the screen.

With the frog scene object selected, open the Edit pane and expand the Components rollout. Next, find the T2DCollisionComponent. In the CollidesWith droplist, select the objCar item and click the green Add button. Also add the objLog and objTurtle items. These items represent the three object types that the player scene object will process collisions with. Next, we need to define what will happen to the player scene object once the collision occurs. In the ResolveCollision listbox, select the RigidCollision item. This will cause the player scene object to react to a collision using rigid physics. When a car, log, or turtle collides with the player scene object, it will push the player off the screen. And when the player reaches the edge of the screen, the T2DWorldLimitsComponent jumps in and kills the player by removing the scene object from the scene.

It's not exactly the same game play as the original *Frogger* game, but it can all be accomplished without a single line of code. In later chapters, you will become more familiar with creating event delegates and mounting. Creating an event delegate will let you add custom code to handle collisions in a very game-specific manner. Mounting will let you take your player scene object and mount it to a log or turtle scene object to hitch a ride.

Running the Game

Now the scene is complete with a Tilemap background, a player, and some moving cars, moving logs, and moving turtles. All that's left to do is save the level file and then recompile the game project from within XNA Game Studio. Again, anytime new graphics are added to Torque X Builder, they must be compiled into the XNA project before the game can be run. After recompiling, you should be able to play *XnaFrogger*. It's not a very exciting game, but it also was accomplished without a single line of code.

Summary

In this chapter you learned about Tilemaps and particle effects. You imported some building block images and assembled them into a simple platformer game level and then enhanced that game level by creating some new particle effects. In the next chapter, we will shift over to the 3D toolset to create a simple scene for a 3D game.

Creating Scenes with Torque X Builder 3D

4

Torque X Builder 3D is a level-design tool used to create 3D scene-data files that are compatible with the Torque X 3D Framework. Level designers can use Torque X Builder 3D to import game assets, such as models, textures, and sounds, into a game project and place them within the scene. Aside from being a very rich scene-data editor, it is also very flexible and lets designers configure the layout in a way that best suits their work flow as shown in Figure 4.1.

Creating a 3D Project

The process of creating a 3D game project begins within XNA Game Studio, just as it does for creating 2D game projects. Once a project is created and compiled into runnable binary, Torque X Builder 3D can step in to help the designer build out 3D scenes. The process begins with the new project.

Choosing a New Project Template

To get started, open XNA Game Studio and select File ➤ New Project from the main menu. Select the Starter Game 3D template and enter a name for the project, such as MyGame3D, as shown in Figure 4.2. Next, press the OK button to create the project.

XNA Game Studio will take the Starter Game 3D template and create the shell for a working 3D game, complete with a terrain and a sky box. You can browse through the solution file to see the source code and art assets that make up the starter game.

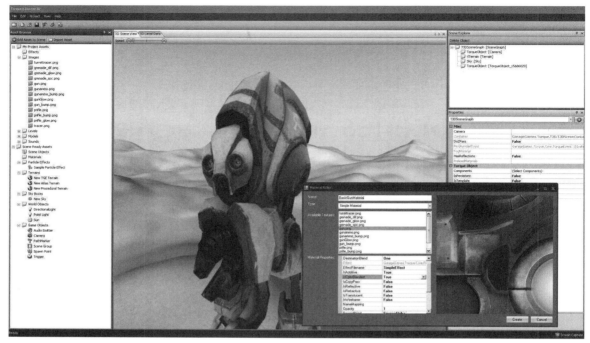

Figure 4.1. Creating 3D scenes with Torque X Builder 3D

With the game project created, the next step is to compile and run the game. Select the Build ➤ Build Solution command from the main menu. After a couple of minutes, the project should fully compile.

In addition to compiling the game code and art assets, this build process also creates a component schema file, which is stored in the myschema.txschema file. Torque X Builder depends upon this file to identify the components available to use. After compiling completes, you can run the game by either pressing F5 or selecting Debug ➤ Start Debugging from the main menu.

Navigating Torque X Builder 3D

After your XNA Game Studio project compiles and successfully runs, you can start Torque X Builder 3D. Begin by selecting the File ➤ Open XNA Game Studio Project… command from the main menu. Browse your Torque X 3D project folder and select the game's .csproj file. Torque X Builder

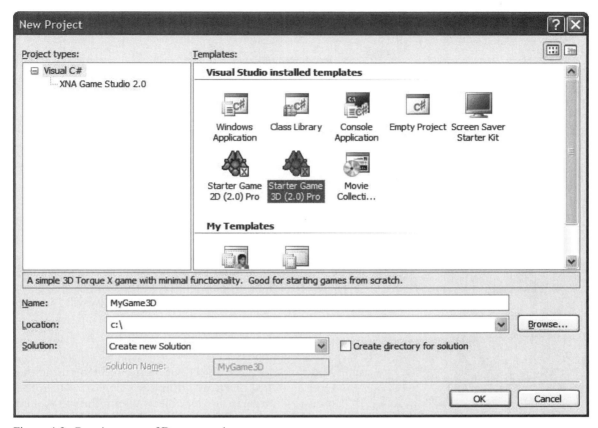

Figure 4.2. Creating a new 3D game project.

3D will begin loading your project's component information and art-asset files.

The Torque X Builder 3D user interface is organized into several different elements, including the viewport, level-data editor, editor panes, and editor dialogs. The positioning of these user interfaces is very flexible. You can easily drag-and-drop panels and reposition windows to best fit your workflow.

The Viewport

The mot important user-interface element is the viewport. It renders the current 3D scene just as it will be rendered when running the game. Also, all lighting, rendering, particle effects, and object placement are exactly how they will appear in the game. Obviously, this excludes any of the editor elements such as the axis gizmo and object position markers.

Figure 4.3. Each axis gizmo represents a different action to be applied.

Moving Around within the Scene

When Torque X Builder initially starts, the camera is positioned in the middle of the scene. You can change the position and orientation of the camera using the mouse and keyboard. If the camera movement is moving too quickly or too slowly for you, you can adjust the camera speed using the Camera Speed slider in the viewport's toolbar.

To move around the scene with the mouse, right-click the Mouse button and then drag the mouse. The camera will pan around in response to the mouse movements. To move forward or backward within the scene, use the mouse's scroll wheel.

To move around the scene with the keyboard, use the arrow keys to pan and pitch the camera. To move the camera forward, left, right, and backwards, use the W, A, S, and D keys, respectively.

Selecting Objects with the Mouse

You can select any object within the scene by using the mouse to click on them within the viewport. When the mouse pointer passes over objects within the scene, they become highlighted. If you click on a highlighted object, it becomes selected. Selected objects can be moved and edited.

Axis Gizmos

Axis gizmos appear over selected scene objects and indicate to the designer that the selected object can be moved, rotated, or scaled directly within the scene. As Figure 4.3 shows, each gizmo has a different visual representation. The gizmo that moves scene objects has arrow end caps, whereas the scaling gizmo has box end caps. The rotation gizmo is represented by rings that rotate the object about each axis. Use the Move, Scale, and Rotate viewport toolbar buttons to activate each gizmo mode.

The axis gizmo provides the designer with precise control over object placement within the scene. To freeform move an object, left-click the center of the gizmo and drag the mouse around. To move the object along a single axis only, left-click on that axis's end cap and drag the mouse. You can also left-click on the plane that joins two axes and drag the mouse to lock movement to only those two planes.

Object Position Markers

Some objects, such as light sources and sound emitters are never visible in the scene, but still have a location. Object position markers are boxes that indicate to the level designer where such objects are positioned. Object position markers can be selected, just like any other scene object, and manipulated by the axis gizmo. A common example of this is resizing and positioning invisible Trigger objects, which are not visible in-game.

Capturing the Viewport to a File

The viewport also includes a screen-capture function that renders the 3D scene to an image file. This is a helpful function for taking screen captures and sharing them with other team members. To capture the screen, click the Screen Capture button at the bottom of the screen and enter a path and filename to save the new image.

The Level-Data Editor

The Torque X Framework persists all scene data to an XML level-data file, which is later loaded by the running game. The purpose of Torque X Builder 3D is to make it as easy as possible to create and edit these XML files. In some cases, it is faster and easier to make changes directly into the XML file, so Torque X Builder 3D provides a rich XML editor. The editor, shown in Figure 4.4, is complete with color-coded syntax, text searching, collapsible tags, and in-place editing.

The level-data editor is updated as new objects are added to the scene. To force an update of the editor, click the Refresh XML but-

Figure 4.4. Editing the XML level-data directly.

ton. As you make changes to the XML file, you can click the Undo and Redo arrow buttons to revert and update your changes. Also, since the XML level-data can grow into a very large file, you can enter a search string and click the Find button to locate specific text within the XML file. Finally, any changes that you manually make to the XML file must be synchronized back to the viewport. Click the Refresh XML button to apply your manual code changes.

The Editor Panes

Torque X Builder 3D also includes a few different editor panes: the Asset Browser, the Scene Explorer, and the Properties pane. By default, these panes appear as a set of tabs anchored to the right side of the viewport. You can customize the layout of these panes by clicking on the pane's caption bar and dragging it around the screen. Blue anchor tags appear where the pane is able to dock.

The Asset Browser

The Asset Browser pane contains a collection of all elements which can be placed into the 3D scene. These elements are divided into assets that belong to your game's project and the general game objects that are packaged with Torque X Builder 3D.

My Project Assets

The My Project Assets tree list is filled when an XNA Game Studio project is selected. It contains a list of images, models, materials, shader effects, and level-data files. These are all objects that are interactive.

Figure 4.5. The Asset Browser editor pane.

The Images node contains all of the texture files currently packaged within your project. Double-clicking an image opens the material editor, where you can create new materials that will be used by other scene objects. As new materials are created, they are added to the Materials node.

The Materials node lists all of the material definitions that exist within the current scene. Material definitions exist on a per level-data file basis, not on a per project basis. Items listed under the Materials node can be applied to other scene-object properties that require a material to be specified, such as the material for a 3D shape object.

The Models node contains a list of all 3D models currently packaged within your project. This includes .dts, .x, .fbx, and .xsi model formats. Double-clicking an entry will automatically add the 3D shape to your scene by creating a Torque Object and adding the necessary component to make the shape appear.

The Shader Effects node contains a list of all shader effects packaged within your project. Double-clicking an entry will open the shader-effect text editor.

Torque X Objects

Torque X Builder 3D simplifies the effort behind adding common game objects to the scene. Instead of mastering the 3D component framework right away, you can simply add the common game elements by their tree-node entry and let Torque X Builder 3D wire all of the component connections behind the scenes.

The Particle Effects node contains a list of particle effect definitions that can be added to the scene. A few sample definitions are provided, and you can build your own re-usable collection of effects. When particle effects are added to the scene, they are saved to the level-data file along with the rest of the scene definition.

The Terrains node contains a list of terrain types that you can add to the scene. These types include TGE, Atlas, and Procedural terrains. Double-clicking any of these nodes will add that terrain type to the scene. Only one terrain can exist within a scene, and you will be prompted to replace any existing terrain.

The Sky Boxes node contains a list of sky boxes that can be added to the scene. A number of sample skies are packaged, and you can easily swap one out for another. Double-clicking a sky box node adds the sky box to the scene.

The Lights node contains a list of different light types, including directional, point, and sun light. Adding lights to the scene is important in order to render any materials that depend upon light. Any number of lights can exist within the scene. Since lights are normally not visible, an object position marker will be displayed to indicate the position of the light.

Under the Game Objects node, there are several additional game-object nodes. The Audio Emitter node adds a basic sound emitter to the scene. You can have several audio emitters within a scene located in different areas.

The Camera node adds a camera object into the scene. Most 3D games make use of a single camera to render the scene, but there are no real limits to the number of camera objects your scene contains.

The Spawner node adds an object spawner to the scene. Spawners in the Torque X 3D Framework work similarly to their counterparts in the 2D Framework. In both cases, you must specify a template object that will be spawned along with other spawning properties.

The Trigger node adds a trigger to the scene. Although triggers are invisible as the game plays, Torque X Builder 3D uses an object position marker to indicate the location and size of the trigger in order to make placement much easier.

Under the 3D Primitives node, there are a few common 3D shapes that can be added to the scene. These shapes include a box, a sphere, and a plane. These common shapes can be helpful for prototyping basic games without 3D art assets and can even be decorated with your own materials.

The Blank Torque Object node is for advanced game designers that want to bypass the macro system and build complex objects manually by attaching the components they want to use.

Importing New Assets into Project

There are two ways to import new art assets into your Torque X game project. The first way is to manually add them as content files within XNA Game Studio. This process is described in detail later in Chapter 11. The second way is to import them with the help of Torque X Builder 3D.

To import new art assets into your XNA Game Studio project, click the Import Asset button or select the Project ➤ Import Assets command from the main menu. The Import Art Assets into Project dialog appears as shown in Figure 4.6. Browse the source location of the art assets and select all the files that you wish to import. Press the Open button to begin the file import.

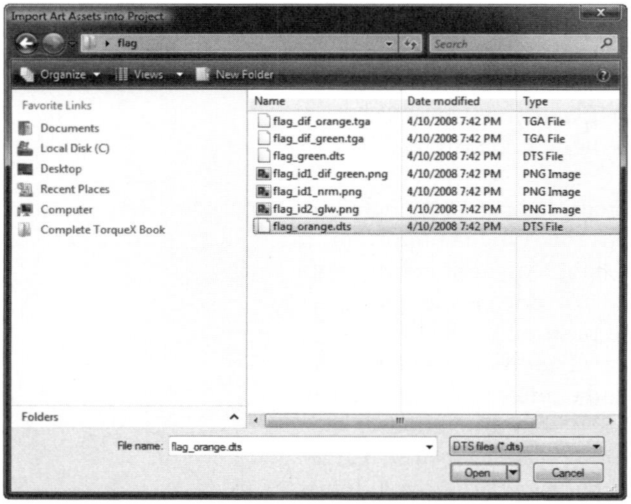

The next time the project is saved, the newly added art assets are written directly to the XNA Game Studio project. As result, XNA Game Studio will detect the project changes and prompt you to reload the project. In order to place the new art assets into your 3D scene, you will need to rebuild the XNA Game Studio project and then reload the changes into Torque X Builder 3D.

Figure 4.6. Importing new assets into Torque X Builder 3D.

The Scene Explorer

The Scene Explorer pane lists all objects that exist within the current 3D scene. Objects are listed by their native object type and assigned a scene name, as shown in Figure 4.7. You can use the Scene Explorer to easily select objects that you want to move or edit.

To bring the viewport camera up to a specific object in your scene, click on the scene object within the Scene Explorer. Then, return to the viewport and click on the Move Camera to Object toolbar button. The viewport camera will be repositioned to the same point as the selected object.

The Properties Window

The Properties window, shown in Figure 4.8, presents all of the editable properties of the currently selected scene object. You can either select a scene object by clicking it in the viewport or by selecting it from the Scene Explorer tree. All object properties are set in real time, so as you edit them you can see the effects within the viewport. Some properties, such as object types and materials, will open separate editors or dialog boxes.

Objects that also have attached components will list their components in the drop-down list at the top of the Properties window. After selecting a component in the drop-down list, that component's properties will be listed. To add or remove components to the selected scene object, click the green Add button to the right of the components drop-down list.

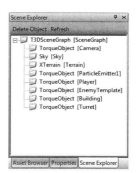

Figure 4.7. The Scene Explorer pane.

The Component Editor

Torque X Builder 3D includes several editors to make 3D scene design easier. The Component Editor, as shown in Figure 4.9, is used to add or remove components to a TorqueObject within the scene. The list on the left contains all of the 3D components discovered when the XNA Game Studio project was loaded. This includes stock Torque X components, as well as components that you created.

The list on the right contains the components that are currently attached to the selected scene object. You can add any number of components to the

Figure 4.8. The Properties window.

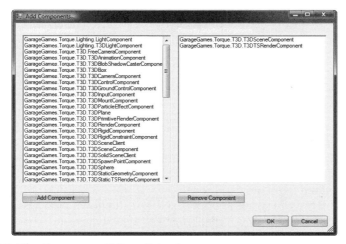

Figure 4.9. The Component Editor dialog box.

scene object to change its behavior. Chapter 13 will go into deeper detail into how to use each component to create specialized game objects.

To add components to the selected scene object, click the Add Component button. An object may have only one instance of any given component. This dialog box may also be used to remove components from an existing scene object by pressing the Remove Component button.

The Material Editor

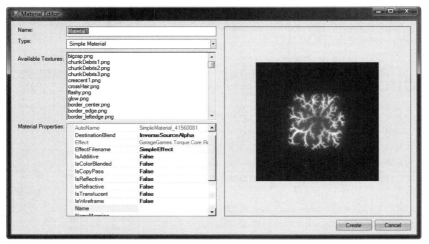

The Material Editor creates material definitions based on image files and material types. In concept, 3D materials work the same way as they do in the 2D Framework. In both cases, they add extended information to a texture about how it should be rendered. The Material Editor, shown in Figure 4.10, creates material definitions based on a name, a material type, and a texture.

Figure 4.10. The Material Editor dialog box.

There are four material types that you can create: simple, detail, lighting, and generic shader materials. Each material type requires its own extended set of properties. The different material types are described in greater detail in Chapter 17.

The Object Type Editor

The Object Type Editor is shown in Figure 4.11 and creates TorqueObjectType definitions that can be attached to game objects. Object types in the 3D Framework behave similarly to those of the 2D Framework. The purpose of this editor is to provide the designer with a way to create the type definitions. You can open the Object Type Editor by selecting the Project ➢ Set Object Types command from the main menu.

The Object Type Editor maintains a list of all known object types within the project. To add a new type, enter the type name and click the Add button. You can have any number of object types registered and a scene object can also have any number of object types assigned to it. Chapter 6 goes into greater detail about how object types can be used within your game. When you are finished editing the list of object types, click the OK button.

Summary

In this chapter, you created a new game project with XNA Game Studio and became familiar with the basics of Torque X Builder 3D, which included how to navigate the program, how to create scene objects, and how to edit them. You successfully imported images, models, and sounds and then added them into scene. Finally, you added basic game play functionality to these objects by attaching components and setting some basic reaction properties—all without writing any code. In the next chapter, we will review the basics of the C# programming language before diving into the Torque X Framework.

Figure 4.11. The Object Types editor.

Programming with Torque X

A C# Primer

5

So far, you have worked with Torque X Builder 2D and 3D to import your graphics and organize them into a scene that represents a game level. In this chapter, we begin the transition in game-development work from the designer to code. This chapter presents an introductory overview to the C# programming language. Once you have a working knowledge of the C# language, you'll be ready to dive into the Torque X Framework classes to start coding your game. If you are already familiar with the C# programming language, feel free to move on to Chapter 6 to begin exploring the Torque X Framework classes.

C# Language Basics

The C# (pronounced *c-sharp*) programming language is a modern, object-oriented programming language. It is type-safe and structurally similar to the C and C++ programming languages. The C# programming language is built on the Microsoft .NET Framework, which includes a common execution engine and a rich class library. The .NET Framework also defines the Common Language Specification (CLS), which is a specification for seamless interoperability between all other CLS-compliant languages and class libraries. Even though C# is a standalone programming language, it has complete access to the same rich class libraries that are used by Visual the Basic .NET and Visual C++ .NET programming languages.

The C# programming language encompasses different language elements, such as keywords, data types, operators, conditional expressions, and control loops. When used along with the rich .NET, XNA, and Torque X class libraries, C# becomes a powerful tool for creating games quickly and easily. Let's begin by examining these different language elements.

Creating a Simple C# Program

A C# program can consist of one or more source code files. Each file can contain one or more declared namespaces. Namespaces can contain custom types, such as classes, structs, interfaces, enumerations, and delegates, in addition to other namespaces. Let's illustrate with a simple C# program.

```csharp
using System;

namespace MyProject
{
   public class MyClass
      {
              private string Name = " ";

      public static void Main()
      {
        MyClass myObject = new MyClass();
        myObject.ProgramName = "My Simple Program";
        myObject.OutputMyMessage();
      }

              public void OutputMyMessage()
              {
                      Console.WriteLine("Welcome to "  + Name );
              }

              public string ProgramName
              {
                      get { return Name; }
                      set { Name = value; }
              }


      }
   }
```

This very simple program illustrates a few fundamental elements of the C# programming language. When it's run, it simply outputs the message "Welcome to My Simple Program" to the screen. It's not a very useful program, but it does illustrate a lot of the elements found in C#.

Namespaces

The first C# element that our simple program illustrates is the use of namespaces. The keyword using indicates that this program will use System namespace. In C#, classes, structs, and enums are typically organized into namespace packages to avoid naming collisions. In this case, the Console class is defined within the System namespace. The Console class includes several methods to interact with a system console. We'll use the Writeline() method output the phrase "Welcome to My Simple Program." Think of namespaces as a way to organize your code library. The using keyword specifies which code library your program will need to reference. This simple program moves on to declare a new namespace, named MyProject.

```
namespace MyProject
{
}
```

Any code, such as the MyClass class, that is defined within this namespace block will belong to the MyProject namespace. Namespaces can be named just about anything, as long as they begin with a letter and are not reserved words, and their names do not need to match the class names that they contain. When you created a new Torque X game in Chapter 2, the default namespace was StarterGame. For now, our namespace only contains a single class, named MyClass.

Classes

A class is a coding construct that organizes related methods and properties together. A class can contain any number of methods and properties. In this case, the MyClass class contains two methods, Main() and OutputMyMessage(); one private field, Name; and one public property, ProgramName. The keyword class is used to define a new class, followed by the class name. Like namespaces, classes can be named just about anything as long as it is not a C# keyword and starts with either a letter or an underscore (_) character.

Another important concept relating to classes is objects. An *object* refers to a created instance of a class, whereas a class only refers to the definition. Typically, an instance of a class must be created before the class can be used. Consider the following code fragment.

```
MyClass myObject = new MyClass();
myObject.OutputMyMessage();
```

In this case, an instance of the MyClass class is created as an object, named myObject. Now that myObject exists in memory, we can call the OutputMyMessage() method, which is attached to the object named myObject.

There are some exceptions, of course. A class can also have one or more static methods and properties. They can be called or referenced directly without creating an object instance of the class. In our preceding simple program, the Main() method is declared with the keyword static. Therefore, we could make the following method call without first creating an object instance.

MyClass.Main();

Methods

Methods perform specific tasks. A method can be defined to perform any logical function you require. In our simple program, the OutputMyMessage() method is tasked with outputting a message to the screen. It accomplishes this task with a call to another method, named Writeline(), that belongs to the Console class.

The Main() method, however, is a special method. It is automatically called when the program is started. In fact, the Main() method will always be the entry point of your program, since it is where the program control starts. It must be declared as static and can have either a void or int return type. The Main() method is where you create objects and call other methods. In this case, the Main() method simply calls our other method, OutputMyMessage().

Private Fields

Private fields of a class typically refer to the internal data values that the class stores. In the preceding sample program, a variable of data type string is created, named Name. Fields can include native data types, enumerations, and even instances of other classes. In the C# programming language, the most common way to expose a private data field to other code elements is to create a public property.

private string Name = "";

Public Properties

Public properties provide a clean and consistent method for accessing private class data. Properties are simply an extension to private fields. Unlike fields, properties do not designate storage locations. Instead of setting an object's private field directly, a property defines accessor methods to provide a layer of abstraction. Other code can then use those accessor methods to get or set the class data.

```
public string ProgramName
{
  get { return Name; }
  set { Name = value; }
}
```

The accessor method of a property contains the executable statements associated with getting or setting the property. The accessor methods include a get accessor, a set accessor, or both. The get accessor is similar to a method and returns a value of the property type. The set accessor is similar to a method that returns void. It uses an implicit parameter called value, whose type is the type of the property. When you assign a value to the property, the set accessor is automatically invoked with an argument that provides the new value.

The Language Keywords

Now that we have an overview of the structure of a C# program, let's take a closer look at specific language elements. Every language has a collection of reserved keywords that the compiler can use to interpret the program's logic. The XNA Game Studio code editor does a great job of color coding all the different programming elements to make the code more readable. Keywords, for example, appear in blue.

abstract	event	new	struct
as	explicit	null	switch
base	extern	object	this
bool	false	operator	throw
break	finally	out	true
byte	fixed	override	try
case	float	params	typeof
catch	for	private	uint
char	foreach	protected	ulong
checked	goto	public	unchecked
class	if	readonly	unsafe
const	implicit	ref	ushort
continue	in	return	using
decimal	int	sbyte	virtual
default	interface	sealed	volatile
delegate	internal	short	void
do	is	sizeof	while
double	lock	stackalloc	
else	long	static	
enum	namespace	string	

Table 5.1. A summary of C# language keywords.

As expected, keywords cannot be used as identifiers, such as variable or method names, in your program. Technically, you can overcome this limitation by including @ as a prefix. For example, @private is a legal identifier, but private is not because it is a keyword. However, it is generally bad practice to use a keyword as an identifier since it quickly can lead to confusion when reading the code. You can always use keywords as part of a valid variable name, such as privateName and publicName. Table 5.1 summarizes the keywords that are reserved by the C# programming language.

The Language Operators

In addition to keywords, C# language also provides a large set of functional operators. These are symbols that specify which operations to perform within a logical expression. C# defines the most common arithmetic and logical operators, as shown in Table 5.2. In addition, you can overload these operators to change their meaning and behavior as they apply to specific classes.

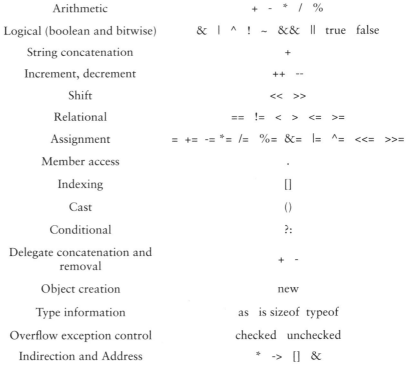

Arithmetic	+ - * / %
Logical (boolean and bitwise)	& | ^ ! ~ && || true false
String concatenation	+
Increment, decrement	++ --
Shift	<< >>
Relational	== != < > <= >=
Assignment	= += -= *= /= %= &= |= ^= <<= >>=
Member access	.
Indexing	[]
Cast	()
Conditional	?:
Delegate concatenation and removal	+ -
Object creation	new
Type information	as is sizeof typeof
Overflow exception control	checked unchecked
Indirection and Address	* -> [] &

Table 5.2. Summary of C# language operators.

Working with Data

Unlike Javascript or TorqueScript, the C# programming language is a strongly typed language. This means that a variable declared as type integer can only store an integer value. Conversely, typeless languages allow a generic variable to store either an integer or a string value.

Creating Variables

Essentially, variables represent storage locations, and every variable has a data type that specifies what kind of values can be stored in the variable. Local variables can be declared within classes and methods. A local variable is defined by specifying a data type and a name, along with an optional initial value.

```csharp
using System;

class Test
{
        static void Main()
        {
                int a;
                int b = 1;
                int c, d = 1;
        }
}
```

In this case, four variables of type integer are created. You can declare a variable with or without an initial value. However, a variable must be assigned to a value before it can be used. You can also declare multiple variables in one statement, as is done for c and d.

A type conversion enables a variable of one data type to be treated as another data type. Conversions can be either implicit or explicit. Consider the following code fragment.

```csharp
int a = 123;
long b = a; //an implicit conversion from int to long
int c = (int) b; //an explicit conversion from long to int
```

In this case, the conversion from type int to type long is implicit, so expressions of type int can implicitly be treated as type long. The opposite conversion, from type long to type int, is explicit, so an explicit cast is required. Some implicit type conversions are already defined by the C# language, and explicit type conversions are very common.

Creating Reference Data Types

C# also differentiates between value data types and reference data types. As we have just seen, a value data type explicitly stores the value of a variable. A reference data type, however, stores a reference to an object. In this case, it is possible for two different variables to reference the same object. In concept, this is similar to pointers in the C++ programming language.

Reference data types are different from value data types. Although the variables of the value data types contain real data values, reference data types store only references to objects. With reference data types, it is possible for two different variables to reference the same object. In this case, changes by one reference variable would ripple over to the other reference variable. However, value data-type variables each have their own copy of the data, so it is not possible for the operations on one to affect the other. The following code illustrates this point.

```
using System;

class SimpleClass
{
        public int Value = 0;
}

class MyTestClass
{
        static void Main()
        {
                int valueType1 = 0;  //set a value type
                int valueType2 = valueType1;  //set a value type to match
                                              //the other value type
                valueType2 = 123;   //set a new value to this value type

                SimpleClass refType1 = new SimpleClass();
                SimpleClass refType2 = refType1; //set this reference type
                                                 //to match the other
                refType2.Value = 123; //change the referenced object

                Console.WriteLine("values: {0}, {1}", val1, val2);
                Console.WriteLine("refs: {0}, {1}", ref1.Value, ref2.Value);
        }
}
```

In this case, a variable of type int—named valueType1—is created and assigned a value of 0. Another variable of the same type is created—

valueType2—and it is assigned the same value as valueType1, which is still 0. Next, valueType2 is set to a new value of 123. Changing valueType2 to 123 does not affect the value of valueType1 because both local variables are of a value type and each has its own storage space.

However, this doesn't work with reference types. A new variable of type SimpleClass is created, named refType1. Next, another variable—refType2—is created and set to point to whatever refType1 is pointed to—in this case, an instance of SimpleClass. But, when refType2 changes a value, it affects the object that refType1 is also pointing to. The end result is that both refType1 and refType2 share the same value. The final output of this program is

values: 0, 123 refs: 123, 123

Language Conditional Expressions

Since most logic involves decision-making code, conditional expressions are very important. The two most commonly used conditional expressions are the *if-else* and *switch* statements. These statements are generally used to branch the flow of execution when logical decisions must be made.

The if-else Statement

The *if-else* statement selects a subsequent line of execution based on the value of a Boolean expression. If the expression is true, the first line is executed. If the optional else clause exists and the expression evaluates to false, then the second line is executed. After executing the if-else statement, control is passed to the next statement.

```
int x = 12;

if (x > 10)
      Console.Write("Statement_1");
else
      Console.Write("Statement_2");
```

In this case, if the variable, named x, has a value of 12, then Statement_1 will be outputted to the screen. However, if x had a value of 6, then Statement_2 would have been displayed. If the result of an if-else statement must execute more than one statement, then multiple statements can be placed into code blocks using curly braces ({ }).

```
if (x > 10)
{
      Console.Write("Statement_1");
```

```
        Console.Write("Statement_2");
    }
```

You can also nest multiple if-else statements within code blocks to finely select a specific condition.

```
if (x > 10)
{
    if (y > 20)
        Console.Write("Statement_1");
}
else
    Console.Write("Statement_2");
```

In this example, Statement_1 is displayed only if the x variable contains a value greater than 10 and the y variable is greater than 20. Another way to express this condition is group the two *if* statements together.

```
if (x > 10 && y > 20)
    Console.Write("Statement_1");
else
    Console.Write("Statement_2");
```

In this case, the AND (&&) operator tests to see if both conditions are true. If both statements within the if clause are true, then Statement_1 is output to the screen. You can also check to see if either statement is true using the OR (||) operator in the same manner.

The switch Statement

The *switch* statement is another control statement that handles multiple selections by passing control to one of the case statements within its body. Control is transferred to the case statement whose constant value matches the switch expression. The switch statement can include any number of case instances, but no two case constants within the same switch statement can have the same value. Execution of the statement body begins at the selected statement and proceeds until the jump-statement transfers control out of the case body.

```
using System;

class SwitchTest
{
    public static void Main()
    {
```

```
        Console.WriteLine("Coffee sizes: 1=Small 2=Medium
            3=Large");
        Console.Write("Please enter your selection: ");
        string s = Console.ReadLine();
        int n = int.Parse(s);
        int cost = 0;

        switch(n)
        {
                case 1:
                        cost += 25;
                        break;

                case 2:
                        cost += 50;
                        break;

                default:

                        Console.WriteLine("Invalid selection.
                            Please select 1, 2, or 3.");
                        break;
        }

        if (cost != 0)
                Console.WriteLine("Please insert {0} cents.",
                    cost);

        Console.WriteLine("Thank you for your business.");
    }
}
```

Notice that the jump-statement is required after each block, including the last block, whether it is a case statement or a default statement. Unlike the C++ switch statement, C# does not support an explicit fall-through from one case label to another.

If the switch expression does not match any constant expression, control is transferred to the statements that follow the optional default label. If there is no default label, control is transferred outside the switch.

Control Loops

Control loops simply repeat lines of execution as long as specific conditions are true. The most common control loops are the *do*, *for*, and *foreach* control loops. Although each version repeats lines of execution, the criteria that determine how they continue to loop are different.

The while Flow Control

The *while* statement executes a statement or a block of statements repeatedly until a specified expression evaluates to false. The while statement requires an expression that can be implicitly converted to bool or a type that contains overloading of the true and false operators. The expression is used to test the loop-termination criteria.

```
using System;

public class TestDoWhile
{
        public static void Main ()
        {
                int y = 0;

                while(y < 5)
                {
                        Console.WriteLine(y);
                        y = y++;
                };
        }
}
```

The do-while Flow Control

The *do-while* statement also executes a statement or a block of statements repeatedly until a specified expression evaluates to false. Unlike the while statement, the body loop of the do-while statement is executed at least once regardless of the value of the expression.

```
using System;

public class TestDoWhile
{
        public static void Main ()
        {
                int y = 0;

                do
                {
                        Console.WriteLine(y);
```

```
                                    y = y++;
                       } while(y < 5);
            }
   }
```

The foreach Flow Control

The *foreach* statement repeats a group of embedded statements for each element in an array or an object collection. The foreach statement is used to iterate through the collection to get the desired information, but it should not be used to change the contents of the collection to avoid unpredictable side effects.

```
foreach( EnemyUnit enemy in AiEnemies )
{
       Position p = enemy.GetPosition();
}
```

- **The iteration variable that represents the collection element.** If the iteration variable is a value type, it is effectively a read-only variable that cannot be modified.

- **Object collection or array expression.** The type of the collection element must be convertible to the identifier type. Do not use an expression that evaluates to null.

- **Evaluates to a type that implements IEnumerable or a type that declares a GetEnumerator method.** In the latter case, GetEnumerator should either return a type that implements IEnumerator or declares all the methods defined in IEnumerator.

The embedded statements continue to execute for each element in the array or collection. After the iteration has been completed for all the elements in the collection, control is transferred to the next statement following the foreach block.

Arrays and Collections

Sometimes it's not enough to just store a single variable. If you need to store data in a series, then an array or collection really comes in handy. Both objects can store large amounts of tabular data, and each has its own special methods to access that data.

Working with Arrays

An array is a data structure that contains a number of variables, called elements. The array elements are accessed through indexes. C# arrays are zero indexed—that is, the array indexes start at zero. All of the array elements must be of the same type, which is called the element type of the array. Array elements can be of any type, including an array type. An array can be a single-dimensional array or a multidimensional array.

Single-dimensional arrays are very easy to define. The following code declares an array of five integers and an array of ten strings.

```
int[] simpleArray = new int [5];
string[] simpleStringArray = new string[4];
```

The integer array contains the elements from simpleArray[0] to simpleArray[4], whereas the string array contains the elements simpleStringArray[0] to simpleStringArray[3]. The operator new is used to create each array and initialize the array elements to their default values.

It is possible to initialize an array upon declaration. You do not need to specify the size of the array because it is already supplied by the number of elements in the initialization list.

```
int[]simpleArray = new int[] {1, 3, 5, 7, 9};
string[] simpleStringArray = new string[] {"John","Paul","George",
    "Ringo"};
```

Now, both arrays are create and initialized with meaningful values at the same time. It is possible to declare an array variable without initialization, but you must use the new operator when you assign an array to this variable.

```
int[] simpleArray;
simpleArray = new int[] {1, 3, 5, 7, 9}; // OK
simpleArray = {1, 3, 5, 7, 9}; // Error
```

Arrays can also hold both value data types and reference data types. In the preceding examples, integer and string value data types were being stored into the array. But when working with arrays of value types, you need to be careful about the data being passed around.

```
SimpleClass refType1 = new SimpleClass();
SimpleClass refType2 = refType1;  //set this reference type to match the
                                  //other

SimpleClass[] valueArray = new SimpleClass[10];
SimpleClass[] referenceArray = new SimpleClass[10];
```

The result of this kind of array assignment varies, depending on whether the contained object is a value type or a reference type. If it is a value type, then the assignment results in creating an array of 10 instances of the type SimpleClass. If it is a reference type, the assignment results in creating an array of 10 elements, each initialized to a null reference.

Arrays can also be passed around as method parameters. You can pass an initialized array to a method, like any other variable. You can also initialize and pass a new array in one step.

```
WorkOnThisArray( simpleArray );
WorkOnThisArray ( new int[] {1, 3, 5, 7, 9} );
```

You might come across the need to store data in a multi-dimensional array. The following code fragment will create an array with 10 rows and 5 columns. Next, an integer value of 100 is stored in the cell (0,20).

```
int[,] multidimArray = new int[10,5];
myArray[0,20] = 100;
```

Initializing a multi-dimensional array is very similar to initializing a basic array. The following statements show two different ways to initialize the array. The first statement uses the new operator and can explicitly set the dimensions.

```
int[,] multidimArray = new int[,] { {1,2}, {3,4}, {5,6}, {7,8} };
int[,] multidim2Array = { {1,2}, {3,4}, {5,6}, {7,8} };
```

If you choose to declare an array variable without initialization, you must use the new operator to assign an array to the variable, such as the following.

```
int[,] multidimArray;
multidimArray = new int[,] {{1,2}, {3,4}, {5,6}, {7,8}}; // OK
multidimArray = {{1,2}, {3,4}, {5,6}, {7,8}}; // Error
```

Sharing Data between Classes

Good coding practice should steer you toward creating modular, reusable code. This means that your game's functionality should be spread out among multiple classes rather than be bundled together in a single class. As result, you will often need to pass data back and forth between classes, and the C# language provides many ways to accomplish this.

Creating Class Properties

Class properties, as we have seen earlier in this chapter, are the easiest way to share data with other classes and methods. When you create a property accessor, any other code can access a class's private data as a member of the class.

```
class Class1
{
```

```
        private int _secretNumber = 5;

        public string SharedNumber
        {
                get { return _secretNumber; }
                set { _secretNumber = value; }
        }
}

class Class2
{
        Class1 myObject = new Class1();
        Console.WriteLine("The secret number is:" + myObject.
            SharedNumber );
}
```

As you can see, the second class has access to the first class's private data by means of a property named SharedNumber. This is probably the easiest way to share data, but it has a limitation: only one value can be accessed at a time.

Passing ref and out Parameters

Accessing one property at a time can be a real pain, especially when it comes to method calls. You may want a method to perform a task and then return two or more values as result. One solution to this situation is to declare a reference parameter.

```
class PlayerPosition
{
    int xPosition = 10;
    int yPosition = 10;
    int zPosition = 10;

    public void GetPosition( ref int x, ref int y, ref int z )
    {
      x = xPosition;
      y = xPosition;
      z = zPosition;
    }
}

class TestClass
{
```

```
public static void Main()
{
    int GetX = 0;
    int GetY = 0;
    int GetZ = 0;

    PlayerPosition pos = new PlayerPosition();
    pos.GetPosition( ref GetX, ref GetY, ref GetZ );
    Console.WriteLine( "x=" + GetX + " y=" + GetY + " z=" + GetZ );
}
}
```

In this case, the PlayerPosition class has three values we are interested in: the X, Y, and Z coordinates of a player. If we create properties to expose these three values, we would have to call this class three times to get each property individually. So, for faster access, we can create a method, such as GetPosition().

The GetPosition() method is different from the other methods we have covered. Instead of having values passed into the method, values will be passed out of the method. This is because the parameters are designated as reference parameters using the keyword ref. Essentially, this method is receiving a reference to the parameter's storage location. When the GetPosition() method assigns a value to this parameter, it is actually changing the originally created variable. A method can mix normal parameters with ref parameters as needed.

Note that in the sample code, each parameter passed into the GetPosition() method was first initialized to 0. An out parameter works exactly like a ref parameter, except that they can accept uninitialized data. This way, a variable can be declared and passed directly into the method.

Creating Interfaces

Sometimes you need to have a consistent way to interact with multiple classes. For example, if you have a variety of vehicles in your game, you might want each vehicle class to have a common Go() method, Stop() method, and Turn() method. You might even want to enforce each vehicle class to have these methods so that you always know they can be called.

One way to enforce that a class has specific methods is to use inheritance. That is, make each vehicle class a descendant of a more basic GenericVehicle class. This way, if the GenericVehicle class has Go(), Stop(), and Turn() methods, then all the descendants of this class will also have those methods. The only problem is that you still need to implement some form of each method in the GenericVehicle parent class, even if you don't want to.

An even better way to enforce that a class has specific methods is to create an interface. An interface is a special class that essentially serves as a template for other classes. An interface is created like a class, complete with a name, a body and members. To create an interface, use the interface keyword instead of the class keyword. By convention, the name of an interface starts with an I.

```
interface IVehicle
{
    void Go();
    void Stop();
    void Turn(int Direction);
}
```

This code fragment declares a new interface, named IVehicle. We can use this interface to ensure that all types of vehicles will have a Go(), Stop(), and Turn() method. You can specify the return types and parameters for any interface method. To have a class implement an interface, add the interface name to the class declaration.

```
class Car : IVehicle
{
}
```

If you try to compile the Car class, the compiler will return an error indicating that the Go(), Stop(), and Turn() methods are not implemented. To successfully compile the code, you must flesh out those methods.

```
class Car : IVehicle
{
    public void Go()
    {
        //add the code to Go
    }

    public void Stop()
    {
        //add the code to Stop
    }

    public void Turn(int Direction)
    {
        //add the code to Turn
    }
}
```

Now everything should compile smoothly. A class may implement multiple interfaces by using a comma to separate the interface names and implementing the necessary methods. Interfaces don't only define methods; they can also contain properties, events, and indexers. Just remember that the interface itself does not provide any implementations for the members that it declares.

Creating Delegates

A delegate allows you to store a reference to a method. Once a delegate is assigned a method, it behaves exactly like that method. The delegate method can be used like any other method, with parameters and a return value. The delegate method can either be a static method or a class-member method. They are very similar to C++ function pointers and are typically used to specify the event handlers. A delegate is declared with any functional code. It is only declared to show what a properly formatted callback function must look like. It simply provides the template for a method, just as an interface provides a template for a class. The delegate reveals the required return type and argument list for a method.

An interesting and useful property of a delegate instance is that it does not know or care about the classes of the methods it encapsulates; all that matters is that those methods are compatible with the delegate's type. This makes delegates perfectly suited for "anonymous" invocation.

Delegate types in C# are name equivalent, not structurally equivalent. Specifically, two different delegate types that have the same parameter lists and return type are considered different delegate types. However, instances of two distinct but structurally equivalent delegate types may compare as equal. The following example declares a delegate.

```
//define the delegate signature
delegate int OnCollide(int i, double d);


//create a test class
class Program
{
    static void Main()
    {
        Console.ReadKey();
    }
}
```

After declaring a delegate, remember that it only provides the template for a method, not an actual implementation for the method. To use it, you must define a separate method to perform the functionality that has the same return type and parameter list. With such a method implemented, you can assign it to the delegate. To use the delegate, create an instance of the delegate, and using the new operator, pass the name of the delegate handler—in this case, Ship1.DestroyShip.

```
//define the delegate signature
delegate void OnCollide(int i, double d);


//create a test class
class Program
{
    static void Main()
    {

        OnCollide collisionHandler = new OnCollide(Ship1.DestroyShip);

        //call the delegate method
        collisionHandler(10, 10);

        Console.ReadKey();
    }
}

class Ship1
{
    //implement the delegate handler
    public static void DestroyShip(int a, double b)
    {
        Console.WriteLine("BOOOOM!!!");

        return;
    }
}
```

You can also declare a delegate that returns a value. When defining a method that would be associated with the delegate, remember that the method must return the same type of value.

You can also combine multiple delegates handlers using the + and += operators. Similarly, a delegate can be removed from a list of delegates, using the - and -= operators. Together, the set of delegate handlers encapsulated by a delegate instance is called an invocation list. When a delegate instance is created from a single method, it encapsulates that method, and its invocation list contains only one entry. The following example adds an additional event delegate to show explosion effects along with the ship's destruction.

```csharp
//define the delegate signature
delegate void OnCollide(int i, double d);


//create a test class
class Program
{
    static void Main()
    {

        OnCollide collisionHandler = new OnCollide(Ship1.DestroyShip);
        collisionHandler += Ship1.ShowExplosion;

        Console.ReadKey();
    }
}

class Ship1
{
    //implement the delegate handler
    public static void DestroyShip(int a, double b)
    {
        Console.WriteLine("BOOOOM!!!");

        return;
    }

    //implement the end game delegate handler
    public static void ShowExplosion(int a, double b)
    {
        Console.WriteLine("* * * SPARKLES * * *");

        return;
    }
```

Now, when the event delegate is called, both delegate handlers will be triggered. The handlers are triggered in the order in which they are added to the delegate. The Torque X Framework makes heavy use of delegates, especially to process events within components, such as collisions. As you create your game, you will be writing your own delegate handlers to events, such as OnCollision.

Creating Events

An event is an action that occurs on an object and affects it in a way that its clients must be made aware of. An event is declared like a pseudo-variable, only based on a delegate. Therefore, to declare an event, you must have a delegate that would implement it. To actually declare an event, you use the event keyword. The attributes factor can be a normal C# attribute. The modifier can be one or a combination of the following keywords: public, private, protected, internal, abstract, new, override, static, virtual, or extern.

```
public static event OnCollide(int i, double d);
```

The event keyword is required, and it is followed by the name of the delegate that specifies its behavior. If the event is declared within a class, it should be made static. Like everything else in a program, an event must have a name. This allows the clients to know which event occurred. After declaring the event, you must define a method that calls the event.

```
//call the delegate methods
OnCollide(10, 10);
```

When the event occurs, its delegate is invoked. When an event occurs, the method that implements the delegate is called. This provides complete functionality for the event and makes the event ready to be used. Before using an event, you must combine it with the method that implements it. This can be done by passing the name of the method to the appropriate delegate, as we learned when studying delegates. You can then assign this variable to the event's name using the += operator. Once this is done, you can call the event.

Summary

In this chapter, we discussed the C# programming language. We started with basic language concepts and finished off with complex class designs. In the next chapter, you will put your new C# knowledge to use by exploring the Torque X Framework. You'll get to know the core classes that make up the framework, and then you will be ready to start creating some real game functionality.

Exploring the Torque X Framework

6

This chapter introduces you to the key classes that make up the powerful Torque X Framework. With a solid understanding of these core classes, you will be able to use them to create new functionality that is specific to your game. Table 6.1 summarizes the Top 10 Framework classes we will concentrate on in this chapter.

TorqueObject	The parent class for any game object added to a scene
TorqueObjectType	Enables the grouping and categorization of TorqueObjects
TorqueObjectDatabase	Manages a collection of all TorqueObjects within the game
TorqueComponent	Adds game-related functionality to a TorqueObject
TorqueSafePtr	A reference pointer to a registered instance of TorqueObject
TorqueGame	The object container that abstracts all game functionality
T2DSceneGraph	The 2D scene graph containing all renderable scene objects
T2DSceneObject	Adds basic functionality for 2D game objects
T2DSceneCamera	The scene camera used by T2DSceneGraph
TorqueFolder	A logical group of TorqueObjects

Table 6.1. Top 10 Torque X Framework classes to know.

Creating a TorqueGame

The TorqueGame class encompasses all of the game functionality within Torque X. When you create a new game using Torque X, your first task is to create a new child class derived from TorqueGame. Fortunately, XNA Game Studio performs this step for you when you select a new project template.

```
public class MyGame : TorqueGame
{
    public static void Main()
    {
        // Create the static game instance.
        MyGame _myGame = new MyGame();

        // begin the game.  Further set-up is done in BeginRun()
        _myGame.Run();
    }

    static MyGame _myGame;
}
```

Your game's life begins when your TorqueGame-derived class is instantiated by the Main() method, which in turn instantiates a variable named _myGame to hold a new instance of the MyGame class. Once initialized, the Run() method is called. The MyGame derived class inherits a lot of functionality from the TorqueGame class, including access to the SceneLoader and the GraphicsDeviceManager, as well as several important methods, including Run, BeginRun, Initialize, LoadGraphicsContent, Update, BeginDraw, Draw, and EndDraw.

The Run() method is called to begin the game. It initializes the game loop and starts processing game events.

Take advantage of XNA Game Studio's code-refactoring functionality to rename classes, methods, and variables. For example, you can replace the stock class name Game to MyCoolGame. Simply left-click the mouse on the class name, and then right-click and select Refactor ➤ Rename. You can also preview all the changes before you commit them.

The BeginRun() method is called after the graphics device is created and before the game starts running. This is typically where game set-up tasks, such as loading the game level, are typically placed.

The Initialize() method is called after the graphics device is created before the LoadGraphicsContent() method.

The LoadGraphicsContent() method is called when graphics resources must be loaded. You can override this method to load game-specific graphics resources.

The Update() method is called when the game logic needs to be processed—typically before the draw method call.

The BeginDraw() method starts the drawing of a frame and is followed by Draw() and EndDraw().

Everything Is a TorqueObject

At the center of the Torque X Framework is the TorqueObject class. All game objects that appear in a scene, from the player and enemy units to projectiles and effects, are descendants of the TorqueObject class. Even the ball scene object presented in the Chapter 2 *XnaBreakout* game was really a T2DStaticSprite object, a child class to TorqueObject.

The TorqueObject class provides basic management services like the ability to be named or looked up by name or ID. To conserve memory, other code may point to a TorqueObject, using a TorqueSafePtr, and that pointer will be valid only as long as the referred TorqueObject is still alive. But, most importantly, TorqueObjects may contain one or more TorqueComponents. As you will soon see, TorqueComponents provide the real functionality behind scene objects.

Creating a TorqueObject

There are many different ways to create a TorqueObject for your game. The easiest way to create one is to open Torque X Builder, drag a material into the scene, and then save the level to a .txscene file. When the level data is loaded from the XML data file, each object is instantiated and becomes available for use. You can also accomplish the same task in code by creating an instance of the T2DSceneObject class, setting its properties, and then registering it with the TorqueObjectDatabase.

```
T2DSceneObject mySceneObject = new T2DSceneObject();
mySceneObject.Position = new Vector2(50, 50);
mySceneObject.Name = "SimpleTemplate";
TorqueObjectDatabase.Instance.Register(mySceneObject);
```

Creating a single-scene object with either code or Torque X Builder is fairly easy. However, if you want to create dozens or even hundreds of identical scene objects, then the most efficient approach is to use Templates.

Managing TorqueObjects with the TorqueObjectDatabase

As its name suggests, the TorqueObjectDatabase manages a collection of TorqueObjects. Every TorqueObject must be registered with the TorqueObjectDatabase before it can be used in a scene. Once a TorqueObject is registered, the scene graph becomes aware of it and can render it within in the scene.

```
T2DSceneObject objPlayer = new T2DSceneObject();
TorqueObjectDatabase.Instance.Register(objPlayer);
```

The TorqueObjectDatabase can be used to look up TorqueObjects by name or ID, along with any other class derived from TorqueBase.

```
T2DSceneObject objCar = TorqueObjectDatabase.Instance.FindObject
    <T2DSceneObject>("car");
```

When a TorqueObject is no longer needed within a scene, it can be unregistered from the TorqueObjectDatabase by setting its MarkForDelete property to true. Once unregistered, any TorqueSafePtr pointing to the TorqueObject becomes null. If the unregistered TorqueObject was marked poolable, then it is added back to the appropriate object pool.

Creating a TorqueObject from a Template

Many games create a lot of identical scene objects, ranging from scattered power-up objects to hordes of enemy units. Rather than creating countless scene objects and setting each of their individual properties, the most efficient way to create them is with a template.

With the template approach, you fully define one scene object, complete with all of its properties and components. Then, you mark it as a template either within code or within Torque X Builder under the Scripting rollout.

Creating a Template

A template for a scene object is really no different from a regular scene object. In fact, the only difference is that its IsTemplate property is set to true. Here is an example of a template created in code.

```
T2DSceneObject aTemplate = new T2DSceneObject();
aTemplate.Position = new Vector2(50, 50);
aTemplate.Name = "SimpleTemplate";
aTemplate.IsTemplate = true;
```

Without the last line of code, this would just create a normal scene object that would appear in a game. But now we have a template! And with this template, we can spawn hundreds of scene objects. Any object cloned from this template will be set to a position of 50, 50. However, it will not have any components, and all the other fields of T2DSceneObject will be set to their default values. You will need a lot more configuration code before you can do anything useful with the cloned objects. The point here is that the only thing special about a template in its definition is that the IsTemplate property is set to true.

Cloning a Template

When you want to create a scene object from a template, all you need to do is clone the template. The object returned by the clone will be identical to the template, except that it will not itself be a template. Since it is not a template, it can be registered with the engine. In code, this means a call to the Clone() method. Within Torque X Builder, you can use a Spawner object and point to the desired template.

Once you have the cloned object, you can position it appropriately within your game and then register it. The following code illustrates the process of finding a template, cloning it, changing a property, and then registering the clone.

```
T2DSceneObject enemyTemplate = TorqueObjectDatabase.Instance.
        FindObject<T2DSceneObject>("SimpleTemplate");

if (enemyTemplate != null)
{
        T2DSceneObject enemy = (T2DSceneObject) enemyTemplate.
            Clone();
        enemy.Position = new Vector2(20, 20);
        TorqueObjectDatabase.Instance.Register(enemy);
}
```

Note that we check to make sure the template is not null before we try to clone it. This is good practice because the template may not exist. If we did not check for null, the game would terminate while trying to clone the template. Another way to find a template object, although a more risky one, looks like this.

```
// unsafe way to find a template object
T2DSceneObject enemyTemplate =
    (T2DSceneObject)TorqueObjectDatabase.Instance.
    FindObject("EnemyTemplate");
```

This version works, but it has the downside that if the template object is found but is not the correct type for the cast, an exception will be thrown and the game will terminate. For this reason, it is advised that you use the parameterized version of FindObject when finding templates and other objects.

When cloning a template object, any data that are associated with an object are copied when the new version of the object is created. This could mean copying a lot of data. In those cases, it is a good idea to separate class data from instance data. This is especially true for data that is constant for all objects of this type versus data that just varies by instance. Simply put the class data in a separate object that can be referenced by all of the instances, so only a single reference to the data must be copied rather than all the data. This saves processing time and spares memory.

Working with Object Pooling

Torque X provides a mechanism for pooling objects for efficient reuse. Object pooling works only when the objects are cloned from a template. When multiple objects are created without using templates, then object pools are wasted and never used. Therefore, you should always clone to create new objects.

Object cloning only requires that you implement the CopyTo() method for all of your objects and components. The CopyTo() method copies all public properties that are not marked with the TorqueCloneIgnore attribute. If your CopyTo() method is missing some code, then an assert failure will appear, telling you what lines of code must be added.

If you choose to use object pooling, then you have to implement the IResetable interface for all of your objects and components. This way, the data can be properly initialized between uses of an object. You should also make sure that your objects are properly reset in the OnRemove() method and that your components are reset within the _ResetComponent() method. With these changes in place, all it takes to turn on object pooling is to set the Pool flag or the PoolWithComponents flag on your object.

You can also set the flag on some objects and not others to get fine-grain control over what objects are pooled. The difference between Pool and PoolWithComponents is that if Pool is set, then your object and components are stored in separate pools. When creating a new object, the object and components are retrieved from their respective pools and assembled like the object from which they are being cloned. The problem with this is that objects and the components can end up on opposite ends of memory, potentially causing poor CPU caching. If PoolWithComponents is set, then the objects and components are pooled together. The pool is on a per-template basis rather than a per-object type or per-component type basis. PoolWithComponents is typically the better choice.

Separating Objects by TorqueObjectType

The TorqueObjectType is an efficient and convenient way to mark objects for specific uses. For example, in a strategy game you might mark all of one side's units with one object type and all of the other side's units with a different object type so that the AI can easily tell friend from foe. Object types are also extremely important for collisions, since they allow you to control which objects can collide with each other. In this case, you might set the projectile objects so that they only collide with enemies, making friendly fire impossible.

A TorqueObjectType can be created from within Torque X Builder or dynamically in code. Using Torque X Builder, click on an empty area of the scene or press the Escape key if a scene object is selected. Next, click the Edit tab and then expand the Scene Data rollout. Finally, enter the name of a new object type and click the green Add button. In code, you can accomplish the same results with the following.

```
TorqueObjectType Unit = TorqueObjectDatabase.Instance.
    GetObjectType("unit");
TorqueObjectType Vehicle = TorqueObjectDatabase.Instance.
    GetObjectType("vehicle");
TorqueObjectType Destructible = TorqueObjectDatabase.Instance.
    GetObjectType("destructible");
```

The GetObjectType() method returns an object type from the TorqueObjectDatabase. If the specified object type does not already exist, this method creates a new type and registers it, always returning a valid object type to use.

Adding Object Types to a TorqueObject

The object database ensures that object type names are unique. The GetObjectType method will create a new TorqueObjectType the first time it sees a particular name, and it will return that same type every time it gets the same name. Object types have some simple operations defined for them.

Suppose we have some TorqueObjects named Helicopter, Tank, Soldier, and Hospital, as well as some useful object types, such as Unit, Vehicle, and Destructible. We can easily associate a TorqueObject with a type as follows.

```
Helicopter.ObjectType += Vehicle;
Tank.ObjectType += Vehicle;
```

We can also associate multiple object types to a single object using a couple of methods as follows.

```
Soldier.ObjectType += Unit;
Soldier.ObjectType += Destructible;

Hospital += (Building + Destructible);
```

Again, we can accomplish the same results from within Torque X Builder by selecting a scene object, clicking the Edit tab, expanding the Scripting rollout, selecting the registered object type, and then clicking the green Add button.

Evaluating a TorqueObject's Object Type

Object types aren't only created in code; they can be created from within Scene rollout and within Torque X Builder. So, it's important to have an easy way to get a registered TorqueObjectType. That's where TorqueObjectDatabase comes in again. Since it manages everything within the Torque X Framework, we can easily query it for our desired object type.

```
//get the EnemyUnit object type
TorqueObjectType typeEnemy =
    TorqueObjectDatabase.Instance.GetObjectType("EnemyUnit");

//create a new enemy object
T2DSceneObject objEnemy = new T2DSceneObject();
TorqueObjectDatabase.Instance.Register(objEnemy);

//set the object type of the enemy
objEnemy.ObjectType += typeEnemy;
```

In this example, a new object type is created, called typeEnemy. We're assuming that this type was created from within Torque X Builder. So instead of creating a new type, we query the TorqueObjectDatabase. Next, we create a new scene object, called objEnemy. After registering the new scene object with the database, we can set its object type to typeEnemy.

Finding TorqueObjects by Object Type

The scene graph can find objects based on their object type. All you need to do is create a TorqueObjectType that matches your search and then pass it to the scene graph's FindObject() method.

```
public List GetLocalEnemies()
{
        TorqueObjectType typeEnemy = TorqueObjectDatabase.Instance.
            GetObjectType("EnemyUnit");

        List listEnemies = new List();

        T2DSceneGraph.Instance.FindObjects(_sceneObject.Position,
            20.0, typeEnemy, (uint)0xFFFFFFFF, listEnemies);

        return listEnemies;
}
```

The FindObjects() method searches for scene objects in the scene graph that match certain parameters. The _sceneObject.Position parameter results in a search based on the position of the owning scene object. A list of scene objects is produced that match the specified object type and are within 20 units of the scene object's position.

Setting Collisions by Object Type

The T2DCollisionComponent exposes a property named CollidesWith that takes a TorqueObjectType value. This property determines which object types a scene object will collide with.

```
TorqueObjectType typeTarget =
    TorqueObjectDatabase.Instance.GetObjectType("ImpactArea");


MyCollidableObject.ObjectType += typeTarget;


Projectile.Collision.CollidesWith = typeTarget;
```

Introduction to TorqueComponents

As mentioned earlier, TorqueComponents are simply packaged elements of game functionality. In Chapter 2, we used the Physics, Collision, and WorldLimits components that come bundled with the Torque X Framework to add some basic game play functionality to the *XnaBreakout* game.

In the following chapters, we will create several additional components, ranging from movement components to weapon components to AI components. Each of these components will be designed to be as generic as possible to add functionality to a wide variety of games. As stated in Chapter 1, the ultimate goal of this book is to teach you how to think about coding game functionality as smaller, more reusable components. You will quickly find that the time you put into well-thought-out and well-designed components will be time well spent.

Code Aggregation versus Code Inheritance

Object-oriented languages, such as C++ and C#, promote the practice of inheritance. In this case, new functionality is added to an existing object by deriving a new class and adding the functionality there. Although this is a great way to evolve an object, it comes with some practical problems. For example, there might be interest in adding that new functionality to another object, such as Class B. In the worst case, the code is simply copied and pasted into the object B, resulting in duplicate code, and possibly duplicate bugs. In the best case, the new functionality is placed into yet another object, such as object C, and then object B inherits from object C. However, even in this case there can be ripple effects to any other class that inherits from object B. Over time, it becomes increasingly complicated to add new functionality to an existing class hierarchy.

An alternative approach is code aggregation. Instead of having objects subclass other objects to get new functionality, each object contains one or more components that provide the new functionality. The object becomes an aggregate of all the components. This way, you can create a vast library of new functionality, implemented in various components.

Component logic is easy to reuse among objects. In many cases, components can be added to the new objects, and they will work just fine. Component reuse can even be extended across different games. You can create a component library that is used from game to game, evolving with each use. That's what we've done with the stock Physics and Collision components in Chapter 2.

TorqueComponents Are Not XNA Components

It is important to know that the XNA Framework has its own concept of Components, outside of the Torque X Framework. Although they share a lot of similar concepts, they are completely different systems. Torque X components make it easier to add functionality to TorqueObjects. In XNA, XNA components make it easier for different vendors to provide subsystems that can be integrated into a single game.

Adding a Component to a TorqueObject in Torque X Builder

In Chapter 2, we put together a simple game by only associating Torque X components to various scene objects. We used stock components, such as the T2DPhysicsComponent, the T2DCollisionComponent, and the T2DWorldLimitComponent.

Adding a component to a scene object is as easy as going to the Edit tab, expanding the components rollout, and then choosing a component from the list and clicking the green Add button. Then it's a simple matter of entering values for the different component parameters.

Adding a Component to a TorqueObject in Code

Associating a Torque X component with a scene object is also easy to do dynamically in code. You could take this approach to add new functionality or special powers to a player when a power-up is collected.

```
T2DStaticSprite ball = new T2DStaticSprite();

ball.ObjectType = TorqueObjectDatabase.Instance.
    GetObjectType("ball");

ball.Components.AddComponent(new T2DPhysicsComponent());
ball.Components.AddComponent(new T2DCollisionComponent());
ball.Components.AddComponent(new T2DWorldComponent ());
```

This code begins by creating a TorqueObject-derived object—in this case, T2DStaticSprite. Next, TorqueObjectDatabase is used to set the new object to the ball scene object. Lastly, three components are added to the ball object's Components collection.

Anatomy of a TorqueComponent

Since most of your Torque X game development will revolve around creating and using multiple components, it's important to fully understand them. So, let's take a component and dissect it into its essentials. Figure 6.1 presents a general anatomy of a component to start with.

When you open the source code for any component, you will typically find it organized into regions of code. In .NET, code can be grouped into blocks that can be easily expanded and collapsed by mouse-click if it is positioned within the #region and #endregion code tags. The five most important elements are private fields, public properties, private methods, public methods, and static methods. Throughout this book, all components will be presented in this order for consistency.

Private fields are generally at the heart of a component. Typically, private fields are prefixed with an underscore (_) to indicate that it is internal to this component only. Private fields generally store the working data for the class instance. For example:

```
private string _username;
```

Public properties expose some, or all, private fields that we want to share with other code. Public properties usually have a more user-friendly name than "private fields." We can also control whether a property can be set (to change a field), get (to return a field), or both. One of the most important reasons for creating public properties is to expose component settings to Torque X Builder.

```
public string UserName
{
    get { return _username; }
    set { _username = value; }
}
```

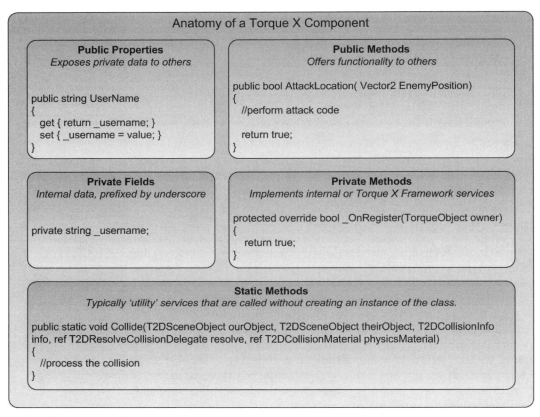

Figure 6.1. The anatomy of a Torque X component.

Private methods usually implement a lot of the internal plumbing for a component. Like private fields, private methods also have an underscore naming prefix. Half of the private methods simply fulfill the duties of a TorqueComponent descendant class, such as register and unregister with the Torque X Framework, register and return interfaces, and process built-in component events. The other half of the private methods will most likely implement internal utility functions and calculations to be used only by this component.

```
protected override bool _OnRegister(TorqueObject owner)
{
    return true;
}
```

Public methods are similar to public properties in that they expose functionality to other code. However, they are different from public properties in that they do not specifically wrap and expose private methods, and they are not visible to Torque X Builder.

```
public bool AttackLocation( Vector2 EnemyPosition)
{
    //perform attack code

    return true;
}
```

Static methods are a special variation of public methods and include the keyword static before their method name. Like public methods, they do expose a component's functionality to other code, but an instance of the component doesn't have to be created first. This comes with both advantages and disadvantages. Here's an example.

```
MyComponent obj = new MyComponent();
obj.MyValue = 1;
obj.DoSomething();
```

In this example, an instance of the MyComponent class is created and assigned to an object name obj. Next, we set a public property, named MyValue, and then call the public DoSomething() method. This is the most common use of a class. With static methods, however, we might see a case like this.

```
MyComponent.DoSomethingElse();
```

The DoSomethingElse() method is a static method and is called without ever really creating the MyComponent class. This is a great way for a component to offer functionality without the overhead of creating an object instance in memory. (We will use static methods a lot when we start creating event delegates, but more about that later.) The downside to using static methods is that they cannot access class instance data. For example, the DoSomethingElse() static method cannot access the MyValue property.

Other code regions will appear in TorqueComponent, but these five elements are really the most important to understand. Let's create a new component and dig even deeper into a component's makeup.

Creating a New TorqueComponent

The easiest way to create a component is from within XNA Game Studio. From the main menu, select Project ➢ Add New Item. Next, select the

T2DComponent template, enter a component name as shown in Figure 6.2, and then click the Add button.

XNA Game Studio creates the shell for an empty component using the filename you specified. As mentioned earlier, the code is organized into code regions, and by default, all regions are collapsed.

The Class Attribute

Class attributes are a new form of providing declarative information. In Torque X, they are frequently used to communicate instructions to Torque X Builder. Consider the following component class declaration.

```
[TorqueXmlSchemaType]
[TorqueXmlSchemaDependency(Type =
    typeof(T2DPhysicsComponent))]
public class MovementComponent : TorqueComponent, ITickObject
{
    //component code
}
```

The [TorqueXmlSchemaType] class attribute specifies that this class should be included in the Torque X schema export process, making this class accessible to Torque X Builder. This is important because a component that is missing the [Torque XmlSchemaType] attribute will not appear within Torque X Builder. The next class attribute, [Torque XmlSchemaDependency], indicates that this class depends on the existence of another component. In this case, the MovementComponent class depends on the T2DPhysicsComponent. If the T2DPhysicsComponent is not present, an Assert will be triggered.

Figure 6.2. Adding a new TorqueComponent to the project.

The Private Fields

As mentioned earlier, private fields are variables used internally by the component. You can have as many private data fields as you need, each declared as any data type you want. Their only limitation is that they are not exposed outside of this class, at least not without some help. A new component does not have any private fields to start with.

The Private Methods

Again, private methods are only exposed to other members of this class. You can add your own private methods to help accomplish the task of your component, or you can override the behavior of already existing private methods. A new component will include three private methods: _OnRegister(), _OnUnregister(), and _RegisterInterfaces(). These three methods are actually declared in the TorqueComponent parent class. But because most components need to implement custom functionality, they are served up to you with the help of the keyword override. This means that your instance of each method will be called instead of TorqueComponent's.

The _OnRegister Method

This method is automatically called when the scene object that owns this component is registered. Any initialization needed by your component should be done here. It is important to first call the base._OnRegister() method belonging to the parent TorqueComponent class and respect its return value.

```
protected override bool _OnRegister(TorqueObject owner)
{
    if (!base._OnRegister(owner) || !(owner is T2DSceneObject))
        return false;

    // todo: perform initialization for the component

    // todo: look up interfaces exposed by other components
    // E.g.,
    // _theirInterface = Owner.Components.GetInterface<ValueInterface
    //<float>> ("float", "their interface name");

    return true;
}
```

In a new component, this method first calls the version of the _OnRegister() method that belongs to the parent class and returns false if the base class returns false. Next, we can add our own component initialization code, such as getting an interface to another component, setting up device input, or kicking off a request for process ticks.

The _OnUnregister Method

This method is automatically called when the scene object that owns this component is unregistered. Any shutdown code that needs to be done by this component should be done here. Calling the _OnUnregister() method that belongs to the parent class should come last.

```
protected override void _OnUnregister()
{
    // todo: perform deinitialization for the component

    base._OnUnregister();
}
```

The _RegisterInterfaces Method

This method is also automatically called after the component has been registered. This is where you register your public interfaces into this class to support intercomponent data sharing. We will go into the details of creating interfaces and registering them in the coming chapters.

```
protected override void _RegisterInterfaces(TorqueObject owner)
{
    base._RegisterInterfaces(owner);

    // todo: register interfaces to be accessed by other components
    // E.g.,
    // Owner.RegisterCachedInterface("float", "interface name", this,
    // _ourInterface);
}
```

The Public Properties

Public properties are a powerful way to expose private fields. Because public properties are exposed to Torque X Builder, a level designer can easily adjust values and test changes to the game rather than change the code and recompile the entire game.

```
public T2DSceneObject SceneObject
{
    get { return Owner as T2DSceneObject; }
}
```

A new component only defines one property, named SceneObject. This property essentially takes its existing Owner property and converts it from a generic TorqueObject into a T2DSceneObject. By doing so, your component can now access more details about the scene object that owns it, such as its position, rotation, and so on.

You can create as many properties as you like and even control how they appear within Torque X Builder. For example, to set a default value for a property, add a [TorqueXmlSchemaType] property attribute.

```
[TorqueXmlSchemaType(DefaultValue = "Kork")]
public string PlayerName
{
        get { return _playerName; }
        set { _playerName = value; }
}
```

In this case, we define a property named PlayerName that exposes a private field named _playerName. We also have set a default player name to Kork.

The Public Methods

Several public methods appear within a new component class. The CopyTo() method is defined in the parent TorqueComponent class. The ProcessTick() and InterpolateTick() methods are defined in the ITickObject interface, which every new component implements by default.

The CopyTo Method

The CopyTo() method is automatically called when a scene object that owns this component is cloned. When cloned, all of the public properties that the Torque X Framework knows about are copied to the new scene object. Those that the Torque X Framework does not know about are not copied. This includes private fields and public properties with the [TorqueCloneIgnore] attribute set.

```
[TorqueCloneIgnore()]
public int PlayerNumber
{
        get { return _playerNumber; }
        set { _playerNumber = value; }
}

private string _playerName;
```

Any time you add a new property to a component, it's good practice to also add it to the CopyTo() method, just to be sure that the component can be perfectly cloned.

For these fields, the CopyTo() method offers a critical service to ensure that the new scene object that is cloned looks exactly like its source object. To make a perfect clone of one scene object to another, you must add your properties into the CopyTo() method.

```
public override void CopyTo(TorqueComponent obj)
{
        base.CopyTo(obj);
        NewComponent obj2 = obj as NewComponent;
        obj2.PlayerNumber = PlayerNumber;
        obj2._playerName = _playerName;
}
```

The ProcessTick Method

The ProcessTick() method is essentially the heartbeat of your component. When ticks are requested, this method is called by the Torque X Framework about 30 times per second to allow the component to update its state. This is where you can implement code that updates the position of the owning scene object. A component registers for process ticks by calling the AddTickCallback() method on the process list.

ProcessList.Instance.AddTickCallback(Owner, this);

This is usually done in the _OnRegister() method of a component. The tick callback for this component is associated with the owning scene object. Therefore, all components attached to a scene object will receive their tick callbacks at the same time.

You can also supply an optional third parameter, a priority, to specify the order in which this callback should occur, relative to other components for the owning scene object. If your component depends on a T2DPhysicsComponent, you might want to assign your component a lower priority to let the physics component process first. However, the most common case of this is when one object is mounted on top of another and you want the mounted object to be processed *after* the object to which it is mounted.

ProcessList.Instance.SetProcessOrder(Owner, SceneObject.MountedTo);

You can also change the priority level at any time with a call to the SetProcessOrder() method. A priority value of 1 will receive ticks first, whereas a priority of 0 will receive them last. By default, all components have a tick priority of 0.5.

The InterpolateTick Method

The Torque X Framework supports both constant and variable time updates. When a constant time update is used, we get the advantage of consistent behavior between different machines. For example, an update routine that is called 100 times per second will behave differently than when called 50 times per second. In fact, you can see this by manually reducing the game's time scale. Try adding the following code to the end of your game's Main() method.

Game.Instance._engineComponent.GameTimeScale = 0.3f;

Now, everything that moves within the scene seems to jump from point to point as time progresses. In between ticks, moving objects are not updated. The solution is to render frames between ticks. This is achieved with the InterpolateTick() method.

When the InterpolateTick() method is called, your component is responsible for interpolating between the last two ticks Usually, this only affects components that need to interpolate things like position and rotation. However, since the InterpolateTick() method is defined by the ITickObject interface, you need to include at least a stub method if you register for ticks.

Intercomponent Communication

Components talk to each other for many reasons. They usually need to work together to accomplish game-related tasks. For example, a projectile component can work with a collision component to determine when it has impacted something. And a projectile component might need to know some properties about the weapon component that fired it. Fortunately, the Torque X Framework addresses the need for intercomponent communication with a couple of key solutions: event delegates and value interfaces.

Calling Methods with Delegates

Delegates define a relationship between a calling entity and the implementation. Rather then defining an entire interface, a delegate defines a single method. The most common delegate this book implements is the T2DOnCollisionDelegate. This delegate, defined by the T2DCollisionComponent, lets you define your own method to respond to a collision. The T2DOnCollisionDelegate delegate is defined as follows.

```
public delegate void T2DOnCollisionDelegate(
        T2DSceneObject ourObject,
        T2DSceneObject theirObject,
        T2DCollisionInfo info,
        ref T2DResolveCollisionDelegate resolve,
        ref T2DCollisionMaterial physicsMaterial );
```

This delegate defines the signature for a callback method that can process the OnCollision event. We can create any method we want to process the onCollision event, as long as its method declaration matches the delegate. The T2DCollisionComponent will call our method when a collision occurs. Here's what our component's implementation might look like.

```
public static void ApplyDamage(
        T2DSceneObject myObject,
        T2DSceneObject theirObject,
        T2DCollisionInfo info,
        ref T2DResolveCollisionDelegate resolve,
```

```
                ref T2DCollisionMaterial physicsMaterial)
{
    //find the scene object's DamageManager component
    DamageManagerComponent enemyDamage =
        theirObject.Components.FindComponent
        <DamageManagerComponent>();

    if (enemyDamage != null)
    {
            enemyDamage.HitPoints--;

            if (enemyDamage.HitPoints <= 0)
            {
                    enemyDamage.MarkForDelete = true;
            }
    }
}
```

Here, we define a method, named ApplyDamage, with a signature that matches T2DOnCollisionDelegate. This example seeks out another component to adjust its damage levels and ultimately deletes it if it has run out of hit points. Now that we have a method that can receive the OnCollision event, we next need to map it to the T2DCollisionComponent. The easiest way to do that is to use Torque X Builder. But first, we need to expose this method as a delegate property as follows.

```
[Torque XmlSchemaType]
public static T2DOnCollisionDelegate Damage
{
    get { return ApplyDamage; }
}
```

Now the ApplyDamage method will become available as an OnCollision event handler, selectable within the T2DCollisionComponent inside Torque X Builder. By using the delegate model, we can create several collision handlers and select the most appropriate one for each scene object within the game.

Sharing Data with Value Interfaces

Another form of intercomponent communication is data sharing. The Torque X Framework shares data between components by means of value interfaces. By declaring a private field as ValueInPlaceInterface, a component can easily share that data with other components. By declaring a private field as a ValueInterface data type, a component can easily access data that is stored in another component.

The ValueInPlaceInterface Interface

When a private field is declared as a ValueInPlaceInterface, the actual storage space for the field is allocated with the declared component. In this case, the field acts as a server for the shared data.

```
ValueInPlaceInterface<float> _speed = new ValueInPlaceInterface<float>
    (0.0f);
```

After an interface is declared, it must be registered so that other components can find it. In the _RegisterInterfaces() method, add a call to the RegisterCachedInterfae() method. This will announce the availability of the interface.

```
protected override void _RegisterInterfaces(TorqueObject owner)
{
        base._RegisterInterfaces(owner);

        Owner.RegisterCachedInterface("float", "Speed", this, _speed);
}
```

In this case, the component's private field, _speed, becomes available to all other interested components, known as Speed.

The ValueInterface Interface

A ValueInterface represents the other side of the communication. A ValueInterface private field holds a reference to an interface obtained from another component. Since this interface is not InPlace, we know that the source of this value comes from another component. In this case, the field acts as a client accessing the remotely owned data.

```
ValueInterface<float> _speed;
```

To connect the local field with the other component, you must first initialize it within the component's _OnRegister() method. The local field must be assigned to the results of a GetInterface() method call to complete the connection.

```
protected override bool _OnRegister(TorqueObject owner)
{
        if (!base._OnRegister(owner) || !(Owner is T2DSceneObject))
                return false;

        speed = Owner.Components.GetInterface<ValueInterface<float>>
            ("float", "Speed");
        return true;
}
```

Now, when changes are made to the source component's _speed field, all connected components will have their local _speed fields automatically updated.

Summary

In this chapter, we learned about the Torque X Framework and the key classes that are used to make a game. Although the TorqueGame class creates and contains our game universe, the TorqueComponent-derived classes you create will implement the real game functionality. We also learned that when designed right, these components can be highly reusable among game projects. With that understanding, we examined the key elements of a TorqueComponent, including its public and private fields and methods. In the next chapter, we will start programming with Torque X game objects, beginning with Tilemaps. We'll create code that manipulates tiles to create a basic Tilemap game.

2D Game Programming

Programming with Tilemaps

7

The Torque X Framework includes powerful tools for working with 2D Tilemaps. As Chapter 3 revealed, Tilemaps make a great solution for rendering a collection of repeated graphics within a scene. Tilemaps are great for more than just classic platformer games. Many popular casual games can be implemented using Tilemaps. In this chapter, we will take a closer look at the Torque X Framework support for Tilemaps and put that knowledge to work by creating a variation of Alexey Pajitnov's classic game of *Tetris*.

Torque X Tilemap Framework

The Torque X Framework support for Tilemaps essentially spans across three key classes: T2DTileLayer, T2DTileObject, and T2DTileType. With these three classes, you can manipulate an entire tile layer and the tiles it contains.

Creating Tilemaps and Tiles

Tilemaps and tiles can be created in code or from within Torque X Builder. Naturally, it's much easier to create a Tilemap in Torque X Builder by dragging a new Tilemap object into the viewport and editing its properties within the Edit pane. However, there are cases in which you might want to create a new Tilemap or tile dynamically. After all, anything you can do within Torque X Builder, you can also do in code.

It's important to always remember that nearly everything in the Torque X Framework is a descendant of the TorqueObject class, including Tilemaps and tiles. As such, these two objects can be created, named, added to the TorqueObjectDatabase, assigned components, deleted, and even made into templates. Therefore, creating them is really no different from creating a simple sprite object.

```
//create the Tilemap
T2DTileLayer _tilemap = new T2DTileLayer();
_tilemap.Position = new Vector2(0, 0);
_tilemap.Name = "MyTilemap";
_tilemap.MapSize = new Vector2(4, 4);
_tilemap.Size = new Vector2(10, 10);
_tilemap.TileSize = new Vector2(5, 5);
```

This code fragment creates a new T2DTileLayer class object and then sets it to the center of the screen, at position (0, 0). Next, a name is assigned to the Tilemap so it can be easily found later by querying the TorqueObjectDatabase. Next, the size of the Tilemap is specified in terms of the number of rows and cells. The Size property specifies the width and height of the whole Tilemap, whereas the TileSize specifies the width and height of each cell. Unfortunately, we can't register a Tilemap that doesn't contain any tiles, so let's create some tiles.

```
T2DTileType _tileType = new T2DTileType();

_tileType.Material = TorqueObjectDatabase.Instance.FindObject
    <GarageGames.Torque.Materials.RenderMaterial>
    ("GGLogoMaterial");

T2DTileObject _newTile = new T2DTileObject();
_newTile.TileType = _tileType;

_tilemap.SetTileByGridCoords(0, 0, _newTile);
_tilemap.SetTileByGridCoords(0, 3, _newTile);
_tilemap.SetTileByGridCoords(3, 0, _newTile);
_tilemap.SetTileByGridCoords(3, 3, _newTile);

TorqueObjectDatabase.Instance.Register(_tilemap);
```

As you can see, creating a single tile takes a little more work because you need to specify a material to render. We can't create a T2DTileObject until we have a T2DTileType. Once created, assign the material for the T2DTileType to the GGLogoMaterial that comes with the StarterGame project template. Of course, you can always change the material name to point to any other material you have created within Torque X Builder. Next, we can create a new T2DTileObject and set its TileType object to the newly created type.

That's all there is to it. The next four lines set the four corners of the Tilemap to the new tile object, as shown in Figure 7.1. Notice that the Tilemap grid coordinates are zero-based, making the first column 0 and the last column 3. The last line registers the new Tilemap to the TorqueObjectDatabase so that it can be rendered to the screen.

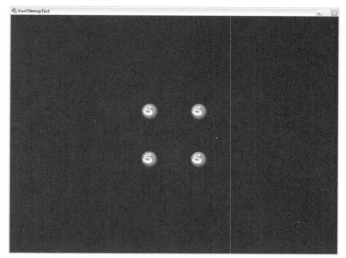

Figure 7.1. Creating a Tilemap and tiles from code.

Working with T2DTileLayer

Now that you have created a Tilemap, you can do a lot with it. The T2DTileLayer class provides a lot of functionality to retrieve individual tiles, as well as move and resize the entire Tilemap. The first task, however, is to get a reference to the Tilemap from the TorqueObjectDatabase.

```
T2DTileLayer tilemap =
    TorqueObjectDatabase.Instance.FindObject<T2DTileLayer>("My
    Tilemap");
```

Now we have a convenient way to access the Tilemap. You can use this reference to perform many common game functions, such as setting visibility, layer position, overall size, cell size, map dimensions, and so on. There are also a few methods available to get and set the individual tiles that are contained within the Tilemap.

```
T2DTileObject myTile = tilemap.PickTile (new Vector2 (2,2) ) ;
```

The PickTile() method returns the specific tile located at the exact world coordinates supplied. This is useful if you're using the position of another scene object, such as a player, to pick a specific tile.

```
T2DTileObject myTile = tilemap.GetTileByGridCoords (2,1);
```

The GetTileByGridCoords() method returns a tile located at specific grid coordinates, determined by column and row. Again, the grid is zero-based, so the preceding statement would return the tile in column 3, row 2. Conversely, you can set a tile by grid coordinates as well. The following code fragment essentially copies the tile in column 3, row 2 into column 1, row 3.

```
T2DTileObject myTile = tilemap.GetTileByGridCoords (2,1);
tilemap.SetTileByGridCoords (0, 2, myTile);
```

Working with T2DTileObject

The T2DTileObject class provides some limited functionality to manipulate individual tiles within a Tilemap. Many methods are available to get a tile's position within the world or parent Tilemap. You can also set the tile's appearance by changing its tile type or by flipping it horizontally or vertically.

In the last section, we found out how to pick an individual tile from an existing Tilemap, using the PickTile() method. The GetWorldPosition() method finds the world position of a tile's center within the supplied Tilemap. Again, the world origin for the Torque X 2D Framework is set as the center of the screen. The GetTileLocalPosition() method works similar to GetWorldPosition() but instead returns coordinates relative to the center of the Tilemap. Knowing the world position of individual tiles is helpful for setting the position of other scene objects. For example, you can move an explosion particle effect to the same position where a tile object is disappearing to create a more interesting disappearing act.

```
//get a reference to a specific tile in cell (2,2)
T2DTileObject myTile = tilemap.PickTile (new Vector2 (2,2) ) ;

//where in the world is this tile
Vector2  posWorld = myTile.GetWorldPosition (tilemap);

//where in the Tilemap is this tile
Vector2 posTileLayer = myTile.GetTileLocalPosition(tilemap);
```

As mentioned earlier, each individual tile has a tile type. You can change tiles within a Tilemap just by changing this tile type. The following example flips two tiles as you might find in a common match-3 game.

```
//get the tilemap
T2DTileLayer tilemapGame = TorqueObjectDatabase.Instance.
    FindObject<T2DTileLayer>("GameBoard");

//define the coordinates to swap
int CurrentPositionX = 0;
int CurrentPositionY = 0;
int ExchangePositionX = 1;
int ExchangePositionY = 1;

//identify tile types to swap
T2DTileType typePlaceHolder;

T2DTileType typeCurrent = tilemapGame.GetTileByGridCoords
    (CurrentPositionX, CurrentPositionY).TileType;
```

```
T2DTileType typeExchangeWith =
    tilemapGame.GetTileByGridCoords(ExchangePositionX,
    ExchangePositionY).TileType;

//perform the tile type swap
typePlaceHolder = typeCurrent;
typeCurrent = typeExchangeWith;
typeExchangeWith = typePlaceHolder;
```

In this example, we first get a reference to the Tilemap by name—in this case, GameBoard. Next, we create a few variables to define the coordinates for the two tiles we will swap. Those coordinates are passed into the GetTileByGridCoords() method to return a reference to a matching T2DTileObject. With the same method call, we append the get accessor to return the TileType for the returned tile. With references to both tiles to be swapped, we can use a placeholder to perform the swap.

Working with T2DTileType

An interesting point to remember about the last code fragment is that we did not swap references to each T2DTileObject. Instead, we just swapped their object types. Think of the T2DTileLayer as a simple container that has a grid of basic T2DTileObjects. The T2DTileObjects really only know about their position within the Tilemap and within the world, but they don't know about the actual tile data it contains. That's where the T2DTileType class comes in; it contains the interesting details about the tile.

> If you are switching a material with a TextureDivider used for celled images, you may need to call T2DTileLayer's UpdateVertexBuffer() method for the material to update its texture coordinates properly.

The T2DTileType class contains the two elements we care about the most: material and the collision polygon.

We can also associate a TorqueObjectType to a T2DTileType, just as we would for any other scene object. This lets you add code that tests the type of tile at a specific position. In the case of the prior tile swap example, we can add a check to see if the tile we are about to swap is a specific object type, such as objWall.

Between the T2DTileLayer, T2DTileObject, and T2DTileType classes, you have an amazing amount of control over Tilemaps within a game. Tilemaps can be as simple as background graphics or as complex as player-interactive elements of a game. In the next section, we'll demonstrate the latter by using Tilemaps to create a basic variation of the game *Tetris*.

Creating XnaTetris

Alexey Pajitnov's classic game of *Tetris* features a series of block shapes falling from the top to the bottom of the scene. The player can rotate and move the shapes to the left and right to position the shape into openings at the bottom of the scene. Each time a row is completed, it is cleared, and the player increases her score. If the stack of shapes reaches the top of the scene, the player loses. Advancing through the levels generally translates into shapes falling faster.

This type of game can be implemented in a variety of different ways. In Torque X we can use either sprites or Tilemaps. Working with sprites could get tricky, because some shapes are concave, but it is not impossible. We'll take the Tilemap approach so we can put our new knowledge of the Tilemap classes to work.

Begin by starting XNA Game Studio and creating a new game project, using the StarterGame project template. Set the name of the game to *XnaTetris*. After the project is created, start Torque X Builder and open the Game.txproj file in the *XnaTetris* project folder.

Creating the Game Level

Creating the *XnaTetris* game can be broken down into several key steps, some in Torque X Builder and some in code. First, we need to create the necessary artwork and then bring it into Torque X Builder. Next, we need to create the necessary game object types. Then, we'll need to create some reference shapes that we can clone at will and add a Spawner to create the clones. Then it's a simple matter of creating the well that contains the shapes and adding any desired background to brighten up the scene.

After wrapping up the Torque X Builder work, we're off to the coding. We need to spawn the new shape, respond to player input, move the shape, detect completed lines, and advance the game forward.

Importing the Tile Art

The first step to creating the *XnaTetris* game is to import all the necessary artwork. Create or download the individual tile images, and then drag them into Torque X Builder to import them as materials. The tiles simply look like square blocks as shown in Figure 7.2. We will use Tilemap objects to form these individual tiles into the necessary shapes, shown in Figure 7.3.

Figure 7.2. The basic tiles that make up the game.

Creating the Object Types

As mentioned earlier, the individual tiles within a Tilemap can be associated with a specific TorqueObjectType. This is helpful since we want to differentiate between the falling shapes and the game well that contains the shapes. From within Torque X Builder, open the Edit pane and deselect any scene object by pressing the Escape key. In the Scene Data rollout, enter "objPiece" in the Object Types field and then press the green Add button. Next, enter "objWell" and then press the green Add button.

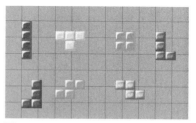

Figure 7.3. Creating shapes from the basic tiles.

Creating Reference Tilemaps

As shown in Figure 7.4, each game shape can be represented by a 4 × 4 Tilemap. From the Create pane in Torque X Builder, drag out a Tilemap shape into the scene. In the Edit pane, expand the Scripting rollout and then enter Tilemap1 for the Name and click the Template checkbox. Next, expand the Tile Map rollout and then enter a tile count of 4 for the X and Y values. Next, enter 3 for the Tile Size X and Y values. This will specify the correct size for the reference Tilemap. Press the Size Object to Layer button to apply the resizing. Finally, click the Edit Tile Layer button to start painting the Tilemap shape.

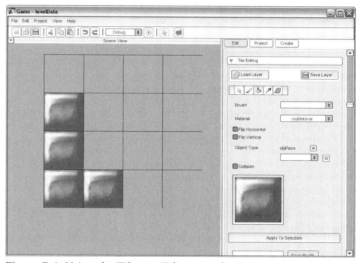

Figure 7.4. Using the Tilemap Editor to edit a game piece.

To start painting the Tilemap shape, choose a graphic from the Material listbox and add the objPiece object type. Next, use the brush tool to paint the tile shape. Repeat this process again to create all seven Tilemaps shown in Figure 7.3.

Creating the Game Well

After you have the seven game shapes created, you can start creating the game well, which will contain all of the falling blocks. Start by creating a new Tilemap with a dimension of 12 × 18 units. Set the individual cell size to 4 × 4. Next, set the Tilemap position to (0, 0). Finally, set the name of the Tilemap to TilemapWell in the Scripting rollout so that you can easily find this object in code.

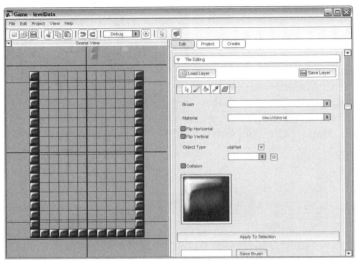

Figure 7.5. Creating the game well.

Now that a new Tilemap for the well exists, let's start painting the walls. Click the Edit Tile Layer button. Select the blackMaterial as the active material, and then add the objWell object type. Now, you're ready to start painting the walls as shown in Figure 7.5.

After you finish creating the well, press the Escape key to return to exit the Tilemap Editor mode. That's it for the basic game elements. You have seven shape reference Tilemaps and one well Tilemap. If you like, you can add a graphic to make the background more attractive; just remember to set its layer value to 30 and to disable collisions. Otherwise, it's time to start adding some game code.

After wrapping up the Torque X Builder work, we're on to the coding. We need to spawn the new shape, respond to player input, move the shape, detect completed lines, and advance the game forward.

Filling in the Code

There are many different ways to code a *Tetris*-style game. One way is to implement each falling piece as an individual game object, complete with its own collision. Another way is to have a set of reference Tilemaps and copy their representations into the well Tilemap. This approach better demonstrates the Torque X Framework's support for Tilemap coding, so we'll go this route.

This game can probably get away without implementing any new components. Components are great for reuse, but functionality we are about to add pretty much applies only to a *Tetris* game. So, we'll just add a series of methods directly into the Game.cs file and call them as needed. Let's start by adding a few private fields.

```
T2DTileLayer _wellTileLayer;
T2DTileLayer _currentShapeTileLayer;

T2DTileObject _clearTile;

int _currentX = 4;
int _currentY = 0;
```

```
int _currentTime;
int _moveInterval = 500;
int _numberOfShapes = 7;

List<int> _rowsCompleted = new List<int>();
```

The _currentShapeTileLayer field will hold a reference to the game piece currently falling, whereas the _wellTileLayer field holds a reference to the well itself. The _clearTile field will hold a reference to a blank tile that will be used when erasing cells within the well Tilemap. The _currentX and _currentY fields hold the current position of the falling shape. We also have some fields relating to game play that can be adjusted to make the game harder or easier. The _currentTime field will track how much time has elapsed since the last game update. The _moveInterval field defines when a game update should happen. A smaller number will make the game go faster, and a higher number will make the game go slower. The _numberOfShapes field will track how many unique pieces we have to pick from. Last, the _rowsCompleted list will help with the scoring and row completion logic.

Setting Up the Game

The game will be started with the BeginRun() method, which is automatically called by the XNA Framework.

```
protected override void BeginRun()
{
    base.BeginRun();

    SceneLoader.Load(@"data\levels\levelData.txscene");

    //set up the well tilelayer
    _wellTileLayer = TorqueObjectDatabase.Instance.FindObject
        <T2DTileLayer>("TilemapWell");

    _currentShapeTileLayer = TorqueObjectDatabase.Instance.FindObject
        <T2DTileLayer>("Tilemap1");

    _clearTile = _wellTileLayer.GetTileByGridCoords(1, 1);

    _SetupInputMap();
}
```

In the BeginRun() method we can accomplish some start-up tasks for the game. This method starts by loading the game level. Once the level is loaded, this method uses the TorqueObjectDatabase to get an object reference to the well Tilemap and one of the shape Tilemaps. Next, this method initializes a clear tile by pulling a known empty cell from the well Tilemap. Last, this method sets up an InputMap to capture the player input. Let's define that method next.

Processing Player Input

Clearly, our game needs a way to capture input from the player. We can create an InputMap object and associate it with the PlayerManager instance. Everything can be set up within a method that is called from the BeginRun() method.

```
private void _SetupInputMap()
{
    InputMap inputMap = PlayerManager.Instance.GetPlayer(0).
        InputMap;

    int gamepadId = InputManager.Instance.FindDevice("gamepad0");
    if (gamepadId >= 0)
    {
        inputMap.BindAction(gamepadId, (int)XGamePadDevice.
            GamePadObjects.LeftThumbX,
                TorqueInputDevice.Action.None, ProcessStickInput);

        inputMap.BindCommand(gamepadId, (int)XGamePadDevice.
            GamePadObjects.A, RotateClockwise, null);

        inputMap.BindCommand(gamepadId, (int)XGamePadDevice.
            GamePadObjects.B, RotateCounterClockwise, null);
    }

    // keyboard controls
    int keyboardId = InputManager.Instance.FindDevice("keyboard0");
    if (keyboardId >= 0)
    {
        inputMap.BindCommand(keyboardId, (int)Keys.Right, MoveRight,
            null);
        inputMap.BindCommand(keyboardId, (int)Keys.Left, MoveLeft,
            null);
        inputMap.BindCommand(keyboardId, (int)Keys.OemComma,
            RotateClockwise, null);
        inputMap.BindCommand(keyboardId, (int)Keys.OemPeriod,
            RotateCounterClockwise, null);
    }
}
```

In the _SetupInputMap() method, we start by creating the InputMap object. We'll add support for both keyboard and game-controller input. For the game controller, we'll use the left thumbstick to let the player move the falling game piece left or right. The game controller's A and B buttons will trigger the rotation of the falling shape. For the keyboard input, everything will be bound to keys. The next chapter explores in more detail the features of the input management framework in Torque X. Next, we need to implement the methods that perform the bound move and rotation actions.

Moving Tilemaps

Obviously, moving the falling game piece is a big part of the game. It will need to move left or right, based on the player input, and move downward as the game progresses. Therefore, we will create a separate method, called Move(), that performs the actual movement. The MoveLeft() and MoveRight() methods that are bound to the InputMap will call the new Move() method.

```
private void MoveLeft()
{
    if (isValidMove(-1, 0, _currentShapeTileLayer))
        Move(-1, 0);
}

private void MoveRight()
{
    if (isValidMove(1, 0, _currentShapeTileLayer))
        Move(1, 0);
}
```

We will also need a method that translates the analog stick input and translates it into specific MoveLeft() and MoveRight() method calls.

```
public void ProcessStickInput(float val)
{
    if (val == -1)
        MoveLeft();

    if( val == 1.0 )
        MoveRight();
}
```

Rotating Tilemaps

Another key function of a *Tetris*-style game is the ability to rotate the falling shape clockwise or counterclockwise. We are not simply rotating the Tilemap for our rotation code. Instead, we will perform a rotation by transposing individual tiles into new positions, based on the direction of rotation.

```
private void RotateClockwise()
{
  // Create a new rotated shape
  T2DTileLayer TempRotationShape = (T2DTileLayer)
    _currentShapeTileLayer.Clone();

  for (int x = 0; x < 4; x++)
  {
    for (int y = 0; y < 4; y++)
    {
      T2DTileObject tile = _currentShapeTileLayer.
        GetTileByGridCoords(3 - y, x);
      TempRotationShape.SetTileByGridCoords(x, y, tile);
    }
  }

  // is it in a valid location?
  if ( isValidMove(0, 0, TempRotationShape) )
  {
    Erase(_currentShapeTileLayer);
    _currentShapeTileLayer = TempRotationShape;
    Draw(_currentShapeTileLayer, "moving");
  }
}
```

The counterclockwise rotation works essentially the same, but it shifts the X component instead of the Y component.

```
private void RotateCounterClockwise()
{
  // Create a new rotated shape
  T2DTileLayer TempRotationShape = (T2DTileLayer)
    _currentShapeTileLayer.Clone();

  for (int x = 0; x < 4; x++)
  {
    for (int y = 0; y < 4; y++)
    {
```

```
            T2DTileObject tile = _currentShapeTileLayer.
                GetTileByGridCoords(y, 3-x);
            TempRotationShape.SetTileByGridCoords(x, y, tile);
        }
    }

    // is it in a valid location?
    if (isValidMove(0, 0, TempRotationShape))
    {
        Erase(_currentShapeTileLayer);
        _currentShapeTileLayer = TempRotationShape;
        Draw(_currentShapeTileLayer, "moving");
    }
}
```

Updating the Scene

The game must be updated regularly to smoothly move the game pieces. Later, you will create TorqueComponents that can request callback ticks. Ticks are update notifications that are sent every few milliseconds to advance the game. Although we're not creating a new component, the TorqueGame class, which our game class inherits from, does receive automatic Update calls. All we need to do is override the behavior of the Update method within our game class.

```
protected override void Update(Microsoft.Xna.Framework.GameTime
gameTime)
{
    base.Update(gameTime);

    // current scene time in miliseconds
    _currentTime += gameTime.ElapsedGameTime.Milliseconds;

    if(_currentTime > _moveInterval)
    {
        if (isValidMove(0, 1, _currentShapeTileLayer))
        {
            Move(0, 1);
        }
        else
        {
            //turn moving shape into fixed
            Draw(_currentShapeTileLayer, "fixed");
```

```
        //test for complete lines
        CheckCompleteLine();

        //move to next shape
        ChangeToNextShape();
    }

    _currentTime = 0;
  }
}
```

Our Update() method first calls the Update() method defined within the parent class. Next, we increment the elapsed time with the amount of time since this method was last called. If this elapsed time reaches our move interval, defined as 500 milliseconds with a private field, then determine if a move is valid. We will create another method called _isValidMove() to determine if a requested move is possible. If the move is possible, then we can call the Move() method. If not, then we can assume that the falling shape has finally reached the bottom. If the shape has reached the bottom, then we can mark it as fixed, check for completed rows, and move on to the next shape.

Drawing the Tilemaps

The next challenge is to draw the falling shape within the well Tilemap. Rather than using a Physics component to just move down a whole Tilemap object, we'll take the classic approach of drawing and erasing individual cells within the well Tilemap, based on another reference Tilemap, to simulate the falling shape, as shown in Figure 7.6.

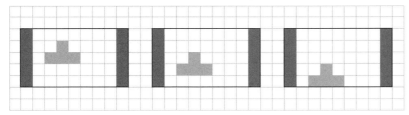

Figure 7.6. Representation of drawing a falling shape.

To simulate the effect of a shape falling down the well, we can create a method that looks at the reference shape and draws it into the well Tilemap at a given position. When the shape falls one block lower, we can erase the shape that has been drawn and then draw a new shape one block lower, as shown in Figure 7.6. To keep everything simple, we can wrap this function within a simple Move() method that takes the current X and Y positions of the shape.

```
    private void Move(int deltaX, int deltaY)
    {
        Erase(_currentShapeTileLayer);
```

```
    _currentX += deltaX;
    _currentY += deltaY;

    Draw(_currentShapeTileLayer, "moving" );
}
```

The Move() method depends on two additional methods: Draw() and Erase(). The purpose of the Draw method will be to take a reference shape and draw it into the well. It accomplishes this by cycling through each column and row of the reference shape and getting the tile object in the particular location. With the tile available, we can then determine the T2DTileType associated with the tile. Now it's an easy matter to assign that T2DTileType to the well Tilemap at a specific position.

```
private void Draw(T2DTileLayer map, string NewTileTypeName)
{
    T2DTileObject tile;

    // get a reference to the tilemap layer
    for (int x=0; x< 4; x++)
    {
      for ( int y=0; y<4; y++)
      {
        if (map.GetTileByGridCoords(x, y) != null)
        {
          tile = (T2DTileObject)map.GetTileByGridCoords(x, y).Clone();
          tile.TileTypeName = NewTileTypeName;
          _wellTileLayer.SetTileByGridCoords(x + _currentX, y +
            _currentY, tile);
        }
      }
    }
}
```

The Erase() method works pretty much the same way. We need to erase the current shape from the Tilemap before it can be drawn into its new position in the well. Otherwise, it would leave a visual trail. The Erase() method works almost exactly like the Draw() method, except that the well Tilemap is drawn with a reference to the _clearTile rather than a tile sampled from the reference shape.

```
private void Erase(T2DTileLayer map)
{
    // get a reference to the tilemap layer
    for (int x=0; x < 4; x++)
    {
```

```
    for (int y=0; y < 4; y++)
    {
      if (map.GetTileByGridCoords(x, y) != null)
        _wellTileLayer.SetTileByGridCoords(x + _currentX, y +
          _currentY, _clearTile);
    }
  }
}
```

The Move(), Draw(), and Erase() methods will position the falling shape anywhere we want, but it won't first check for collisions with the floor of the well or with other shapes. So, we'll need to add another method to check for valid moves.

Performing a Move Check

Determining if we can make a valid move is a tricky task. We need to check for collisions between the falling shape and well or other landed shapes. Since a shape that is falling will eventually become a landed shape at the bottom of the well, we will need a way to identify the shapes as being different. This is where the TileTypeName property can come in handy.

The isValidMove() method begins by creating variables set to the proposed location of the shape. Next, the method cycles through each column and each row and evaluates the well tile in the tested position. The first test determines if the tested tile is not null. Next, the method tests to see if the shape collides with the side walls of the game well. Next, the method checks to see if the new shape position collides with a landed tile shape, now marked as fixed. If none of these tests fail, then it is assumed that the shape is safe to move into the new location.

```
    private bool isValidMove(int deltaX, int deltaY, T2DTileLayer tileLayer)
    {
      int newX = _currentX + deltaX;
      int newY = _currentY + deltaY;

      for( int x = 0; x < 4; x++)
      {
        for( int y = 3; y >= 0; y--)
        {
          if ( tileLayer.GetTileByGridCoords(x, y) != null)
          {
            // check for collisions with the side walls of the well
            if ( newX + x <= 0 || newX + x >= _wellTileLayer.
              MapSize.X-1)
                return false;
```

```
            // does the block collide with an existing block
            T2DTileObject tile = _wellTileLayer.
            GetTileByGridCoords(newX + x, newY + y);

            if (tile != null)
            {
               if (tile.TileTypeName == null)
                  return false;

               if (tile.TileTypeName.CompareTo("fixed") == 0)
                  return false;
            }
         }
      }
   }

   return true;
}
```

Detecting Completed Rows

Now that we have shapes falling down into place and the player moving and rotating them to fit openings, we need to test for completed rows. The CheckCompleteLine() method does just that. It begins by scanning the well Tilemap from left to right, tile by tile. If there are any holes in a row or if a game piece is still falling, then the check fails. However, if a row is filled with pieces marked fixed, then the row is added to a list collection of completed rows. After the Tilemap scan is completed, a call to the EraseLines() method is made to remove the completed rows from the Tilemap and pull everything down.

```
private void CheckCompleteLine()
{
   for (int y = 0; y < 4; y++)
   {
      //assume we have a complete row
      bool rowComplete = true;

      for (int x = 1; x < _wellTileLayer.MapSize.X - 1; x++)
      {
         T2DTileObject tile = _wellTileLayer.GetTileByGridCoords(x,
            _currentY + y);

         if (tile == null || tile.TileTypeName == null || (tile.TileTypeName.
            CompareTo("fixed") != 0 &&
```

```
                tile.TileTypeName.CompareTo("moving") != 0))
        {
          rowComplete = false;
          break;
        }
      }

      if (rowComplete)
      {
        // add line to completed line list for later removal
        _rowsCompleted.Add(_currentY + y);
      }
    }

    if (_rowsCompleted.Count > 0)
    {
      //if we've completed any lines we need to award points

      // delete the lines that have been completed
      EraseLines();
    }
  }
```

The EraseLines() method tracks how many rows have been completed in order to drop the entire well contents by the correct amount. The method cycles through the List collection. The actual process of removing a line simply involves copying the contents of the row above the line being erased. However, we also need to account for cases in which multiple lines are deleted at once. In this case, we might need to copy rows even higher. That's where the dropBy variable comes in. This value indicates how much higher we need to copy a line.

```
private void EraseLines()
{
  // starting with the bottom complete line and working backward
  // we'll move all lines down by N place. Each time we reach a
  // complete line we move all subsequent lines down by N+1
  int dropBy = 0;
  int currentLine = _rowsCompleted[_rowsCompleted.Count - 1];

  while( currentLine >= 0 )
  {
    // if we're on a line that has been completed increase dropBy and
```

```
        // erase it
        if( _rowsCompleted.Contains(currentLine) )
        {
            // delete line
            for( int x = 1; x < _wellTileLayer.MapSize.X-1; x++)
                _wellTileLayer.SetTileByGridCoords(x, currentLine,
                    _clearTile);

            // remove line from toErase list
            _rowsCompleted.Remove(currentLine);

            // increase drop by
            dropBy++;
        }
        else
        {
            //shift the current line down by %dropBy number of lines
            for ( int x = 1; x < _wellTileLayer.MapSize.X-1; x++)
            {
                T2DTileObject tile = _wellTileLayer.GetTileByGridCoords(x,
                    currentLine);
                _wellTileLayer.SetTileByGridCoords(x, currentLine + dropBy,
                    tile);
                _wellTileLayer.SetTileByGridCoords(x, currentLine,
                    _clearTile);

            }
        }

        currentLine--;
    }
}
```

At the end of an update cycle, when a game piece has finally reached the bottom, we need to pick the next shape to start falling. The ChangeToNextShape() method accomplishes this by picking a random number between zero and the number of reference shapes available. Next, the method queries the TorqueObjectDatabase for the shape template that matches the random selection and sets that shape to the current shape reference. Finally, the current shape position is reset to the top of the well Tilemap, and the entire game update process starts again.

```
private void ChangeToNextShape()
{
    Random randomizer = new Random();
```

```
int nextShapeID = randomizer.Next(1, _numberOfShapes);
string nextShape = "Tilemap" + nextShapeID;
_currentShapeTileLayer = TorqueObjectDatabase.Instance.FindObject
    <T2DTileLayer>(nextShape);

_currentX = 4;
_currentY = 0;
}
```

Figure 7.7. Running the *XnaTetris* game.

That's it for the coding. Now it's time to rebuild the project and run. Figure 7.7 reveals our simple version of the game. Remember that you have a lot of ways to customize the game. You can make the blocks move faster or slower, add a next shape preview, and add a nice background image or scrollers.

XnaTetris is a fun way to test the flexibility of the Torque X Tilemap Framework. There is so much that you can do by organizing graphics into cells with custom collisions and object types.

Summary

In this chapter, we took a deeper look into the Torque X Framework support for Tilemaps. A lot of great functions are available to control the entire Tilemap or just the individual tiles it contains. We have so much control that we can fully implement a variation of the classic game of *Tetris*. In the next chapter, we will create a few player-specific components that can be used in many different types of games.

Creating a Robust
Player Object

8

Many games have some sort of on-screen representation of the player, whether it be a soldier, a vehicle, a spacecraft, or even a chomping yellow circle. For these types of games, the player-character is one of the most important game elements with many responsibilities. Some of these responsibilities include responding to player input, positioning the player on the screen, animating the player, and interacting with other game elements. This chapter takes a close look at these responsibilities and examines how they can be implemented with the Torque X Framework.

Responding to Player Input

The Torque X Framework provides several layers of input management. This multilayered solution offers a lot of flexibility and allows your code to interact with services ranging from low-level device events to high-level responses (Figure 8.1).

Device Input

The lowest layer of interaction is the device level input. These are low-level methods that interact with input coming into the Torque X Framework and generate input events. All input passes through the input system so it can journal the input and deterministically play it back later for debugging. It also makes all input, whether from a mouse, keyboard, or gamepad, look the same at the lowest level. This is useful, since it allows you to listen for input events and monitor all input coming into the system.

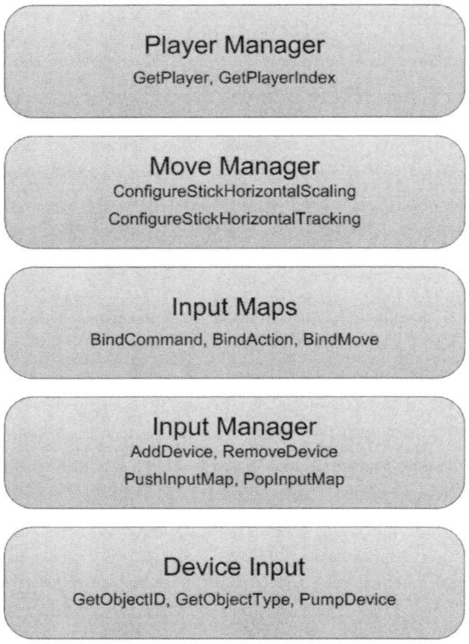

Figure 8.1. The layered input management of Torque X.

Input Manager

The next layer of interaction is the input manager. The input manager listens for all device input events and routes them to input maps and the GUI system. There is normally no need to interact with input within this layer.

Input Maps

Input maps are the first high-level layer of interaction that deals with input. Input maps allow you to easily map input events to specific callback methods. The MoveComponent that is packaged with every Torque X StarterGame template interacts with the component's owner using input maps. In this case, the input map is created within the _SetupInputMap() method, which is called by the _OnRegister() method when the component is first initialized.

```
// Get input map for this player and configure it
InputMap inputMap = PlayerManager.
Instance.GetPlayer(playerIndex).InputMap;

//keyboard controls
int keyboard = InputManager.Instance.
FindDevice(keyboard);

if (keyboard >= 0)
{
        //Mapping Arrow Keys

        inputMap.BindMove(keyboard, (int)Keys.Right, MoveMapTypes.
           StickDigitalRight, 0);
        inputMap.BindMove(keyboard, (int)Keys.Left, MoveMapTypes.
           StickDigitalLeft, 0);
        inputMap.BindMove(keyboard, (int)Keys.Up, MoveMapTypes.
           StickDigitalUp, 0);
        inputMap.BindMove(keyboard, (int)Keys.Down, MoveMapTypes.
           StickDigitalDown, 0);

        // Mapping WASD Keys
        inputMap.BindMove(keyboard, (int)Keys.D, MoveMapTypes.
           StickDigitalRight, 0);
        inputMap.BindMove(keyboard, (int)Keys.A, MoveMapTypes.
            StickDigitalLeft, 0);
```

```
    inputMap.BindMove(keyboard, (int)Keys.W, MoveMapTypes.
        StickDigitalUp, 0);
    inputMap.BindMove(keyboard, (int)Keys.S, MoveMapTypes.
        StickDigitalDown, 0);
}
```

First, an InputMap object is declared and initialized by the PlayerManager object. Next, the keyboard identifier is determined, in case multiple keyboards are connected. If a valid keyboard identifier exists, then the input map is filled with calls to the BindMove() method. Each call to BindMove() passes along the keyboard identifier, the key that is being mapped, the type of device move occurring, and the index of the stick, trigger, or button.

In addition to moving an object using keyboard keys, this component also accepts input from a connected gamepad.

```
int gamepadId = InputManager.Instance.FindDevice(gamePad);

if (gamepadId >= 0)
{
        inputMap.BindMove(gamepadId, (int)XGamePadDevice.
            GamePadObjects.LeftThumbX,
            MoveMapTypes.StickAnalogHorizontal, 0);

        inputMap.BindMove(gamepadId, (int)XGamePadDevice.
            GamePadObjects.LeftThumbY,
            MoveMapTypes.StickAnalogVertical, 0);

        inputMap.BindAction(gamepadId, (int)XGamePadDevice.
            GamePadObjects.Back, OnBackButton);
}
```

Again, we start by first finding the connected gamepad ID; it's more likely that there will be multiple gamepads connected. Next, we again call the BindMove() method, passing the gamepad ID as the first parameter. For the next parameter, we use an enumerated type to identify which gamepad input element was fired.

This code fragment illustrates another important method. The BindAction() method maps input to a specific class method. In this case, the _OnBackButton() method is called when the gamepad's Back button is pressed (Figure 8.2).

You can always create different input maps and push and pop them as you transition from one part of the game to another. The input map stack is kept on the input manager. If you wanted to push the above input map onto the stack, you would call the following.

Figure 8.2. An Xbox 360 gamepad.

InputManager.Instance.
PushInputMap(inputMap);

When you want to remove input map, even while others have been pushed in the meantime, you would call this.

InputManager.Instance.
PopInputMap(inputMap);

Move Manager

Input maps provide a nice high-level mapping for input events to actions. But we want to connect the movement of a game object to input. The MoveManager provides an even higher level of interaction that translates device input into on-screen player movement. You simply create an input map that maps to the MoveManager and then associate your game object with the MoveManager. Then, you configure the MoveManager to perform the type of move you want and let it remap keyboard input to stick input as needed.

```
// Get input map for this player and configure it
InputMap inputMap = PlayerManager.Instance.GetPlayer(playerIndex).
    InputMap;

int gamepadId = InputManager.Instance.FindDevice(gamePad);

if (gamepadId >= 0)
{
    //bind the thumbsticks
    inputMap.BindMove(gamepadId, (int)XGamePadDevice.
        GamePadObjects.LeftThumbX,
        MoveMapTypes.StickAnalogHorizontal, 0);

    inputMap.BindMove(gamepadId, (int)XGamePadDevice.
        GamePadObjects.LeftThumbY,
        MoveMapTypes.StickAnalogVertical, 0);

    inputMap.BindMove(gamepadId, (int)XGamePadDevice.
        GamePadObjects.RightThumbX,
        MoveMapTypes.StickAnalogHorizontal, 1);

    inputMap.BindMove(gamepadId, (int)XGamePadDevice.
        GamePadObjects.RightThumbY,
        MoveMapTypes.StickAnalogVertical, 1);
```

```
        //bind the buttons
        inputMap.BindMove(gamepadId, (int)XGamePadDevice.
            GamePadObjects.A, MoveMapTypes.Button, 0);

        inputMap.BindMove(gamepadId, (int)XGamePadDevice.
            GamePadObjects.B, MoveMapTypes.Button, 0);

        inputMap.BindMove(gamepadId, (int)XGamePadDevice.
            GamePadObjects.X, MoveMapTypes.Button, 0);

        inputMap.BindMove(gamepadId, (int)XGamePadDevice.
            GamePadObjects.Y, MoveMapTypes.Button, 0);
}

//keyboard controls
int keyboard = InputManager.Instance.FindDevice(keyboard);

if (keyboard >= 0)
{
        //Mapping Arrow Keys
        inputMap.BindMove(keyboard, (int)Keys.Right, MoveMapTypes.
            StickDigitalRight, 1);
        inputMap.BindMove(keyboard, (int)Keys.Left, MoveMapTypes.
            StickDigitalLeft, 1);
        inputMap.BindMove(keyboard, (int)Keys.Up, MoveMapTypes.
            StickDigitalUp, 1);
        inputMap.BindMove(keyboard, (int)Keys.Down, MoveMapTypes.
            StickDigitalDown, 1);

        // Mapping WASD Keys
        inputMap.BindMove(keyboard, (int)Keys.D, MoveMapTypes.
            StickDigitalRight, 0);
        inputMap.BindMove(keyboard, (int)Keys.A, MoveMapTypes.
            StickDigitalLeft, 0);
        inputMap.BindMove(keyboard, (int)Keys.W, MoveMapTypes.
            StickDigitalUp, 0);
        inputMap.BindMove(keyboard, (int)Keys.S, MoveMapTypes.
             StickDigitalDown, 0);
}
```

First, the code binds the gamepad thumbsticks to the MoveManager, and the same is done for the keyboard. Now, the move manager will generate moves that have the thumbsticks and keyboard bound to sticks on the move. The MoveMapTypes enumerator specifies which element of the gamepad is bound. Typically, the choice is between an analog or digital binding. A thumbstick is an analog device that provides a continuous range of values, so it is bound using analog mapping. A button and keyboard key are digital devices, either up or down, so it is bound using a digital mapping. The keyboard and thumbstick are both mapped to a move a virtual "stick."

After you have set up the MoveManager to generate moves signals the way you want them, you can receive moves. To receive moves, your component needs to receive tick callbacks. Any component can request ticks by calling the AddTickCallback() method from within the component's _ OnRegister() method.

```
ProcessList.Instance.AddTickCallback(Owner, this);
```

The ProcessTick() method becomes the recipient of MoveManager updates. If no input was detected from the gamepad and keyboard, then the Move object will be null. However, if input was detected, then the Move object will indicate which input was recorded.

```
public void ProcessTick(Move move, float elapsed)
{
    if (move != null)
    {
        // set our test object's Velocity based on stick/keyboard //
        // input
        _sceneObject.Physics.VelocityX = move.Sticks[0].X *
            20.0f;
        _sceneObject.Physics.VelocityY = -move.Sticks[0].Y *
            20.0f;
        if (move.Buttons[1].Pushed)
            _myMethod1();
        else if (move.Buttons[2].Pushed)
            _myMethod2();
        else if (move.Buttons[3].Pushed)
            _myMethod3();
        else if (move.Buttons[4].Pushed)
            _myMethod4();
    }
}
```

In this case, the component checks for a valid Move object. When one arrives, this code takes the recorded value from move.Sticks[0], which was mapped to the left thumbstick. This value is multiplied and set to a property of the attached Physics component to result in acceleration in the X or Y direction, moving the owned game object. Similarly, this code checks for button presses. Depending on which button is pressed, a class method is called to take action in response. These buttons could map to weapon selections, special moves, and so on.

You have a lot of control over how your game receives input from devices, such as a gamepad. This can help you fine-tune the sensitivity of the input controls and their impact on your game. The MoveManager is used to configure the gamepad and keyboard inputs. Analog input to a move stick can be rescaled by setting a function curve on it. The following code configures the MoveManager to square the input on the horizontal stick.

```
float [] scalevalues = { 0, 0.25f, 1.0f };
MoveManager.Instance.ConfigureStickHorizontalScaling(0,scalevalues);
```

The ConfigureStickHorizontalScaling() method receives specific X-Y coordinates (0, 0), (0.5, 0.25), and (1, 1). They are used to scale the input. You can supply more than three values in the scale function. If you supplied four values, then the X coordinates assumed would be 0, 0.33, 0.66, and 1.0.

Similarly, you can configure how long it takes a button press to change the move stick tracked by the MoveManager.

```
float [] rampUpValue = null;
float rampUpTime = 0.25f;
float [] rampDownValue = {1, 0.25, 0 };
float rampDownTime = 0.5f;

MoveManager.Instance.ConfigureStickHorizontalTracking( 0,
    rampUpTime, rampUpValue, rampDownTime, rampDownValue );
```

This code tells the MoveManager to take 0.25 second to move the stick all the way in one direction or another. No curve is supplied for the ramp-up value, so it is done linearly. It takes a half-second to return the stick to the center position. Since we pass in a ramp-down function, we can see that in half this time (a quarter-second), we should return almost the entire way, from 1.0 to 0.25, and that over the next quarter-second we'll return the rest of the way to 0.

Using the PlayerManager Class

The PlayerManager class saves you the work of binding a MoveManager to an input map, configuring the MoveManager, and associating it with a game object.

```
// Set playerObject as the controllable object
PlayerManager.Instance.GetPlayer(playerIndex).ControlObject =
    playerObject;
```

```
// Get input map for this player and configure it
InputMap inputMap = PlayerManager.Instance.GetPlayer(playerIndex).
    InputMap;

// Get MoveManager for this player and configure it
MoveManager moveManager =
    PlayerManager.Instance.GetPlayer(playerIndex).MoveManager;
```

With the PlayerManager, you don't have to worry about how the input map, MoveManager, and the player object interact. Simply set the input map on a player in the PlayerManager. You can either use the one that initially exists for that player or set your own. Setting the control object on a player object makes that object the recipient of that player's moves.

The PlayerManager also provides a convenient place to associate data with players in the game. You can associate data directly with the player.

```
String name;
PlayerManager.Instance.GetPlayer(0).SetData("score",1000);
PlayerManager.Instance.GetPlayer(0).GetData("name", out name);
PlayerManager.Player player = PlayerManager.Instance.
    GetPlayer(killedObject);

if (player != null)
{
    // our player was killed...decrement lives and respawn
    int lives;
    player.GetData("lives",out lives);
    player.SetData("lives",--lives);

    if (lives>0)
            RespawnPlayer(player);
    else
            GameOver(player);
}
```

Positioning the Player On the Screen

Now that we can capture player input from a keyboard or gamepad, we need to translate that into the action of moving the player around on the screen. As we just reviewed, the existing basic MovementComponent simply slides its owner around the screen, using a velocity value. Depending on the type of game you are creating, you will probably need more player-movement capability.

Setting the player's orientation on-screen in response to input depends heavily on the type of game you are creating. In a classic side-scroller game, the player typically faces only left or right, depending on the input. Conversely, in a top-down game, the player typically faces any rotational angle, depending on the input.

Vertical and Horizontal Orientation

A very simple method of setting player orientation, commonly found in classic platformer games, such as *Defender*, is sprite flipping. The Torque X Framework has the capability of horizontally and vertically flipping static and animated sprites with a property. The ProcessTick() method defined earlier can be modified to orient the player as follows.

```
public void ProcessTick(Move move, float elapsed)
{
        if (move != null)
        {
                // set our test object's Velocity based on stick/keyboard /
                // input
                _sceneObject.Physics.VelocityX = move.Sticks[0].X *
                    20.0f;
                _sceneObject.Physics.VelocityY = -move.Sticks[0].Y *
                    20.0f;

                //horizontally flip a sprite
                if (move.Sticks[0].X < 0)
                        _sceneObject.FlipX = true;
                else
                        _sceneObject.FlipX = false;

                //vertically flip a sprite
                if (move.Sticks[0].Y < 0)
                        _sceneObject.FlipY = true;
                else
                        _sceneObject.FlipY = false;
        }
}
```

The flipping effect works only for a sprite or animation that can be flipped and still looks right. In *Defender*, the ship looks great facing left or right. However, it looks strange when flipped upside down. For cases like this, it might be better to use an animation that represents the player, or ship, in all different orientations. We'll cover this condition with a single-state animation shortly.

Rotational Orientation

Aside from simply flipping a sprite or animation, another method of setting the orientation of a player is to rotate it. This approach was used in popular games like *Asteroids*, and it works for most games that offer an overhead look of the world. The following code differs from the preceding example in that we use the scene object's Rotation property instead of its FlipX/Y properties.

```
public void ProcessTick(Move move, float elapsed)
{
    if (move != null)
    {
        _sceneObject.Rotation += (move.Sticks[0].X * 10.0f);

        //get a vector from the current angle of the ship
        Vector2 direction = T2DVectorUtil.VectorFromAngle
            (_sceneObject.Rotation);
        _sceneObject.Physics.VelocityX = direction.X * (move.
            Sticks[0].Y * 20.0f);
        _sceneObject.Physics.VelocityY = direction.Y * (move.
            Sticks[0].Y * 20.0f);
    }
}
```

Input is driven by a mapped thumbstick to set the rotation and forward movement of the scene object. Rotation is specified by the left and right movement of the stick, along the X-axis. Since the value returned from the input manager will be a floating point number between −1.0 and +1.0, we take that number and multiply it by a factor of 10 and assign it as the incremental angle of rotation. So, if an object was currently rotated to 30 degrees and the player slams the stick to the far right, the input manager may send back a value between 0.0 and 1.0. If the returned value is 0.5, then this code will rotate the scene object 10 degrees clockwise:

0.5 input × 10.0 unit scalar + 30 degrees currently = 35 degrees.

Rotating the game object is the easy part. The next step is to move the ship forward. To do that, we need to know the object's current angle of rotation and then translate that into a Vector. The T2DVectorUtil has a lot of great methods that convert angles to vector and back. The VectorFromAngle() method takes the new angle of our object and returns a two-dimensional Vector. And now that we have an X and Y component, we can multiply the forward thrust of the thumbstick by a multiplier of 20 units to get the resulting X and Y velocities.

Animating the Player

Player objects that are animated function similarly to their static sprite counterparts. In fact, there are a couple of different ways to use animations to represent the player's current state. One way is to use one single animation file to represent different viewing angles of the player and then just change the displayed frame based on different actions—for example, a car that banks as it makes turns.

Another way to use animations is to have several animation files to represent the motion of the player from different angles, such as a running animation, a jump animation, an idle animation, and so on. Both approaches have their merits, depending on the type of game you are making.

In the preceding code sample, letting go of the stick brings the game object to an immediate stop. To get the idea of the effect of *Asteroids*, consider using the ApplyImpulse() method instead of setting velocities.

```
_sceneObject.Rotation += (move.
    Sticks[0].X * 10.0f);
Vector2 direction;
direction = T2DVectorUtil.
    VectorFromAngle(_sceneObject.
    Rotation);
direction.X *= move.Sticks[0].Y * 2.0f;
direction.Y *= move.Sticks[0].Y * 2.0f;
_sceneObject.Physics.
ApplyImpulse(direction);
```

Single-State Animation

A single-state animation uses an animation to represent different positions of an object without cycling through the animation frames. An equivalent approach would be to have several static sprites in memory and swap out each sprite image for each pose. Using an animation instead, however, is more efficient and easier to manage in code. In Figure 8.3, a simple animation depicts a car that is banked to the left in cell 0, then level in cell 1, and then banked to the right in cell 2. We'll use these different positions of the car to make it look like the car us responding to turns by banking.

We start by adding the graphic to the project as a new material. In the Create pane, expand the Materials rollout and double-click the new car material to open the Material Builder. Click the Animation checkbox, set the Cell Count X to 3 and Cell Count Y to 1, and then click the Save button. In the Create pane, click the Create a New Animation button and choose the carMaterial. Click the green Add button, set the Frames Per Second to 1, and then click the Save button. Now you can add the car animation to the scene.

That's all the Torque X Builder changes for now; time to switch over to the code. Instead of creating a new component, this example will simply modify the existing MovementComponent that comes with the StarterGame template. Add the following line.

```
T2DAnimatedSprite _animation;
```

Figure 8.3. A simple banked car animation.

This component will only apply to animations, and the _animation variable will act as our reference point into this component's owner animation. Next, change the _OnRegister() method to properly set up this component.

    Assert.Fatal(_sceneObject is T2DAnimatedSprite,
        "Alert: Component not attached to T2DAnimatedSprite.");

    _animation = _sceneObject as T2DAnimatedSprite;

    _animation.PauseAnimation = true;

Since this component only works with T2DAnimatedSprites, adding an Assert will generate an error if the component is accidentally attached to a scene object other than animation object. It is better to fail an assert than to generate an unhandled exception at runtime. Then, this code initializes the recently added T2DAnimatedSprite variable so that it can easily access all of the T2DAnimatedSprite properties and methods. Finally, set the PauseAnimation property to true. We don't want the normal animation controller to set which frame is visible. Instead, we'll leave that to the user input.

Since the AddTickCallback() method was already added to the _OnRegister() method for this component, we know this component is receiving ticks. So, the next step is to modify the ProcessTick() method to take the user input and update the player animation state.

```
public void ProcessTick(Move move, float elapsed)
{
    if (move != null)
    {
        if (move.Sticks[0].Y != 0)
        {
            _sceneObject.Rotation += (move.Sticks[0].X * 2.0f);

            //get a vector from the current angle of the ship
            Vector2 direction = T2DVectorUtil.VectorFromAngle(
                _sceneObject.Rotation);
            _sceneObject.Physics.VelocityX = direction.X * (move.
                Sticks[0].Y * 20.0f);
            _sceneObject.Physics.VelocityY = direction.Y * (move.
                Sticks[0].Y * 20.0f);

            if (move.Sticks[0].X > 0)
                _animation.SetAnimationFrame(0);
            else if (move.Sticks[0].X < 0)
                _animation.SetAnimationFrame(2);
            else if (move.Sticks[0].X == 0)
                _animation.SetAnimationFrame(1);
        }
    }
}
```

The ProcessTick() method is where everything comes together. First, we check to make sure that a valid move structure was received and that there is movement on the Y-axis of the thumbstick. The only reason for checking the Y-axis of the thumbstick is that it wouldn't make sense to rotate a car if it wasn't already moving forward or backward.

The next task is to set the rotation of the car. The code should be familiar from the *Asteroids*-like rotational orientation code presented earlier. The only difference is that the multiplier is set to 2.0 instead of 20.0 to better match a car's turning ability. Otherwise, the same principles of forward thrust are applied by creating a directional vector and multiplying the stick value by a multiplier.

The last task is to set the static animation frame. In this case, it's fairly easy. If the stick value is greater than zero, then the car is turning right, and we need to set the current animation frame to 0. If the stick value is less than zero, then the car is turning left, and we need to set the animation to frame 2. Otherwise, if there is no stick input—a value of zero—then set the level car state, frame 1.

You can easily add more animation frames that show more degrees of banking and even some frames with the car dipping due to a hard stop. Just compare the stick value, or even button values, and map them to ranges that translate into different frames.

Multistate Animations

Single-state animations can certainly add some interest that a static sprite can't. However, an even more interesting character is one that seems alive with many different animations that reflect different movements, such as running, jumping, and sitting idle. Naturally, accomplishing this is a little more involved but not too much. It starts with the animation graphics. Figure 8.4 illustrates a small collection of animations that feature Kork running in different directions.

An animation set like this can be created in many ways. Some people use 2D art tools, such as *Mirage Studio* and *ToonBoom*, to create 2D vector images that are tweened. I prefer to create a 3D animated model and use a tool, such as *SpriteForge*, to take snapshots of the character in various poses of the animation. Or, you can simply hand-draw each animation cell using classic onion-skinning techniques. In any case, you need to end up with a single graphic file that contains all the animation cells. Once you have that, you can drag the file into Torque X Builder to create a material and then use the Animation Editor to create a useful animation, as shown in Figure 8.5. Once you have an animation ready to use, drag one into the scene to represent your player character—ideally an idle animation. That's it! Now it's time to switch over to the code.

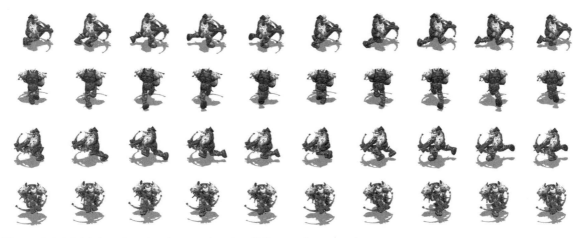

Figure 8.4. Multiple animation frames showing different player motions.

Having multistate animations for characters is probably something that is highly reusable for other parts of your game and a great candidate for a component. Open XNA Game Studio, and add a new T2DComponent, named AnimatedCharacterComponent. Add the following private fields to the component's source.

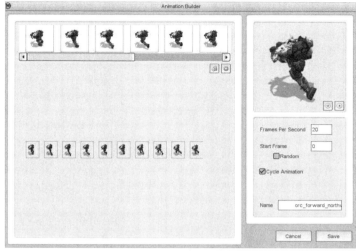

Figure 8.5. Defining a player motion animation.

```
private T2DSceneObject
  _sceneObject;
private T2DAnimationData
  _animNorth;
private T2DAnimationData
  _animNorthWest;
private T2DAnimationData
_animWest;
private T2DAnimationData _animSouthWest;
private T2DAnimationData _animSouth;
private T2DAnimationData _animSouthEast;
private T2DAnimationData _animEast;
private T2DAnimationData _animNorthEast;
```

These private fields will hold the animation data for the different animations we are interested in. In this case, each animation refers to a forward-walking movement in a specific direction; north represents up, south represents down, east represents right, and west represents left. If your game requires other character animations, simply add more T2DAnimationData fields. Next, we need to expose those private fields to Torque X Builder by means of public properties.

```
public T2DAnimatedSprite AnimatedSprite
{
   get { return Owner as T2DAnimatedSprite; }
}

public T2DAnimationData AnimNorth
{
   get { return _animNorth; }
   set { _animNorth = value; }
}
public T2DAnimationData AnimNorthWest
```

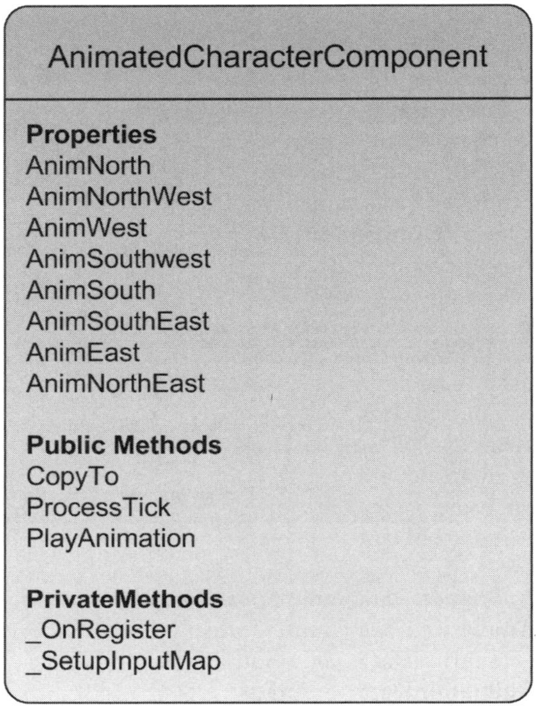

Figure 8.6. The AnimatedCharacterComponent diagram.

```
{
    get { return _animNorthWest; }
    set { _animNorthWest = value; }
}
public T2DAnimationData AnimWest
{
    get { return _animWest; }
    set { _animWest = value; }
}
public T2DAnimationData AnimSouthWest
{
    get { return _animSouthWest; }
    set { _animSouthWest = value; }
}
```

```
public T2DAnimationData AnimSouth
{
  get { return _animSouth; }
  set { _animSouth = value; }
}
public T2DAnimationData AnimSouthEast
{
  get { return _animSouthEast; }
  set { _animSouthEast = value; }
}
public T2DAnimationData AnimEast
{
  get { return _animEast; }
  set { _animEast = value; }
}
public T2DAnimationData AnimNorthEast
{
  get { return _animNorthEast; }
  set { _animNorthEast = value; }
}
```

Adding these public properties is going to make this component very easy to interact with. When you edit this component within Torque X Builder, all available animations will appear in a friendly drop-down list. This results in a significantly faster level design. And since we have so many private fields, it's a great idea to include them in a CopyTo() method so that we can set up one character and then clone many more without having to set all their individual properties.

```
public override void CopyTo (TorqueComponent obj)
{
        base.CopyTo(obj);

        AnimatedCharacterComponent obj2 = obj as
        AnimatedCharacterComponent;
        obj2._animNorth = _animNorth;
        obj2._animNorthWest = _animNorthWest;
        obj2._animWest = _animWest;
        obj2._animSouthWest = _animSouthWest;
        obj2._animSouth = _animSouth;
        obj2._animSouthEast = _animSouthEast;
        obj2._animEast = _animEast;
        obj2._animNorthEast = _animNorthEast;
}
```

The added assignments to the CopyTo() method will ensure that the cloned objects are exactly the same. Next, let's update the _OnRegister() method with a couple of necessary steps.

```
protected override bool _OnRegister(TorqueObject owner)
{
        if (!base._OnRegister(owner) || !(Owner is T2DSceneObject))
                return false;

        // retain a reference to this component's owner object
        _sceneObject = owner as T2DSceneObject;
        _SetupInputMap(_sceneObject, 0, "gamepad0", "keyboard");

        // tell the process list to notify us with ProcessTick and
        // InterpolateTick events
        ProcessList.Instance.AddTickCallback(Owner, this);

        return true;
}
```

This method is similar to the _OnRegister() method for the standard MovementComponent, since it needs to do the same thing. After ensuring that this is a valid component, this method associates the owner of the component with a specific data type. Then, this method calls _SetupInputMap to map out the user input. Finally, this method requests ticks with a call to the AddTickCallback() method. With ticks coming in, we can fill out the ProcessTick() method.

```
public void ProcessTick(Move move, float elapsed)
{
    if (move != null)
    {
        if ((move.Sticks[0].X > 0) && (move.Sticks[0].Y > 0))
        {
            PlayMyAnimation (_animNorthEast);
        }
        else if ((move.Sticks[0].X > 0) && (move.Sticks[0].Y < 0))
        {
            PlayMyAnimation (_animSouthEast);
        }
        else if ((move.Sticks[0].X < 0) && (move.Sticks[0].Y > 0))
        {
            PlayMyAnimation (_animNorthWest);
        }
        else if ((move.Sticks[0].X < 0) && (move.Sticks[0].Y < 0))
```

```
        {
            PlayMyAnimation (_animSouthWest);
        }
        else if (move.Sticks[0].X > 0)
        {
            PlayMyAnimation (_animEast);
        }
        else if (move.Sticks[0].X < 0)
        {
            PlayMyAnimation (_animWest);
        }
        else if (move.Sticks[0].Y > 0)
        {
            PlayMyAnimation (_animNorth);
        }
        else if (move.Sticks[0].Y < 0)
        {
            PlayMyAnimation (_animSouth);
        }
        else
        {
            AnimatedSprite.PauseAnimation = true;
        }
        // set our test object's Velocity based on stick/keyboard input
        _sceneObject.Physics.VelocityX = move.Sticks[0].X * 25.0f;
        _sceneObject.Physics.VelocityY = -move.Sticks[0].Y * 25.0f;
    }
}
```

Since the ProcessTick() method receives a regular heartbeat, it's a great place to check the state of the player input. In this case, we can evaluate the state of the thumbstick. If the X-axis (left-right direction) of the stick is less than zero, then the stick is pointing left and we need to play the _animWest animation. If the X-axis is greater than zero, then the stick is pointing right and we need to play the _animEast animation. The same holds true for the Y-axis and for combinations of the X- and Y-axes. We pass the appropriate animation data structure to a new method named PlayMyAnimation().

```
public void PlayMyAnimation( T2DAnimationData animationData )
{
    if (AnimatedSprite.AnimationData != animationData ||
        AnimatedSprite.PauseAnimation)
    {
        AnimatedSprite.PlayAnimation(animationData);
```

```
        AnimatedSprite.PauseAnimation = false;
    }
}
```

The PlayMyAnimation() method is reduced to something very simple. It accepts the T2DAnimationData object that represents the desired animation. Next, the method checks to see if the passed animation data matches the animation data currently assigned to the parent animation game object or if the current animation is still paused. If the passed animation data is different, then the T2DAnimatedSprite method PlayAnimation() is called and the animation is unpaused. The only task remaining is to add the input map that controls this object.

```
private void _SetupInputMap(TorqueObject player, int playerIndex,
String gamePad, String keyboard)
{
    // Set player as the controllable object
    PlayerManager.Instance.GetPlayer(playerIndex).ControlObject =
        player;

    // Get input map for this player and configure it
    InputMap inputMap = PlayerManager.Instance.
        GetPlayer(playerIndex).InputMap;

    int gamepadId = InputManager.Instance.FindDevice(gamePad);
    if (gamepadId >= 0)
    {
        inputMap.BindMove(gamepadId,
            (int)XGamePadDevice.GamePadObjects.LeftThumbX,
            MoveMapTypes.StickAnalogHorizontal, 0);

        inputMap.BindMove(gamepadId,
            (int)XGamePadDevice.GamePadObjects.LeftThumbY,
            MoveMapTypes.StickAnalogVertical, 0);

        inputMap.BindAction(gamepadId, (int)XGamePadDevice.
            GamePadObjects.Back, _OnBackButton);
    }

    // keyboard controls
    int keyboard = InputManager.Instance.FindDevice(keyboard);
    if (keyboard >= 0)
    {
        inputMap.BindMove(keyboard, (int)Keys.Right, MoveMapTypes.
```

```
      StickDigitalRight, 0);
    inputMap.BindMove(keyboard, (int)Keys.Left, MoveMapTypes.
      StickDigitalLeft, 0);
    inputMap.BindMove(keyboard, (int)Keys.Up, MoveMapTypes.
      StickDigitalUp, 0);
    inputMap.BindMove(keyboard, (int)Keys.Down, MoveMapTypes.
      StickDigitalDown, 0);

    // WASD
    inputMap.BindMove(keyboard, (int)Keys.D, MoveMapTypes.
      StickDigitalRight, 0);
    inputMap.BindMove(keyboard, (int)Keys.A, MoveMapTypes.
      StickDigitalLeft, 0);
    inputMap.BindMove(keyboard, (int)Keys.W, MoveMapTypes.
      StickDigitalUp, 0);
    inputMap.BindMove(keyboard, (int)Keys.S, MoveMapTypes.
      StickDigitalDown, 0);
  }
}
```

After the code changes are made, the component is ready to use. Select the player animation object added to the scene earlier. In the Edit tab, open the components rollout. In the drop-down list, click the AnimatedCharacterComponent component and press the green Add button. Last, assign each of the animations by choosing the matching list box values as shown in Figure 8.7. After you save the level and run, you should see the animated Kork character running around the screen based on your input.

It doesn't take long to run out of area for the Kork character to run around in, so the next section introduces the Torque X camera system and implements a method to track the player's movements on the screen.

Following the Player with a Custom Camera

As we have seen, Torque X objects are created within a scene. What you see on the screen at any given time is a view into that scene. This allows Torque X to support games of many different types, ranging from a platformer game where a character must move through a large horizontal level to a strategy game where the player scrolls around a large map to a puzzle game where the entire scene is the same size as the screen. The camera controls which part of the scene you see on the screen at any given moment.

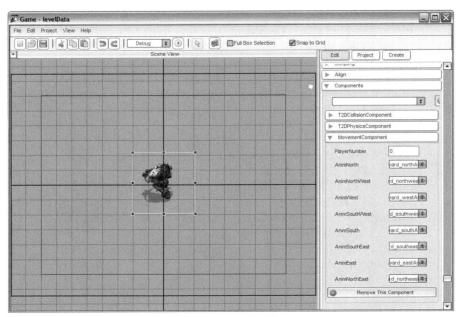

Figure 8.7. Setting the different animations to the MovementComponent.

The Torque X 2D camera has two main parameters: the CenterPosition, which specifies where in the scene the camera is pointed, and the Extent, which specifies the width and height of the scene. By setting the CenterPosition of the camera, you can control which part of the scene you are displaying on the screen. By setting the Extent, you can control how much of the scene shows up on the screen, similar to zooming in and out.

If the camera's Extent is set to an aspect ratio that doesn't match the aspect ratio of the screen, then the scene will seem squashed or stretched in the X or Y directions. The ResizeToDisplayAspectRatioWithFixedWidth parameter will cause the height of the camera's view area to be set based on the width and the aspect ratio.

The good news is that the T2DSceneCamera object is derived from T2DSceneObject, so you have a lot of control over it. You can even mount the camera to another T2DSceneObject, such as the player. Doing so will result in the player remaining in a fixed position on the screen while the game world appears to move around it.

Let's put that to the test. Start by opening Torque X Builder. Click an empty area to make certain that no scene object is selected. Open the Edit tab and expand the camera rollout. Enter SceneCamera for the camera's

Name property. The player scene object should still have its name set to Player. Next, we need some sort of background for the player to walk on. Return to the Create tab and drag the GGLogoMaterial into the scene. We'll enlarge the logo and use it as the background for now. With the new logo scene object selected, return to the Edit tab and expand the Scene Object rollout. Set the logo's size to 250 units width and 250 units height. Also, set its Layer property to 31 so that the logo appears under everything else in the scene. Finally, uncheck the Collision Enabled property; we don't want the player to collide with the background he's walking on.

That's it for now, save the level and open up XNA Game Studio. The code changes are very simple. Open the Game.cs file and the following private fields.

```
T2DSceneCamera _camera;
T2DAnimatedSprite _player;
```

These two fields will hold a reference to the camera and player scene objects and allow our code to access their properties and methods. Next, find the BeginRun() method and make the following changes.

```
protected override void BeginRun()
{
    base.BeginRun();

    SceneLoader.Load(@"data\levels\levelData.txscene");

    //get a hold of the camera object
    T2DSceneObject _camera =
        TorqueObjectDatabase.Instance.FindObject<T2DSceneCamera>
        ("SceneCamera");

    //get a hold of the player object
    T2DAnimatedSprite _player = TorqueObjectDatabase.
        Instance.FindObject<T2DAnimatedSprite>("player");

    _camera.Mount(_player, "", true);
}
```

The .txscene game-level file that was saved in Torque X Builder automatically includes a T2DSceneCamera. By giving it the name SceneCamera, we have an easy way to get a reference to it. The TorqueObjectDatabase returns the reference to the camera with the help of the FindObject() method. The same method is called again to obtain the player object. Since our player object is a T2DAnimatedSprite, we set that as the data type that the FindObject() method must return. Finally, we call the Mount() method attached to the camera object to mount the camera onto

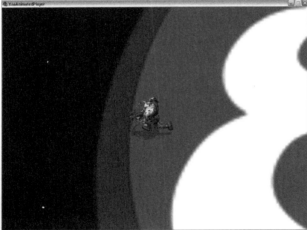

Figure 8.8. A camera mounted to the player follows the player's every movement.

the player object. Now, every time the player moves, the camera follows, as depicted in Figure 8.8.

It's also worth mentioning that mounting the camera to the player object is not the only way to have the camera follow the player. In fact, one of the side benefits of mounting the camera is when the player object rotates, the camera view rotates with it. In the preceding example, we never rotate the player object, but we simply play a different animation to represent movement in different directions.

Suppose your game has a top-down view of the world, one that is not isometric. You might want to have the player rotate and not the camera. For this case, you can simply instruct the camera to ignore the rotation by setting the TrackMountRotation property.

```
protected override void BeginRun()
{
  base.BeginRun();

  SceneLoader.Load(@"data\levels\
    levelData.txscene");

  T2DAnimatedSprite _player =
    TorqueObjectDatabase.
    Instance.FindObject
    <T2DAnimatedSprite>
    ("player");

  //get a hold of the camera object
  T2DSceneObject _camera =
    TorqueObjectDatabase.Instance.FindObject
    <T2DSceneCamera>("SceneCamera");

  //ignore the rotation
  _camera.TrackMountRotation = false;

  //add a delay to the camera movement
  camera.UseMountForce = true;
  _camera.MountForce = 2.0F;
```

```
_camera.Mount(_player, " ", false);
}
```

The code to prevent the camera rotation can be accomplished in one additional line of code. Since the camera object is mounted to the player, we can set other mount properties as we like. To prevent the camera from rotating, set the TrackMountRotation property to false. This property works for other mounted objects, too, such as a turret on a moving tank.

We can also produce other interesting camera effects by setting mount properties. By setting the UseMountForce property to true, we can also set a MountForce value that results in a lagging camera follow. Now, when the player moves around, there's a slight delay before the camera follows.

It might be tempting to find the camera in response to player input during a ProcessTick() method call. Keep in mind that the ProcessTick() method is called continuously—about 30 times a second—and we only need to find the camera once. So, it makes more sense to find the camera object when the component is initialized within the _OnRegister() method. Adding a lot of unnecessary code to the ProcessTick() method is the fastest way to kill you game's performance. Also, keep in mind that updating the camera position during ProcessTick() locks the camera motion to the tick rate and it won't interpolate. As a result, the world will move smoothly at the frequency of the frame rate while the camera updates move at 30 hertz.

Target Crosshairs

In a top-down shooter type of game, you might want to take advantage of the Xbox 360 game controller's dual analog stick input. You could map the left stick to move the player around the screen and map the right stick to move separate crosshairs around the screen. Then, when the player fires his weapon, the projectile follows the path from the player to the crosshairs (Figure 8.9).

Instead of creating a new component to do this, we can modify the existing MovementComponent that is provided with the StarterGame project. We start by adding a private field to the MovementComponent.

```
T2DSceneObject _target;
```

Next, we add some public properties to expose this object.

```
public T2DSceneObject
TargetObject
{
    get { return _target; }
    set { _target = value; }
}
```

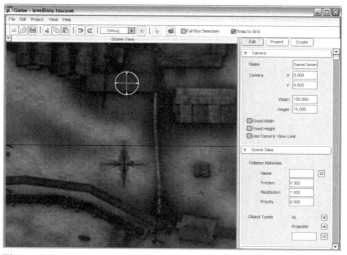

Figure 8.9. Representation of a game featuring dual analog sticks.

Next, change the existing _SetupInputMap() method to bind the right thumbstick to a move index. The move index is the last parameter passed into the BindMove() method. In this case, we bind the left thumbstick to 0 and the right thumbstick to 1. By binding to different move indexes, we can process the state of both thumbsticks simultaneously.

```
private void _SetupInputMap(TorqueObject player, int playerIndex,
String gamePad, String keyboard)
{
    // Set player as the controllable object
    PlayerManager.Instance.GetPlayer(playerIndex).ControlObject =
        player;

    // Get input map for this player and configure it
    InputMap inputMap = PlayerManager.Instance.
        GetPlayer(playerIndex).InputMap;

    int gamepadId = InputManager.Instance.FindDevice(gamePad);
    if (gamepadId >= 0)
    {
        inputMap.BindMove(gamepadId, (int)XGamePadDevice.
            GamePadObjects.LeftThumbX,
            MoveMapTypes.StickAnalogHorizontal, 0);

        inputMap.BindMove(gamepadId, (int)XGamePadDevice.
            GamePadObjects.LeftThumbY,
            MoveMapTypes.StickAnalogVertical, 0);

        inputMap.BindMove(gamepadId, (int)XGamePadDevice.
            GamePadObjects.RightThumbX,
            MoveMapTypes.StickAnalogHorizontal, 1);

        inputMap.BindMove(gamepadId, (int)XGamePadDevice.
            GamePadObjects.RightThumbY,
            MoveMapTypes.StickAnalogVertical, 1);
    }
}
```

Next, change the ProcessTick() method to move the target object in response to the move input. Moving the crosshair object is the same as moving the player object. We simply set a velocity that corresponds to the amount of movement in the thumbstick. However, since the thumbstick range is from –1.0 to +1.0, we need to multiply the value by 20 to see observable movement. If 20 is too fast, try a smaller value, like 5.

```
public void ProcessTick(Move move, float elapsed)
{
    if (move != null)
    {
        //left stick moves the player
        _sceneObject.Physics.VelocityX = move.Sticks[0].X * 20.0f;
        _sceneObject.Physics.VelocityY = -move.Sticks[0].Y * 20.0f;

        //right stick moves the crosshairs
        _target.Physics.VelocityX = move.Sticks[1].X * 20.0f;
        _target.Physics.VelocityY = -move.Sticks[1].Y * 20.0f;
    }
}
```

That's it for the code. Now rebuild the project and open Torque X Builder. Begin by dragging your crosshairs graphic into the scene. Next, go to the Edit tab and open the Scripting rollout and enter the name "target" into the Name field.

Select your player object (which should have the MovementComponent attached). Next, within the Edit tab, open the Components rollout. Under the MovementComponent, there should be a new field called TargetObject. In that list you should be able to select "target" that references your crosshairs object.

That's it. Now save everything and run. If all goes well, the left thumbstick should move the player around and the right thumbstick should move the crosshairs around. And the best part of this approach is that the MovementComponent has a quick reference to the player object and the target object, so it's quick and easy to get an angle between the two as your direction of weapons fire.

Summary

This chapter focused mostly on the player character because it is one of the most important parts of the game. These functions include responding to player input, positioning the player on the screen, animating the character, and interacting with other game elements. We used Torque X Components to implement these features so that we can easily use them with Toque X Builder.

At this point, you should have sufficient knowledge to build a playable game. You can create a new game project and create a game level filled with sprites, animations, tilemaps, and particles. You can assign stock Torque X components to your scene objects. You also have a familiarity with the C# programming language and an understanding of the many Torque X classes.

And now you can create fully functional game components that can drive a character in the game, complete with properties you can assign from Torque X Builder. In the next chapters, we will continue to build on this foundation and create even more useful game components.

Adding Game Functionality

9

In this chapter, we'll add some more common game functionality as components. In doing so, we'll uncover more useful Torque X Framework classes and reveal best practices for designing and creating your own game components. We'll start with the heart of any combat game: projectiles. Next, we'll build on projectiles to create a destructible component that allows scene objects to be destroyed. Then, we'll create an inventory manager to collect objects found within a game and then conclude by taking a look at a method for managing the overall game state, such as player score.

Adding 2D Game Components

Building a game with Torque X really requires a high comfort level with building TorqueComponents. An important lesson to learn is how to identify functionality that fits well into a component paradigm. Let's create a new 2D air combat game that features some useful components.

Start by launching XNA Game Studio and creating a new game, called *XnaChopperStrike*, using the StarterGame template. The game will be pretty simple: a helicopter flies around, picks up ammunition, and shoots down other helicopters.

From the description alone, you can tell that we need a few components. Since the game involves destroying enemy units, we'll need some sort of destructible component. Since the destruction is the result of shooting, we'll need some sort of weapon component. And since we need to pick up ammo to shoot with, we'll need to create inventory and pick up item components.

Creating XnaChopperStrike

From XNA Game Studio, create a new project, using the StarterGame project template called XnaChopperStrike. Build the project, and then open Torque X Builder to import your game's art. You can either create new graphic files or download them from the TorqueXBook.com website. From within Torque X Builder, add the background texture with collision disabled. Next, add the player and a couple of enemy helicopters, mounting the rotor animated sprite to the helicopter's body. Also, add the explosion effect that was described in Chapter 3. Finally, set the player helicopter's object name to "player" and add the MovementComponent to its components rollout. Now you can save the game, overwriting the existing levelData.txscene file, and rebuild the game (Figure 9.1).

Figure 9.1. The *XnaChopperStrike* game.

Now we have the foundation for a top-down aerial combat game. You should make the player-tracking camera changes described in the last chapter. You can fly around the scene, but that's about it. So, let's add the ability to destroy some of those enemy helicopters.

Making Something Destructible

If you want to make any scene object in your game destructible, one way to go about it is to create a destructible component. You can make the component track the health of its owner, emit smoke particles when

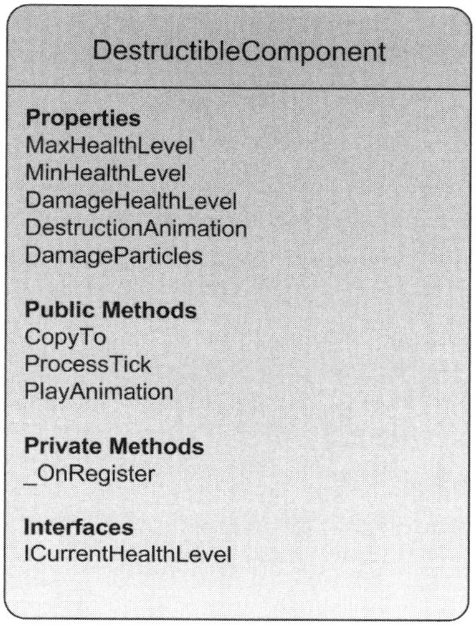

Figure 9.2. Diagram of the DestructibleComponent.

damaged, and then remove the owner from the scene when it's completely destroyed. We'll create this component so that it can be attached to any scene object in our game, including the player, AI units, and even buildings or other structures. Figure 9.2 illustrates the properties and method of this component.

Creating the Destructible Component

Open your XNA Game Studio project and add a new component called DestructibleComponent. At the heart of this component, we will track the health level of the component owner. So let's start adding some private fields.

```
float _health;
float _maxHealth;

T2DParticleEffect _destructionEffect;
```

The _health field will track the current health value of the component owner, whereas the _maxHeath will indicate the highest possible health value. We've also added a T2DParticleEffect field that will point to a particle effect. We will add code that plays back this particle effect, such as an explosion effect, when the owning scene object is finally destroyed. Next, let's wrap these private fields within some public properties.

```
[TorqueXmlSchemaType(DefaultValue = "10")]
public float Health
{
   get { return _health; }
   set { _health = value; }
}

[TorqueXmlSchemaType(DefaultValue = "10")]
public float MaxHealth
{
   get { return _maxHealth; }
   set { _maxHealth = value; }
}

public T2DParticleEffect DestructionEffect
{
   get { return _destructionEffect; }
   set { _destructionEffect = value; }
}
```

This provides a clean method for other code to access this component's private data. This also gives us a chance to specify default values that will appear within Torque X Builder when this component is assigned to a scene object. Next, let's add the public methods.

```
public override void CopyTo(TorqueComponent obj)
{
   base.CopyTo(obj);
   DestructibleComponent obj2 = (DestructibleComponent)obj;
   obj2.MaxHealthLevel = MaxHealthLevel;
   obj2.DamageHealthLevel = DamageHealthLevel;
   obj2.T2DParticleEffect = T2DParticleEffect;
}
```

The CopyTo() method is required, especially if this component is attached to a template object that will be cloned. All we're doing here is making sure the private fields are properly copied.

```
public void ReduceHealth(float value, TorqueObject damageSource)
{
   //perform the adjustment
   _health -= value;

   //destroy object if below minimum health
```

```
    if (_health <= 0.0F)
    {
        if (_destructionEffect != null)
        {
            T2DParticleEffect explosion = _destructionEffect.Clone() as
                T2DParticleEffect;
            explosion.Position = ((T2DSceneObject)Owner).Position;
            TorqueObjectDatabase.Instance.Register(explosion);
        }

        Owner.MarkForDelete = true;
    }

    return;
}
```

The ReduceHealth() method will be called when a projectile hits a scene object that has this component. This method decreases the health level of the component by the value passed as a parameter. The other parameter points back to the object that inflicted the damage. First, the _health field is reduced, and then we check whether the reduced value is still above zero. If the _health field is at or below zero, then set the MarkForDelete property to inform Torque X that this object should be deleted from the scene. Otherwise, check to see if a destruction particle effect exists. If one does exist, then clone a new instance of the effect and position it with this component's owning scene object.

```
public void IncreaseHealth(float value, TorqueObject providingSource)
{
    //perform the adjustment
    _health += value;

    //cap the health level
    if (_health >= _maxHealth)
        _health = _maxHealth;

    return;
}
```

The IncreaseHealth() method does essentially the opposite of the DecreaseHealth() method. It is typically called when a scene object runs into a power-up or collectible object that intends to help restore health. This method first increases the _health field with the amount passed into the method. If the amount passed into this method exceeds the maximum health limit, then the _health field is simply set to that limit.

Processing the Collision

There are many ways to design a destructible component. One way is to set a current health level and a minimum health level. On each ProcessTick() method call, you can check to see if the current health level is at or below the minimum health level to indicate that the object is destroyed and should be removed. The problem, however, is that 99% of the time the ProcessTick() method is called, there may be no change in health. This inefficiency can be replaced by a delegate that adjusts the health level in response to a specific event, such as a collision with a weapon projectile.

Adding the Destructible Component

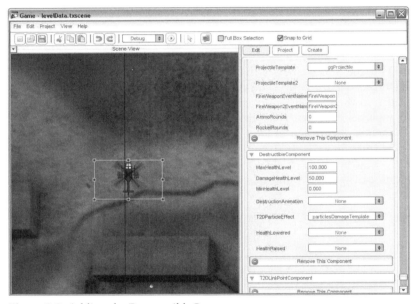

After you rebuild your game code in XNA Game Studio, Torque X Builder will detect the changes and prompt you to reload the component schema. After reloading, select each enemy helicopter and go to the components rollout within the Edit pane. Add a DestructibleComponent to each enemy helicopter, as shown in Figure 9.3. You can set the MaxHealthlevel to 100, the DamageHealthLevel to 50, the MinHealthLevel to 0, and the T2DParticleEffect to the explosion particle effect.

Figure 9.3. Adding the DestructibleComponent.

Creating Projectiles

We can define weapon projectiles by two important elements: the visible projectile element and the logical weapon component that fires it.

Creating the Projectile Template

Most combat games use some form of projectile implementation to carry out attacks between players. In the Torque X world, we can think of a projectile as a template scene object that is spawned, moves toward a target, and processes a collision. It sounds like another great use of the component framework!

From the Create pane, drag a projectile image into the scene and edit its collision polygon. The polygon will represent where the collisions can happen. Without a collision polygon, the entire square border of the projectile image would count as part of the projectile (Figure 9.4).

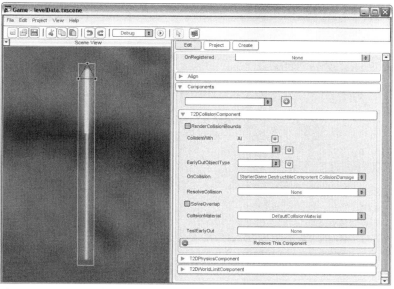

Figure 9.4. Setting the projectile's collision polygon.

Projectiles are a type of scene object we will probably have a lot of in a game. So it's important to plan for this in a few different ways. For starters, be sure to specify world limits for the projectile. This way, when a projectile is fired, it doesn't continue flying forever. Instead, once it reaches the world limits, we can kill it. To change the world limits, select the projectile scene object and click on the Change the World Limits for This Object quick-edit button. Next, drag the corners of the gray rectangle to resize it so that it is bigger than the viewable area. Click the Selection Tool button to finish editing the world limits.

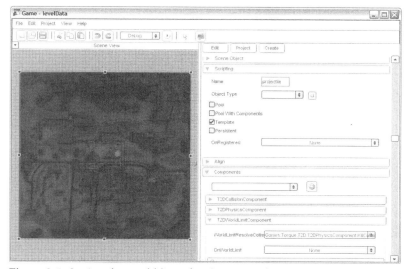

Figure 9.5. Setting the world limit for the projectile.

Torque X Builder will automatically add a T2DWorldLimitComponent to the projectile scene object. Next, open the Edit pane and expand the T2DWorldLimitComponent rollout. Set WorldLimitResolveCollision to GarageGames.Torque.T2D.T2DPhysicsComponent.KillCollision.

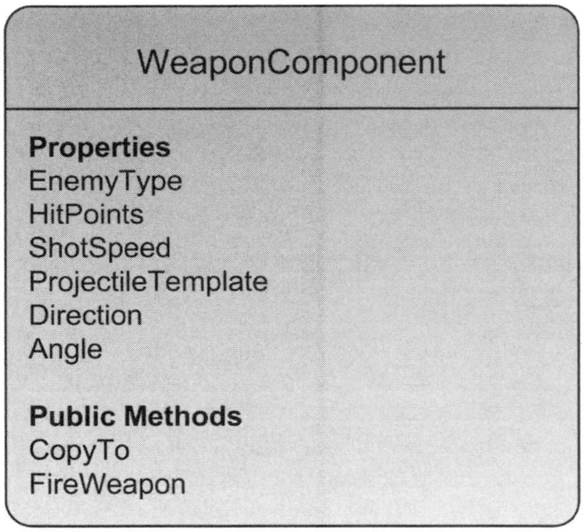

WeaponComponent

Properties
EnemyType
HitPoints
ShotSpeed
ProjectileTemplate
Direction
Angle

Public Methods
CopyTo
FireWeapon

Figure 9.6. The WeaponComponent diagram.

Now, when the projectile collides with the edge of the world limit rectangle, it will be removed (Figure 9.5).

Next, expand the Scripting rollout and enter "projectile" for the scene object's Name property. Set the Template checkbox to true to turn the projectile into a template. This way, it won't automatically show up in the scene, but it can be cloned as many times as we want with the weapon component.

Creating a Weapon Component

Now that we have a projectile, it's time to create a weapon component that is capable of firing the projectile. This component can be added to a player or an AI scene object to give it the ability to fire projectiles. Figure 9.6 illustrates the core properties and methods of the WeaponComponent.

Begin by adding a new component to the project, named WeaponComponent. Next, add the private fields that define the behavior of the weapon component.

```
TorqueObjectType _enemyType;
int _hitPoints;
float _shotSpeed;
Vector2 _direction;
T2DSceneObject _projectileTemplate;
```

The _enemyType field will hold a reference to an object we designate as an enemy. The _hitPoints field will track the damage strength of this weapon. The _shotSpeed field will set the projectile velocity. The _direction field holds a vector that represents the 2D direction of fire for the weapon. Last, the _projectileTemplate points to a scene object template that will be cloned as the projectile.

By storing these weapon attributes within a component, we can define multiple weapons, each with its own unique characteristics. The next step is to expose these private fields to the level designer by creating matching public properties with default values.

```
public TorqueObjectType EnemyType
{
  get { return _enemyType; }
  set { _enemyType = value; }
}
```

```
[TorqueXmlSchemaType(DefaultValue = "5")]
public int HitPoints
{
  get { return _hitPoints; }
  set { _hitPoints = value; }
}


[TorqueXmlSchemaType(DefaultValue = "160")]
public float ShotSpeed
{
  get { return _shotSpeed; }
  set { _shotSpeed = value; }
}
public T2DSceneObject ProjectileTemplate
{
  get { return _projectileTemplate; }
  set { _projectileTemplate = value; }
}

public Vector2 Direction
{
  set { _direction = value; }
}

public float DirectionAngle
{
  set { _direction = T2DVectorUtil.VectorFromAngle(value); }
}
```

Next, implement the CopyTo() method to support a clean cloning process. All of the private fields within this component must be copied.

```
public override void CopyTo(TorqueComponent obj)
{
  base.CopyTo(obj);

  WeaponComponent obj2 = obj as WeaponComponent;

  obj2.EnemyType = EnemyType;
  obj2.HitPoints = HitPoints;
  obj2.ShotSpeed = ShotSpeed;
  obj2.ProjectileTemplate = ProjectileTemplate;
  obj2.FireWeaponEventName = FireWeaponEventName;
}
```

Next, add the method that creates and sends off the projectile. The FireWeapon() method begins by taking the _projectileTemplate and cloning a new instance of it. Next, the position of the projectile is set to match the position of the owning scene object. The collision object list needs to be set to enable the collision with the designated enemy type. Next, both the rotation of the projectile and the velocity of the projectile are set. Finally, the projectile is brought into existence by registering it with the TorqueObjectDatabase.

```
public void FireWeapon()
{
    T2DSceneObject projectile = _projectileTemplate.Clone() as
        T2DSceneObject;
    projectile.Position = SceneObject.Position;
    projectile.Collision.CollidesWith = _enemyType;
    projectile.Rotation = SceneObject.Rotation;
    projectile.Physics.Velocity = _direction * _shotSpeed;
    TorqueObjectDatabase.Instance.Register(projectile);
}
```

That's it for the WeaponComponent. Now we need a way to trigger the weapon to fire. After rebuilding your project, add the WeaponComponent to your player object. You can modify your MovementComponent and add a BindCommand() method call to map the player input to the firing action.

```
inputMap.BindCommand(keyboardId, (int)Keys.Space, Fire, null);
```

Now, the keyboard's Space key is mapped to a local Fire() method. The next step is to create that method. Since the Fire() method will exist as a member of the MovementComponent class, we need to get a reference to the WeaponComponent class. This is where the FindComponent() method comes in handy. After an object reference is obtained, we can set the DirectionAngle property and then call the public FireWeapon() method.

```
public void Fire()
{
    WeaponComponent weapon =
        Owner.Components.FindComponent<WeaponComponent>();

    weapon.DirectionAngle = ((T2DSceneObject)Owner).Rotation;
    weapon.FireWeapon();
}
```

Now that the weapon is fired and the projectile is on its way, we need to apply some damage to the target object. We can accomplish this by creating a collision delegate handler with the WeaponComponent. Add a new method that implements the T2DOnCollisionDelegate signature, named ApplyDamage. This method will find the DestructibleComponent we created earlier and then reduce its health level by the amount defined by the weapon's properties.

```
public static void ApplyDamage(
T2DSceneObject ourObject,
T2DSceneObject theirObject,
T2DCollisionInfo info,
ref T2DResolveCollisionDelegate resolve,
ref T2DCollisionMaterial physicsMaterial)
{
    DestructibleComponent enemyDamage = ourObject.Components.
        FindComponent<DestructibleComponent>();

    if (enemyDamage != null)
    {
        enemyDamage.ReduceHealth(_hitPoints, theirObject);
    }
}
```

We can also expose this delegate with a public property, so it can easily be attached to a scene object from within Torque X Builder as a custom collision delegate, as shown in Figure 9.7. The name

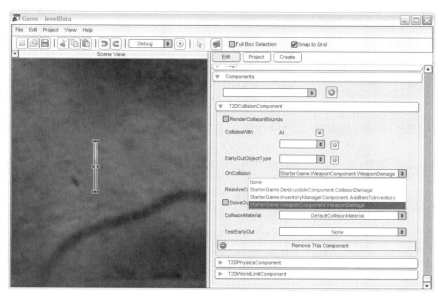

Figure 9.7. Specifying a custom collision delegate.

WeaponDamage becomes the public alias for the ApplyDamage delegate method.

```
[TorqueXmlSchemaType]
public static T2DOnCollisionDelegate WeaponDamage
{
    get { return ApplyDamage; }
}
```

Responding to TorqueEvents

You can enable components to interact with each other in a few different ways. We've already used the most common method of intercomponent communication: delegates. We have been using delegates in one component to respond to collision events in another component.

Events allow one component to talk to another component asynchronously. A component can listens for a specific event while one or more other components send them. We'll use a TorqueEvent to allow other components to signal our WeaponComponent when to fire. The first step is to add the private fields that define the event.

```
string _fireweaponEventName;
TorqueEvent<string> _fireweaponEvent;
```

The _fireWeaponEventName is a variable that specifies the name of the event. Usually, event names are constant, like OnCollision, so you always know what event name you need to send. However, to keep our WeaponComponent flexible, we'll allow the name to be set by the designer. The _fireweaponEvent field creates a strongly typed TorqueEvent. In this case, we will only process an event that is based off the int data type. Next, let's expose these private fields to Torque X Builder.

```
[TorqueXmlSchemaType(DefaultValue = "FireWeapon")]
public string FireWeaponEventName
{
    get { return _fireweaponEventName; }
    set { _fireweaponEventName = value; }
}
```

Now a level designer should be able to specify its own event name. The next step is to register the event listener when the WeaponComponent is created. Change the _OnRegister() method to create the new event and to begin listening for it.

```
protected override bool _OnRegister(TorqueObject owner)
{
```

```
    if (!base._OnRegister(owner) || !(owner is T2DSceneObject))
        return false;

    //register the fire weapon event
    _fireweaponEvent = new TorqueEvent<string>
        (_fireweaponEventName);

    //map the event to the event handler
    TorqueEventManager.Instance.MgrListenEvents<string>
        (_fireweaponEvent, FireEventHandler, null);

    return true;
}
```

Now the WeaponComponent has its own event and is actively listening for it. When a matching event is received, it will call the FireEventHandler() method in response. All that remains is to implement the FireEventHandler() method.

```
protected void FireEventHandler(string eventName, string
ProjectileTemplateName )
{
    //check to see if selected weapon has changed
    if( ProjectileTemplateName != null )
        ProjectileTemplate = TorqueObjectDatabase.Instance.FindObject
            <T2DSceneObject>(ProjectileTemplateName);

    FireWeapon();
}
```

The FireEventHandler() method is pretty simple. It just calls the local FireWeapon() method to perform the actual weapon firing. Keep in mind that there is no requirement to use an event to fire, but it does provide us with a lot of options. Now any code within our game can fire the weapon by creating an event and sending it.

Giving the Player a Weapon

With a weapon component and projectiles to be fired, it's time to give your game player some firepower. Select the player object and expand the components rollout. Add the WeaponComponent to the player as shown in Figure 9.8. Set the HitPoints to 10, the ShotSpeed to 160, the ProjectileTemplate to the bullet scene template, the FireWeaponEventName to FireWeapon, and the AmmoRounds to 500.

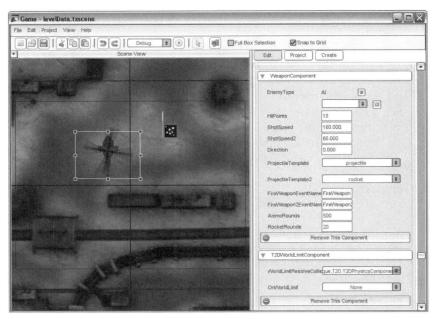

Figure 9.8. Adding the WeaponComponent to the player.

Managing Player Inventory

Many types of games have some sort of inventory-management system. Such a system allows a player to collect different types of objects throughout a game and then use them as desired. These collectibles can be anything, including weapons, magic spells, pieces of a puzzle, and so on. Inventory management systems usually have a few things in common. They typically have several slots, or categories of items. And each slot can accommodate a maximum amount of items. Such systems also typically add items based on a player collision. This sounds like a great use for components. In this case, it makes sense to have two different components, one for the inventory manager and one for the inventory item being added.

Creating an Inventory Item Component

Let's begin by creating the InventoryItemComponent component (Figure 9.9). This component will be attached to a scene object, such as a weapon, a healthpack, or a coin, that you designate as a pickup item. This will make it easy for a level designer to use Torque X Builder to designate a pickup object.

After you add a new component to your solution, add the following private fields.

```
private int _itemCount;
private int _itemCapacity;
private string _itemName;

private string _useItemEventName;
private string _useItemEventData;
```

These private fields describe the inventory item's characteristics. The _itemCount field identifies how many units of this item are attached to this pickup item. If this was a box of ammunition, you could set this value to 50 to indicate that 50 rounds are now in hand. If this was a magic potion, you could simply set this value to 1. The _itemCapacity field indicates how many of these items the inventory manager can hold. Again, if this item was a box of ammunition, you might indicate that the inventory manager can only hold 250 rounds. The _itemName field will be a player-friendly name for the item in case you want to display the name of this pickup item on screen.

The last field is the most interesting. Our inventory system will include a mechanism to use the items that are held. We won't just decrement the amount as we use an item, but we'll also fire an event that should be implemented by the item. (More on that later.) For now, we'll just need a variable to serve as a placeholder for that event name.

Next, we need to add the public properties to expose these private fields to Torque X Builder.

```
public int ItemCount
{
    get { return _itemCount; }
    set { _itemCount = value; }
}

public int ItemCapacity
{
    get { return _itemCapacity; }
    set { _itemCapacity = value; }
}

public string ItemName
{
    get { return _itemName; }
    set { _itemName = value; }
}

public string UseItemEventName
{
```

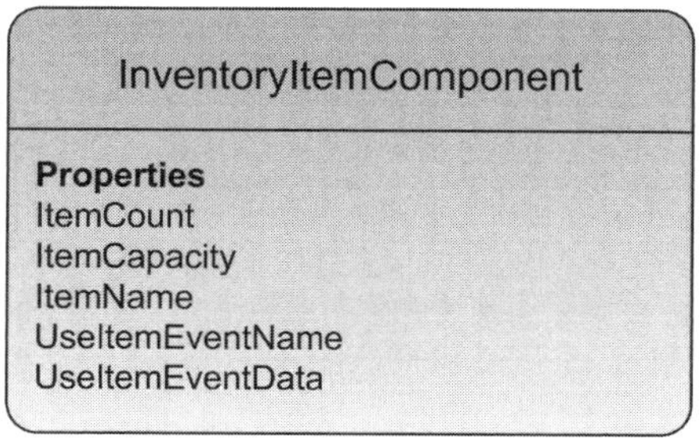

Figure 9.9. The InventoryItemComponent diagram.

```
    get { return _useItemEventName; }
    set { _useItemEventName = value; }
}

public string UseItemEventData
{
    get { return _useItemEventData; }
    set { _useItemEventData = value; }
}
```

That's it for this component. There's really no functionality, only properties that will turn a scene object into a collectible pickup item.

Creating the Inventory Manager Component

The InventoryManagerComponent will be attached to the player (Figure 9.10). It maintains a strongly typed list of InventoryItemComponent objects. You can use this component to get and set an active item, like a selected weapon slot. You can also use an item in the collection, reducing its count within an item slot.

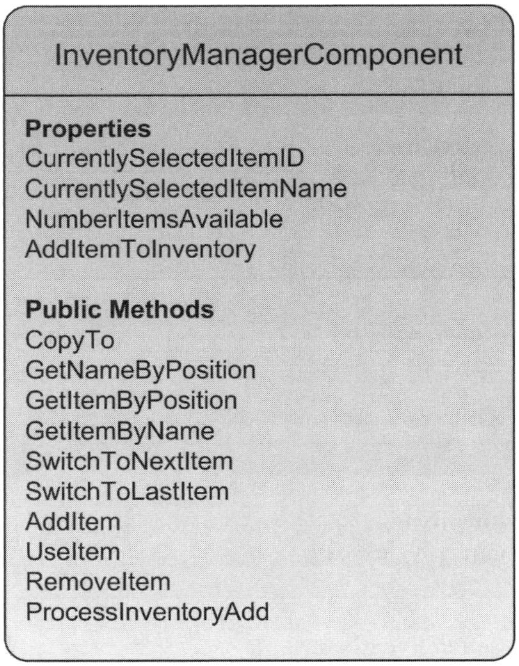

Figure 9.10. The InventoryManagerComponent diagram.

Add the following private fields to the component.

```
private List<InventoryItemComponent> _listItems = new
List<InventoryItemComponent>();
private int _itemSelectedID = -1;
private int _maxItems = 0;
```

Next, add public properties that expose the private fields to make them accessible to Torque X Builder.

```
[System.Xml.Serialization.XmlIgnore]
public int CurrentlySelectedItemID
{
    get { return _itemSelectedID; }
    set { _itemSelectedID = value; }
}

public string CurrentlySelectedItemName
{
    get { return GetNameByPosition(_itemSelectedID); }
}

public int NumberItemsAvailable
{
    get { return _listItems.Count; }
}

public static T2DOnCollisionDelegate AddItemToInventory
{
    get { return ProcessInventoryAdd; }
}
```

TorqueXmlSchemaField allows you to hide fields and properties from a parent class. Hidden fields are not exported in the schema. We use the XmlIgnore attribute from System.Xml.Serialization, not the TorqueXmlSchemaField attribute. You may need to add a reference to the System.Xml namespace in your project to get access to System.Xml. Serialization.

Add the following public methods to interact with the inventory manager. The GetNameByPosition() method returns the name of the item held within the specified inventory slot. This is useful for updating a user interface label.

```
public string GetNameByPosition(int index)
{
```

```
      return _listItems[index].Name;
}
```

The GetItemByPosition() method returns the inventory item held within a specific slot position.

```
public InventoryItemComponent GetItemByPosition(int index)
{
   return _listItems[index];
}
```

The GetItemByName() method also returns the inventory item, except by Name instead of slot position.

```
public InventoryItemComponent GetItemByName(string name)
{
   foreach (InventoryItemComponent item in _listItems)
   {
      if (item.ItemName.CompareTo(name) == 0)
         return item;
   }
   return null;
}
```

The SwitchToNextItem() and SwitchToLastItem() methods set the actively selected inventory item. These helper methods are intended to assist a user interface that cycles through an inventory selection.

```
public void SwitchToNextItem()
{
   if (CurrentlySelectedItemID + 1 >= _maxItems)
      CurrentlySelectedItemID = 0;
   else
      CurrentlySelectedItemID++;
}

public void SwitchToLastItem()
{
   if (CurrentlySelectedItemID - 1 < 0)
      CurrentlySelectedItemID = _maxItems - 1;
   else
      CurrentlySelectedItemID--;
}
```

The AddItem() method performs the task of adding a new item into the inventory collection.

```
public void AddItem(string name, int amount, int capacity, string
eventName, string eventData)
{
    //check our inventory for this item
    InventoryItemComponent item = GetItemByName(name);

    //if this item is not already in the inventory, add it
    if (item == null)
    {
        item = new InventoryItemComponent();
        item.ItemName = name;
        item.ItemCapacity = capacity;
        item.UseItemEventName = eventName;
        item.UseItemEventData = eventData;

        //item.OnUseItem = useDelegate;


        _listItems.Add(item);
        _maxItems++;

        //if this is the first item, then select it
        if (_listItems.Count == 1)
            CurrentlySelectedItemID = 0;
    }

    //increment the amount
    item.ItemCount += amount;

    //prevent inventory overflow
    if (item.ItemCount > capacity)
        item.ItemCount = capacity;
}
```

The UseItem() method reduces the amount of an inventory item by the specified amount. It also sends a use message to the inventory item to trigger its item function.

```
public void UseItem(int itemID, int amount)
{
    //check our inventory for this item
    if (itemID >= 0)
    {
        InventoryItemComponent item = GetItemByPosition(itemID);
```

```
if (item != null && item.ItemCount >= amount)
{
    //raise use event
    TorqueEvent<string> useEvent =
        new TorqueEvent<string>(item.UseItemEventName);

    TorqueEventManager.Instance.MgrPostEvent<string>
        (useEvent, item.UseItemEventData);

    //item.OnUseItem(); //delegate

    //reduce inventory amount
    item.ItemCount -= amount;
}
}
}
```

The RemoveItem() method removes an item from the inventory collection. This method is called when an item is meant to be removed from an inventory slot. This is a useful method to call when a player is killed and subsequently loses her inventory.

```
public void RemoveItem(string name)
{
    //check our inventory for this item
    InventoryItemComponent item = GetItemByName(name);

    _listItems.Remove(item);
    _maxItems--;

    if (_itemSelectedID - 1 >= 0)
        _itemSelectedID--;
    else
        _itemSelectedID = -1;
}
```

Finally, let's add the collision delegate handler that will process the collision between the player and the pickup item.

```
public static void ProcessInventoryAdd(T2DSceneObject
    ourObject, T2DSceneObject theirObject, T2DCollisionInfo info,
    ref T2DResolveCollisionDelegate resolve, ref T2DCollisionMaterial
    physicsMaterial)
{
```

```
InventoryItemComponent item = ourObject.Components.
    FindComponent<InventoryItemComponent>();

InventoryManagerComponent inventoryManager = theirObject.
    Components.FindComponent<InventoryManagerComponent>();

//only process this collision if there is an inventory manager found
if (inventoryManager != null)
{
    inventoryManager.AddItem(item.ItemName, item.ItemCount, item.
        ItemCapacity, item.UseItemEventName,
        item.UseItemEventData);
    ourObject.MarkForDelete = true;
}
}
```

Turning Scene Objects into Pickup Items

Now that we have our two inventory management components, let's put them to work. Open Torque X Builder and select a scene object that will be a pickup item, such as a weapon. Make sure that the Collision Enabled property is checked within the Scene Object rollout. Next, open the Components rollout and edit the T2DCollisionComponent and set the OnCollision property to InventoryManagerComponent. AddItemToInventory. Next, add the InventoryItemComponent. Edit the properties for the InventoryItemComponent by setting the ItemCount to 15, the ItemCapacity to 50, the ItemName to Gun, and the UseItemEventName to FireGun.

Using Items

To use inventory items, you need to bind a button event to one of our inventory manager method calls. You can do this by modifying your InputMap bindings within the MovementComponent. Add the following bindings to the _SetupInputMap() method.

```
inputMap.BindCommand(keyboardId, (int)Keys.Space,
    UseInventoryItem, null);
inputMap.BindCommand(keyboardId, (int)Keys.OemPeriod,
    NextInventoryItem, null);
inputMap.BindCommand(keyboardId, (int)Keys.OemComma,
    LastInventoryItem, null);
```

Next, we need to implement the actual methods required by the BindCommand() mappings.

```
public void UseInventoryItem()
{
   //get the selected inventory item
   TorqueObject player = PlayerManager.Instance.GetPlayer(0).
      ControlObject;
   InventoryManagerComponent inventoryManager = player.
      Components.FindComponent<InventoryManagerComponent>();

   inventoryManager.UseItem(inventoryManager.
      CurrentlySelectedItemID, 1);
}

public void NextInventoryItem()
{
   //get the next inventory item
   TorqueObject player = PlayerManager.Instance.GetPlayer(0).
      ControlObject;
   InventoryManagerComponent inventoryManager = player.
      Components.FindComponent<InventoryManagerComponent>();

   inventoryManager.SwitchToNextItem();
}

public void LastInventoryItem()
{
   //get the last inventory item
   TorqueObject player = PlayerManager.Instance.GetPlayer(0).
      ControlObject;
   InventoryManagerComponent inventoryManager = player.
      Components.FindComponent<InventoryManagerComponent>();
   inventoryManager.SwitchToLastItem();
}
```

Managing the Game State

During the course of a game, you will normally want to track the game state. Data, such as player score, number of lives remaining, and the current spawn point, are important to track as the player advances through the game. There are a number of different ways to implement this feature. The approach we'll take is to create a GameState class and set it as a property of the Game class.

Creating a Game State Class

Begin by creating another component, named GameState. The class does not need to inherit from any other classes or implement any interfaces. Add the following private fields to the component.

```
int _numberOfLivesRemaining = 3;
int _score = 0;
T2DSceneObject _currentSpawner;
```

Next, add the public properties that expose these private fields so that other games can get and set them.

```
public int NumberOfLivesRemaining
{
    get { return _numberOfLivesRemaining; }
    set { _numberOfLivesRemaining = value; }
}

public int Score
{
    get { return _score; }
    set { _score = value; }
}

public T2DSceneObject CurrentSpawner
{
    get { return _currentSpawner; }
    set { _currentSpawner = value; }
}
```

That's it. We'll keep this class small and to the point. You can always add additional fields and properties that match your specific game. The next question to answer is, what code will own this class? For most games, the best exposure for this type of component is the top-level TorqueGame class. Games that are created from the StarterGame template define a derived class, named Game, within the Game.cs file. Add the following private field.

```
GameState _gameState;
```

Next, create an accessor property that exposes this component to other game codes.

```
public GameState GameState
{
    get { return _gameState; }
}
```

Finally, in the BeginRun() method, bring this component to life by creating a new instance of it and assigning it to _gameState.

```
_gameState = new GameState();
```

Because the Game class has wide exposure to other game codes, you can easily get and set game state values. This can be applied to user interface updates, custom collision handling, or other game-changing events. Here's an example of setting a string value in one component to the value of the Score property in the GameState class.

```
string displayScore = "Score: " + Game.Instance.GameState.Score.
ToString();
```

Since the Game class is a top-level class, you should be able to access it from just about anywhere.

Summary

In this chapter, we learned how to design and create game components that implement specific game behaviors. The underlying goal of this chapter was to demonstrate a process for taking game functionality, breaking it down into discrete components, and implementing those components with Torque X Framework code. This whole process will represent the bulk of your coding effort for a Torque X game. Along the way, we introduced a new game project as a platform for testing our new components. In the next chapter, we will tackle the problem of Artificial Intelligence in a Torque X game and break down that feature into additional components.

10

Adding 2D Artificial Intelligence

In this chapter, we will continue to create additional components that enhance game play features. We will create three new components that implement some basic artificial intelligence for our game enemies. In addition to adding some interesting game functionality, these components demonstrate a couple of important lessons. The first lesson is reusability. With some good up-front planning, components can be highly reusable. These AI components should be applicable to several different types of 2D games. The second lesson is interoperability. Components should be designed to work well with other components. The three AI components created in this chapter can be applied individually, together, or in different combinations to an enemy scene object to create different AI behaviors.

Getting to Know Vector Math Tools

XNA and the Torque X Framework have a lot of great tools for solving vector mathematics. Two classes in particular include the Vector2 class and the T2DVectorUtil class. Both classes contain a number of great vector mathematics methods.

The XNA Framework provides the **Vector2** class. It can be instantiated as a standalone object, or you can call a number of useful static methods. Here are some of these methods.

- **Add:** Adds two different vectors to produce a new vector.

- **Subtract:** Subtracts two different vectors to produce a new vector.

- **Multiply:** Multiplies two different vectors to produce a new vector.

- **Divide:** Divides two different vectors to produce a new vector.

- **Distance:** Determines the absolute distance between two vector points.

- **Clamp:** Restricts a vector to a specified range.

You can use these methods to perform quick vector calculations, such as the distance between your player object and another scene object. For example, here's a method that you can write to get the closest EnemyType scene object to the player.

```
public T2DSceneObject GetClosestEnemy()
{
    float MaxRange = 1000.0f;

    TorqueObjectType typeEnemy =
        TorqueObjectDatabase.Instance.GetObjectType("EnemyType");

    List<ISceneContainerObject> listEnemies = new
    List<ISceneContainerObject>();

    T2DSceneGraph.Instance.FindObjects(SceneObject.Position,
        MaxRange, typeEnemy, (uint)0xFFFFFFFF, listEnemies);

    float closestDistance = MaxRange;
    T2DSceneObject closestEnemy = null;

    foreach (T2DSceneObject enemy in listEnemies)
    {
        float distance = Vector2.Distance(SceneObject.Position, enemy.
            Position);

        if (distance < closestDistance)
            closestEnemy = enemy;
    }

    return closestEnemy;
}
```

The Torque X Framework adds some additional capability with its **T2DVectorUtil class,** which has the following static methods that can be accessed without creating an instance of the class:

- **AngleFromInput:** Calculates the clockwise angle from analog stick input. Positive Y-axis (0, 1) is 0 degrees rotation, so an object drawn with the returned rotation will have its top pointing in the direction of the input stick. (Note: In T2D −y is up, but on the thumbstick +y is up.) Return value is in degrees.

- **AngleFromTarget:** Calculates the clockwise angle of the vector between two points. Negative Y-axis (0, −1) is 0 degrees rotation, so an object drawn with the returned rotation will have its top pointing from the source position to the target position. (Note: In T2D −y is up.) Return value is in degrees.

- **AngleFromVector:** Calculates the clockwise angle from an offset vector assuming T2D coordinates. Negative Y-axis (0, −1) is 0 degrees rotation, so an object drawn with the returned rotation will have its top pointing along the vector. (Note: In T2D −y is up.) Return value is in degrees.

- **VectorFromAngle:** Calculates vector pointing in the given angle. Angle is in clockwise degrees from "up" (negative y (0, −1) is up).

- **VelocityFromInput:** Converts a vector from an input stick into a velocity. Converts from "plus y-up" space of input controller to "minus y-up" screen space.

- **VelocityFromTarget:** Converts an offset vector to a velocity that will move toward the target at the given speed.

The foreach operator is a convenient way to cycle through a list. However, it comes with a high performance cost because it creates a new enumerator instance at the start of each foreach, resulting in extra garbage collection cycles. Instead of this

```
foreach (T2DSceneObject enemy in
    listEnemies)
{
    float dist = Vector2.
        Distance(SceneObject.Position,
        enemy. Position);
}
```

you can also use a traditional for loop.

```
T2DSceneObject enemy;
for(int index = 0; index < listEnemies.
    Count; index++)
{
    enemy = (T2DSceneObject)
        listEnemies[index];
    float dist = Vector2.
        Distance(SceneObject.Position,
        enemy. Position);
}
```

This chapter deals with manually setting the position and orientation of scene objects to accomplish AI functionality. Since most of these properties are expressed as vectors, it's a good idea to become familiar with these available methods.

Path-Following AI

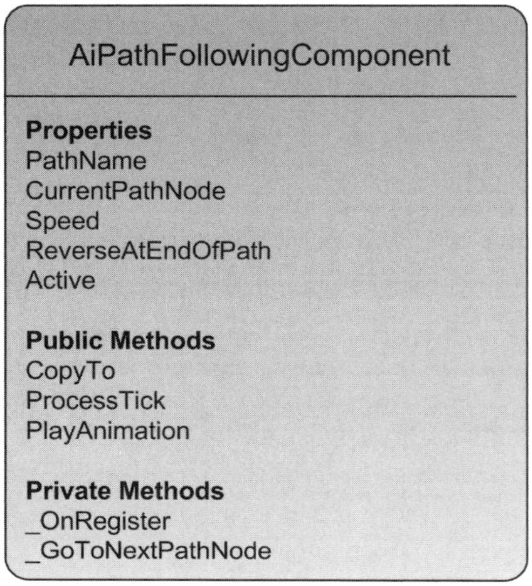

AiPathFollowingComponent

Properties
PathName
CurrentPathNode
Speed
ReverseAtEndOfPath
Active

Public Methods
CopyTo
ProcessTick
PlayAnimation

Private Methods
_OnRegister
_GoToNextPathNode

Figure 10.1. The AiPathFollowingComponent diagram.

The most basic form of artificial intelligence in games is simple path-following. Although it barely qualifies as AI, it can be used to drive NPC (nonplayer character) objects around the scene. This bundled functionality is a perfect candidate for a Torque component. The code will look for scene objects scattered around a level that follows a specific naming convention and then move from one to the next along the path (Figure 10.1).

Creating the Component Data

Begin by creating a new T2DComponent class, named AiPathFollowingComponent. We first add some private fields that will manage the state of the component.

```
T2DSceneObject _sceneObject;
T2DSceneObject _targetObject;

string _pathName;
int _currentPathNode = -1;
float _speed = 5.0f;
bool _reverseAtEnd = true;
bool _movingForward = true;
bool _destinationReached = true;
bool _active = true;
```

The _sceneObject field will hold a reference to the actual scene object that owns this component, such as a patrolling enemy. The _targetObject field will hold a reference to the next path node for which this component is heading. The _pathName field will hold the name of the path, whereas the _currentPathNode will indicate the currently targeted path node. The _reverseAtEnd field will determine what happens when the AI reaches the end of the path: turn back, or return to the first node. The _movingForward field indicates which direction the component is moving (used if _ reverseAtEnd is true). The _destinationReached field informs the component that it's time to go to the next node, and the _active field indicates if the component is ready for use.

These fields will certainly help drive the component along the path. But, we're going to need some help from Torque X Builder to set these properties and create the path. In fact, we will define the path for this AI to follow by dropping blank scene objects that define the path, like breadcrumbs. Therefore, we need to expose some of those private fields to Torque X Builder, using public properties.

```
public string PathName
{
      get { return _pathName; }
      set { _pathName = value; }
}

public int CurrentPathNode
{
      get { return _currentPathNode; }
}

[TorqueXmlSchemaType(DefaultValue = "10.0")]
public float Speed
{
      get { return _speed; }
      set { _speed = value; }
}

[TorqueXmlSchemaType(DefaultValue = "1")]
public bool ReverseAtEndOfPath
{
      get { return _reverseAtEnd; }
      set { _reverseAtEnd = value; }
}

[TorqueXmlSchemaType(DefaultValue = "1")]
public bool Active
{
      get { return _active; }
      set { _active = value; }
}
```

The PathName component property will identify the name of the path. If we use the name MyPath, then each blank scene object we place must have the name MyPath0, MyPath1, MyPath2, and so on. The Speed property identifies how fast the AI will travel between nodes and the ReverseAtEndOfPath property tells the AI to either backtrack along the path when the end is reached or complete a circle by returning to the first node (Figure 10.2).

Adding the Component Set-Up Methods

Now that the private fields and properties are set, let's start adding methods. This component must make some decisions as time progresses. Specifically,

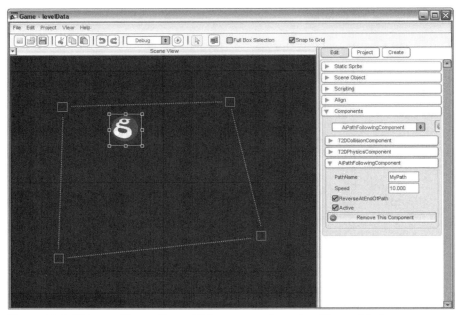

Figure 10.2. Using an Empty Scene Object as a path marker (lines added).

the component will need to know when it reaches its destination and then decide what action to take next.

There are two ways to accomplish this. The first is to regularly check the position and distance from the component to the current destination. The second is to set a destination and go; then generate a message event when the destination is reached. Both approaches are valid. The continuous checking can add some unnecessary processing during the AI's journey. However, if you simply set a destination and go, when the destination moves, the event will never be generated. The following example takes the first approach and uses the ProcessTick() method to regularly check the component's status.

```
public virtual void ProcessTick(Move move, float dt)
{
    if (!_active)
        return;

    _GoToNextPathNode(dt);
    return;
}
```

Again, the ProcessTick() method is called continuously to let you update the state of the component. We use this opportunity to verify that the component is active and then call _GoToNextPathNode(), a method that we will create shortly to advance the AI forward.

```
public override void CopyTo(TorqueComponent obj)
{
    base.CopyTo(obj);
    AiPathFollowingComponent obj2 = (AiPathFollowingComponent)
        obj;

    obj2.PathName = PathName;
    obj2.ReverseAtEndOfPath = ReverseAtEndOfPath;
}
```

Again, we add our important properties to the CopyTo() method to ensure that a cloned instance of this component is correctly set up. Next, we need to register the component and request tick processing.

```
protected override bool _OnRegister(TorqueObject owner)
{
    if (!base._OnRegister(owner) || !(owner is T2DSceneObject))
        return false;

    _sceneObject = Owner as T2DSceneObject;

    // register for ProcessTick callback
    ProcessList.Instance.AddTickCallback(Owner, this, 0.8f);

    return true;
}
```

We need to update the _OnRegister() method to register for tick callbacks. If we don't request ticks, then the ProcessTick() method will never be called, and we won't be able to advance the AI.

Performing the Path Follow

Now we get to the real meat of this component. Every component will have a method or two that will ultimately define the purpose of the component. The _GoToNextPathNode() method is called on every tick and determines if the component has reached its destination, which direction it should be moving, where it should be going, and which way it should be facing.

```
private void _GoToNextPathNode(float elapsed)
{
    if (_destinationReached)
```

```
        {
                //get next destination
                if (_movingForward)
                        _currentPathNode++;
                else
                        _currentPathNode--;

                string strNextPathNode = _pathName +
                    _currentPathNode.ToString();

                _targetObject = TorqueObjectDatabase.Instance.
                    FindObject<T2DSceneObject>(strNextPathNode);

                //end reached
                if (_targetObject == null)
                {
                        //toggle the direction
                        if (_reverseAtEnd)
                        {
                                _movingForward = !_movingForward;

                                if (_movingForward)
                                        _currentPathNode += 2;
                                else
                                        _currentPathNode -= 2;
                        }
                        else
                                _currentPathNode = 0;

                        strNextPathNode = _pathName +
                            _currentPathNode.ToString();

                        _targetObject = TorqueObjectDatabase.Instance.
                            FindObject<T2DSceneObject>
                            (strNextPathNode);
                }

                _destinationReached = false;
        }
        else
        {

                // determine angle to point our object to the target
                float angle = T2DVectorUtil.AngleFromTarget
```

```
            (_sceneObject.Position, _targetObject.Position);

            // set the rotation of our owner
            _sceneObject.Rotation = angle;

            // set our owner on its way toward the path node
            _sceneObject.Physics.Velocity =
                T2DVectorUtil.VelocityFromTarget(_sceneObject.
                Position, _targetObject.Position, _speed);

            //determine the distance
            float Distance = Vector2.Distance(_sceneObject.Position,
                _targetObject.Position);

            //is target within range
            if (Distance <= 1)
                    _destinationReached = true;
        }


    return;
}
```

Our first task is to determine if the component has arrived at a node point. If a node has been reached, then we determine if the component is moving forward or backward and either increment or decrement the next target node value. This target node value is paired with the path name to create the object name that should match the name set within Torque X Builder. We query the TorqueObjectDatabase for a T2DSceneObject with a name that matches our target node. If there is no match, then _targetObject is set to null, and we assume that we're at the end of the path. So the next task is to check the component settings, via the _reverseAtEnd field, to determine if this component should go backward along the path or complete the circle and return to the first path node. Based on that decision, the next node identifier either decrements or goes to zero.

If, however, the destination has not yet been reached, we use an important T2DVectorUtil method, AngleFromTarget(), to get the angle between our component's owner and the next node. Based on the resulting angle, the Rotation property of the owning scene object is set. Next, a velocity is applied to the owning object to drive it to the next node. Last, we perform a quick distance calculation to see how far the component is from the next path node. When the component is about 1 unit away, we set the flag that indicates that the component has arrived at the next path node. You can also replace the constant value of 1 with a field value that is exposed to the level designer to add more flexibility.

In the preceding code sample, the AiPathFollowingComponent searches for blank scene objects that had a consistent naming convention. Another approach to designating destinations is to add a strongly typed List collection that contained references to specific destination scene objects, regardless of name.

AIProximityAttackComponent

Properties
TargetObject
AttackDistance
Active

Public Methods
CopyTo
ProcessTick

Private Methods
_OnRegister
_UpdateAttack
_PerformAttack

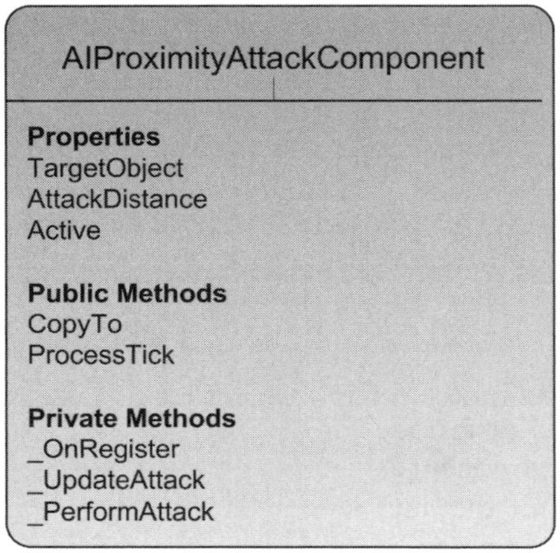

Figure 10.3. The AIProximityAttackComponent diagram.

Proximity Attack AI

The Proximity Attack AI component continuously sweeps the local area for an enemy within a specific distance, presumably attack range. The enemy is identified by object type. If an enemy is detected within range, the component will launch an attack. The attack will involve a projectile launch against its target. The results of the attack will be driven by component properties, such as accuracy, so that you can use the same component to set one enemy soldier as a novice with 50% accuracy and another soldier to veteran with 95% accuracy.

This component can be attached to a fixed-position standalone object to represent a turret, used with the path-following AI component to represent a patrolling guard, or have a zero attack distance and a high attack value to represent a mine (Figure 10.3).

Creating the Component Data

Begin by creating a new T2DComponent class, called AIProximityAttackComponent. Add the following private fields.

```
T2DSceneObject _sceneObject;
T2DSceneObject _targetObject;
int _attackDistance;
bool _active = true;
bool _attackInProgress;
float _accuracy;
```

The _targetObject field will hold a reference to the scene object that this AI should attack. The _attackDistance field indicates the distance at which this component should begin attacking the target, presumably set to the range of the selected weapon. And just like the last component, an _active field indicates that this component is active and ready to perform. Your game might have to pause the attack and set the _active field to false could ensure that. Next, let's expose these private fields to Torque X Builder, using public properties.

```
public T2DSceneObject TargetObject
{
    get { return _targetObject as T2DSceneObject; }
    set { _targetObject = value; }
}
```

```
[TorqueXmlSchemaType(DefaultValue = "20")]
public int AttackDistance
{
      get { return _attackDistance; }
      set { _attackDistance = value; }
}

 [TorqueXmlSchemaType(DefaultValue = "1")]
public bool Active
{
      get { return _active; }
      set { _active = value; }
}

public bool IsAttackInProgress
{
   get { return _attackInProgress; }
}

[TorqueXmlSchemaType(DefaultValue = "0.50")]
public float Accuracy
{
   get { return _accuracy; }
   set { _accuracy = value; }
}
```

Exposing some of our private fields will help the level designer set and fine-tune this component. Next, add the public methods to help drive this component.

Adding the Component Set-Up Methods

Since this component is designed to attack a target when it becomes in range, the component needs a heartbeat to continuously perform an action. Again, that will take the form of tick processing.

```
public virtual void ProcessTick(Move move, float dt)
{
      if (!_active)
              return;

      _UpdateAttack(dt);
}
```

The ProcessTick() method is called on every update tick, and for this component, we simply call the _UpdateAttack() method to perform its function. But before implementing that, let's make sure that this component can be cloned properly by filling out the CopyTo() method.

```
public override void CopyTo(TorqueComponent obj)
{
    base.CopyTo(obj);
    AIProximityAttackComponent obj2 =
        (AIProximityAttackComponent)obj;
}
```

The CopyTo() method ensures a clean copy by setting all the properties of the newly cloned object to those of the source object. Next, let's add the private methods that get everything done. We'll start with the component's initialization code.

```
protected override bool _OnRegister(TorqueObject owner)
{
    if (!base._OnRegister(owner) || !(Owner is T2DSceneObject))
        return false;

    // our owner
    _sceneObject = Owner as T2DSceneObject;

    // register for ProcessTick callback
    ProcessList.Instance.AddTickCallback(Owner, this, 0.8f);
    return true;
}
```

In the _OnRegister() method, we simply add the AddTickCallback() method to request tick calls into our component. The ProcessTick() method simply calls a new method, _UpdateAttack().

```
public virtual void ProcessTick(Move move, float dt)
{
    _UpdateAttack(dt);
}
```

Performing the Attack

The _UpdateAttack() method is at the core of this component and is responsible for evaluating proximity and carrying out the attack.

```
private void _UpdateAttack(float elapsed)
{
    // determine angle to point our ship to the player
    float angle = T2DVectorUtil.AngleFromTarget(_sceneObject.
```

```
        Position, _targetObject.Position);

    // set the rotation of our ship
    _sceneObject.Rotation = angle;

    //determine the distance
    float Distance = Vector2.Distance(_sceneObject.Position,
        _targetObject.Position);

//determine the chance of hit based on accuracy
Random randomizer = new Random();
float chance = ((float)randomizer.Next(_accuracy, 100)) / 100;
angle = angle*chance;

    //is enemy within range
    if (Distance <= _attackDistance)
    {
            WeaponComponent weapon =
                Owner.Components.FindComponent
                <WeaponComponent>();

            weapon.Direction = angle;
            weapon.FireWeapon();
    }
}
```

The _UpdateAttack() method is where everything gets done. All this method does is determine the angle between the component's owner and the target, rotate the owner to aim at the target, and then calculate the distance between the two. When the distance falls within the specified attack distance, this component gets a reference to the WeaponComponent. It uses that reference to set the angle of fire to match the angle of the player and then fires.

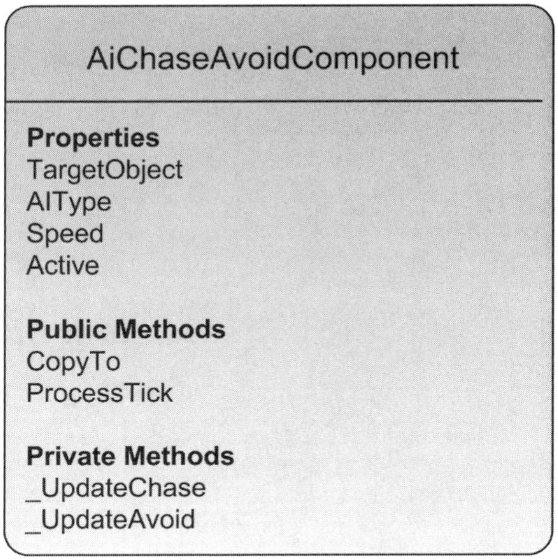

Chasing and Avoiding AI

The player-interactive AI can be configured to either follow or avoid the player. It effectively works by searching the scene graph for the player object, rotating to an angle pointing toward the player, and setting a velocity. By repeating these basic steps at regular intervals, such as a tick, we can accomplish

AiChaseAvoidComponent

Properties
TargetObject
AIType
Speed
Active

Public Methods
CopyTo
ProcessTick

Private Methods
_UpdateChase
_UpdateAvoid

Figure 10.4. The AiChaseAvoidComponent diagram.

a convincing player-chase effect. By packaging this code into a component, we can easily add the player-chase capability to just about any scene object (Figure 10.4).

Creating the Component Data

We begin by creating another T2DComponent class, called AiChaseAvoidComponent. Next, add the following private fields to designate a T2DSceneObject target to follow. We also add a field of type EnemyAITypes, an enumerated type that we'll create next. Last, add a field to track the speed of the chasing or fleeing AI units.

```
T2DSceneObject _sceneObject;
T2DSceneObject _TargetObject;
EnemyAITypes _aiType;
float _speed = 5.0f;
bool _active = true;
```

Next, let's expose these private fields to make them customizable from within Torque X Builder. The level designer will definitely want to specify a target object for the attacking AI unit, as well as move speed.

```
public enum EnemyAITypes
{
        Chase,    // follow the player
        Avoid,     // avoid the player
}

public T2DSceneObject TargetObject
{
        get { return _TargetObject as T2DSceneObject; }
        set { _TargetObject = value; }
}

 [TorqueXmlSchemaType(DefaultValue = "Chase")]
public EnemyAITypes AIType
{
        get { return _aiType; }
        set { _aiType = value; }
}

[TorqueXmlSchemaType(DefaultValue = "10.0")]
public float Speed
{
```

```
        get { return _speed; }
        set { _speed = value; }
}


[TorqueXmlSchemaType(DefaultValue = "1")]
public bool Active
{
        get { return _active; }
        set { _active = value; }
}
```

Adding the Component Set-Up Methods

On each tick, the AI unit must decide if it is in a mode to chase or flee. Depending on its active mode, either the _UpdateChase() method is called to pursuit the player or the _UpdateAvoid() method is called to move away from the player.

```
public void ProcessTick(Move move, float elapsed)
{
        if (!_active)
                return;

        switch (_aiType)
        {
                case EnemyAITypes.Chase:
                        _UpdateChase(elapsed);
                        break;

                case EnemyAITypes.Avoid:
                        _UpdateAvoid(elapsed);
                        break;
        }

        return;
}
```

Again, the CopyTo() method must change to ensure a complete cloning of an object containing this component.

```
public override void CopyTo(TorqueComponent obj)
{
        base.CopyTo(obj);

        AiChaseAvoidComponent obj2 = (AiChaseAvoidComponent)obj;
```

```
        obj2.AIType = AIType;
        obj2.Active = Active;
        obj2.Speed = Speed;
}
```

The protected _OnRegister() method sets up the component. After initializing the parent class, we set a type-casted reference to the scene object that owns this component. This makes it easy to get and set the owner's position and rotation. Last, a call to AddTickCallback() ensures the flow of ticks.

```
protected override bool _OnRegister(TorqueObject owner)
{
        if (!base._OnRegister(owner) || !(Owner is T2DSceneObject))
                return false;

        // our owner
        _sceneObject = Owner as T2DSceneObject;
        // register for ProcessTick callback
        ProcessList.Instance.AddTickCallback(Owner, this, 0.8f);

        return true;
}
```

Performing the Player-Interactive Tasks

Two methods accomplish the real task of following or avoiding the player. The _UpdateChase() method, called by the ProcessTick() method, will perform the task of chasing the player. This method begins with a call to the AngleFromTarget() method, found within the T2DVectorUtil class. It is used to get the angle between this component's parent scene object and the designated target scene object, measured in degrees. Next, the owning scene object is set to match that angle so it points to the enemy it is chasing. Finally, we use another T2DVectorUtil method to help set a velocity toward the target object.

```
private void _UpdateChase(float elapsed)
{
        // determine angle to point our ship to the player
        float angle = T2DVectorUtil.AngleFromTarget(_sceneObject.
            Position, _TargetObject.Position);

        // set the rotation of our ship
        _sceneObject.Rotation = angle;

        // set the ship on its way towards the player
        _sceneObject.Physics.Velocity =
            T2DVectorUtil.VelocityFromTarget(_sceneObject.Position,
```

```
        _TargetObject.Position, _speed);

    return;
}
```

As you might guess, the _UpdateAvoid() method works the opposite way. We start off by determining the velocity, angle, and distance between the owning scene object and the target. Next, we determine how far this AI object is from the player. If this component is less that 30 units from the target object, then a velocity is set to the opposite of the earlier calculated velocity. However, if the distance is greater than 30 units, then the velocity for this component is set to zero. Again, you can create a field that holds the distance value and add properties to allow the level designer to adjust the value within Torque X Builder. There's no need to keep moving away once out of danger.

```
private void _UpdateAvoid(float elapsed)
{
    Vector2 target = T2DVectorUtil.VelocityFromTarget(_sceneObject.
        Position, _TargetObject.Position, _speed);

    float angle = T2DVectorUtil.AngleFromTarget(_sceneObject.Position,
        _TargetObject.Position);

    _sceneObject.Rotation = angle;

    //how far away is the player?
    float dist = Vector2.Distance(_TargetObject.Position, _sceneObject.
        Position);

    // check distance from player, if we are too close then we want to
    move away
    if (dist < 30.0f)
        _sceneObject.Physics.Velocity = Vector2.Negate(target);
    else
        _sceneObject.Physics.Velocity = Vector2.Zero;
}
```

The AI chase and avoid methods work very similarly. Although these methods can move an AI unit around the screen, they still don't easily qualify as artificially intelligent. The next step is to give the AI unit some smarts by creating an AiBrainComponent that can be added.

Creating an AI Brain

Depending on the sophistication of your game, you can add a lot more to the AI system. The proximity attack AI can be enhanced to not only scan an area

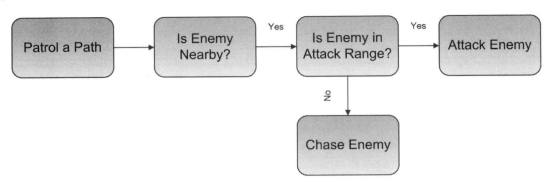

Figure 10.5. Basic AI logic flowchart.

for an enemy but to add a line of sight capability so that AI players can't see through walls. You might also want to have an AI player react to a situation by changing state. For example, an AI player may change state from a path follower to a player chaser when it detects a nearby enemy. To facilitate changes in state, we can create a new component, AiBrainComponent, that encapsulates the individual AI components and directs the overall behavior of the AI.

When creating an AI brain, it's helpful to start with a flowchart or state diagram that maps out the expected behavior. Figure 10.5 summarizes the general flow of logic for our simple AI brain.

This basic AI logic fits well with the components we now have in our collection. An AI unit using this component should follow a preset path around the scene. Then, when an enemy is nearby, such as the player, its proximity attack code kicks in to attack the enemy and chase it until it's destroyed.

You can certainly create more complex AI logic that also determines if the AI unit has enough ammo before committing the attack. Next, let's create the AiBrainComponent as described in Figure 10.6.

Creating the AiBrainComponent

To give the AI some really intelligent behavior, let's create another component, AiBrainComponent. You can add this component along with the other AI components to create a more robust behavior.

Since this component depends on the presence of the other components, be sure to include [TorqueXmlSchemaDependency] class attributes. This will help Torque X Builder to verify that the other components have already been added.

```
[TorqueXmlSchemaType]
[TorqueXmlSchemaDependency(Type =
    typeof(AiPathFollowingComponent))]
[TorqueXmlSchemaDependency(Type =
    typeof(AiChaseAvoidComponent))]
[TorqueXmlSchemaDependency(Type =
    typeof(AiProximityAttackComponent))]
public class AiBrainComponent : TorqueComponent,
    ITickObject
{
}
```

Now, if you try to add the AiBrainComponent to a scene object from within Torque X Builder, a message box will appear, as shown in Figure 10.7. The message box prompts you to add the components, and clicking the Yes button will automatically add the missing components to your scene object.

To help keep our AI logic organized, we can create our own enumerated data type, called AiState. An enumerated data type lets us create our own easy-to-understand representation of values. Instead of testing if state = 1, we can test if state = AiAttack. It's really all the same to the game code, but it definitely makes your code a lot easier to read.

```
public enum AiState
{
    AiPatrol,
    AiAttack
};
```

AiBrainComponent

Properties
AiProximityAttackComponent
AiPathFollowingComponent
AiPlayerChaseComponent
AiState

Public Methods
CopyTo
ProcessTick

PrivateMethods
_OnRegister

Figure 10.6. The AiBrainComponent diagram.

Figure 10.7. Torque X Builder warning about a component dependency.

The brain is going to need a few internal fields to help the component along. First, we create three reference fields that will point to the other required components. This way, we don't need to look them up on every tick. We also need a field to track the current state of the brain.

```
AiProximityAttackComponent _proximityAI;
AiPathFollowingComponent _pathAI;
AiChaseAvoidComponent _playerchaseAI;
AiState _aiState = AiState.AiPatrol;
```

As for private methods, we need only to update the component's initialization code. The first change sets the local reference to the other AI components required by this component. The second change is simply to request ticks to this component.

```
protected override bool _OnRegister(TorqueObject owner)
{
    if (!base._OnRegister(owner) || !(owner is T2DSceneObject))
        return false;

    //get references to the components
    _proximityAI = Owner.Components.FindComponent
        <AiProximityAttackComponent>();
    _pathAI = Owner.Components.FindComponent
        <AiPathFollowingComponent>();
    _playerchaseAI = Owner.Components.FindComponent
        <AiChaseAvoidComponent>();


    //request ticks
    ProcessList.Instance.AddTickCallback(owner, this);

    return true;
}
```

Again, the objective of the AiBrainComponent is to direct the activity of an AI unit. Specifically, the AI unit will follow a path and then chase and attack an enemy when one approaches.

The AiBrainComponent can also accomplish its purpose within the ProcessTick() method. The first task is to update the state of the brain. Since the AiProximityAttackComponent has the ability to detect the presence of an enemy unit, we'll use that to determine if an attack is in progress. Next, we activate or deactivate components based on the state of the AI. If the AI is in its patrol state, then the AiChaseAvoidComponent should be deactivated. Similarly, if the AI is in its attack state, the AiPathFollowingComponent should be deactivated.

```
public virtual void ProcessTick(Move move, float dt)
{
    //use the proximity attack range detector to set the state
    if (_proximityAI.IsAttackInProgress)
        _aiState = AiState.AiChase;
    else
        _aiState = AiState.AiPatrol;

    switch (_aiState)
    {
        case AiState.AiPatrol:
            _pathAI.Active = true;
            _proximityAI.Active = true;
```

```
            _playerchaseAI.Active = false;
            break;
        case AiState.AiAttack:
            _pathAI.Active = false;
            _proximityAI.Active = true;
            _playerchaseAI.Active = true;
            break;
        }
    }
```

When you compile the AiBrainComponent and attach it to a scene object from within Torque X Builder, be sure to set all the properties of the required components.

Summary

In this chapter, we created several reusable components that can add some basic artificial intelligence to the game. By implementing each AI behavior as a component, we can combine them to create different types of AI units that behave differently, with the ultimate goal of providing a fun and challenging game. Also, by creating another component that represents the AI brain, we're also able to introduce the ability to orchestrate the use of the other components. In the next chapter, we will migrate from the world of 2D games to the world of 3D games. Creating a 3D game is significantly more complicated than a 2D game. Fortunately, the Torque X Framework has a rich library of features that help make 3D game creation much easier.

3D Game Programming

IV

3D Programming with Torque X

11

This chapter dives into the world of 3D game programming with the Torque X Framework. Torque X offers many classes that enable 3D game creation and gives you fine control over how scenes are created and rendered. This chapter begins with a review of core 3D concepts, such as 3D coordinate systems and modeling, then examines the key 3D classes provided by the Torque X Framework, and finally walks through the creation of a simple 3D scene that renders your game's player model.

Introduction to 3D Shapes

The key to successful 3D game programming is in understanding how shapes are organized and positioned into a scene. Let's start by taking a 3D shape and breaking it down into its core elements.

The 3D Mesh Basics

Any given 3D shape is essentially a collection, or mesh, of triangles. These triangles are commonly referred to as polygons. Each polygon has three distinct corners, each referred to as a vertex. An edge connects each pair of vertices together. The closed polygon also has a filled surface, commonly referred to as a face. These elements are illustrated in Figure 11.1. A mesh of

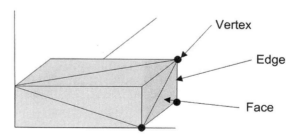

Figure 11.1. The basic elements of a 3D mesh.

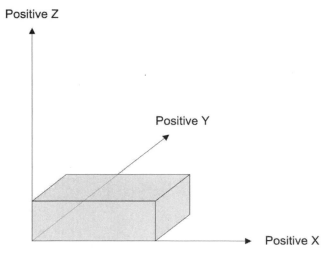

Positive Z

Positive Y

Positive X

Figure 11.2. Axis orientation within the Torque X Framework.

thousands of differently shaped and sized polygons combined together can produce amazing 3D shapes.

The 3D Coordinate System

All 3D shapes, from a simple box to a complex humanoid character, are little more than a collection of points. These points map to the X, Y, and Z coordinates of a vertex in world space. World space is defined as a 3D area with an arbitrary origin; 3D objects are positioned with a 3D coordinate system.

The Torque X coordinate system is slightly different from the standard XNA coordinate system. In Torque X, the X-axis points to the right, the Y-axis points forward, and the Z-axis points upwards, as shown in Figure 11.2.

Object Coordinates and World Coordinates

One of the most important elements of a coordinate system is the designation of the origin, where the value along each axis is zero. In 3D game programming, there are usually two separate coordinate systems: object coordinates and world coordinates.

Object coordinates refer to a coordinate system that is relative to a single 3D shape. It is used to identify each vertex position that composes the 3D shape. The origin of the object coordinates is typically designated at the center of the 3D shape but can be arbitrarily set to be anywhere within the shapes bounds. Figure 11.3a illustrates a simple box shape that is four units wide, two units deep, and two units high. As you can see, the origin of the object coordinates is in the center of the shape.

World coordinates refer to a coordinate system that applies to all of the 3D objects within a scene. The origin of the world coordinates is some arbitrary point in space and all 3D shapes that are placed into the 3D scene need to have their vertices mapped into world coordinates in order to render on screen. In Figure 11.3b, the same box shape is placed into a scene in which its geometric center is positioned at (7,6,11) and is indicated by a dark gray square. As you can see, the vertices have been converted from object-space coordinates to world-space coordinates.

Both coordinate systems are equally important. Since the object-coordinate system applies to a single 3D shape, it is used mostly during the shape-creation process. The 3D modeling tool that creates the shape works

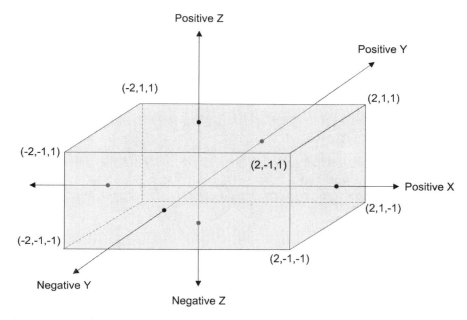

Figure 11.3a. A box's vertices marked in object coordinates.

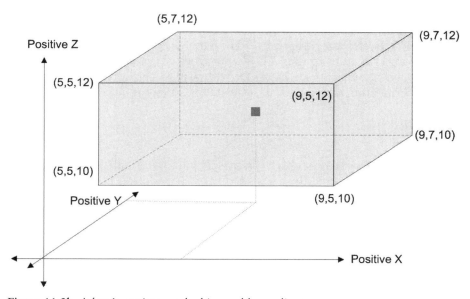

Figure 11.3b. A box's vertices marked in world coordinates.

exclusively in object coordinates to define each vertex position. World coordinates are necessary for rendering a complete 3D scene that contains multiple 3D shapes. Each vertex from every 3D shape must be transformed into world coordinates. Vertices are often, but not always, stored in object space. On each frame, the video card's Graphics Processor Unit (GPU) transforms the shape's vertices from object space to world space then to screen space.

3D Transformation

3D transformation refers to the process of mapping the model's object coordinates to world coordinates. This mapping process can also factor in changes to the shape's position, including scale, translation, and rotation.

Vectors

A vector is a mathematical construct that is used to describe a position and a magnitude in 3D space. We've already worked with 2D vectors and the Vector2 class while interacting with 2D scenes. Now, we'll work with 3D vectors and the Vector3 class. As you can guess, the Vector3 class is used because it has three properties to hold: X, Y, and Z values.

In XNA, the Vector3 class is a lot smarter than a simple data structure that holds three positions. It also has a number of powerful vector-mathematics functions that can compute the addition, subtraction, multiplication, and division between two vectors. In addition, it includes a number of advanced mathematical functions: dot-product, cross-product, clamp, and of course transform. Fortunately, Torque X does most of the hard work of transforming 3D shapes from object coordinates to world coordinates. But, in many cases, we will want to perform our own specific transformations, including scale, translation, and rotation, using the Vector3 class.

Scale

Scale is the most basic form of transformation and refers to the change in size of a model. Typically, a scale value of 1.0 indicates no change in size. Scale values greater than 1.0 will result in an increase in object size. For example, a scale value of 2.0 doubles the size of the 3D shape. Values less than 1.0 indicate a decrease in object size. For example, 0.5 will halve the size of the 3D shape.

From a vector mathematics perspective, a vector scalar is multiplied against each vertex position that makes up the object. To double the size of a shape, you can cycle through every vertex point and multiply it by a vector with a value of 2.0.

```
Vector3 vertexA = new Vector3(2, 1, 1);
Vector3 vertexNew = Vector3.Multiply(vertexA, 2);
```

As this code fragment shows, a vertex point at position (2,1,1) can be multiplied by a value, in this case 2. The result is a new vertex value of (4,2,2). When this process is applied to every vertex that makes up the mesh, the result is a mesh that is twice the size of its original.

Translation

Translation is another simple form of transformation and refers to the change in position of a model. However, instead of multiplying each vertex by a value, we simply add each vertex to a new vector. The new vector represents the amount of offset from the current position to the new position.

```
Vector3 vertexOffset = new Vector3(5, 4, 3);
Vector3 vertexA = new Vector3(2, 1, 1);
Vector3 vertexNew = Vector3.Add(vertexA, vertexOffset);
```

In this code fragment, we first specify the offset from the current position to the new position. In this case, the offset is +5 units along the X-axis, +4 units along the Y-axis, and +3 units along the Z-axis. This vector offset is added to the vertex at position (2,1,1) and a new vertex position is returned. The new vertex position becomes (7,5,4). As you can imagine, by adding the offset vector to every vertex point within the mesh, the end result is that the mesh will be moved, or translated.

Rotation

Rotation is a much more complex form of transformation and refers to the change in orientation of a model in all three directions. Unfortunately, rotating a vertex around an axis takes much more work than simply adding or multiplying vectors. In fact, it requires the use of trigonometry to determine a new position based upon angles.

```
Vector3 vertexA = new Vector3(2, 1, 1);
Vector3 vertexRotationAmount = new Vector3(30, 60, 90);
Vector3 vertexNew;

//Rotation about the X-axis:
vertexNew = new Vector3(vertexA.X,
    (float)((Math.Cos(vertexA.X) * vertexA.Y) -
    (Math.Sin(vertexA.X) *vertexA.Z)), (float)((Math.Sin(vertexA.X) *
    vertexA.Y) + (Math.Cos(vertexA.X) * vertexA.Z)));
```

```
//Rotation about the Y-axis:
vertexNew = new Vector3((float)((Math.Cos(vertexA.Y) * vertexA.X) +
    (Math.Sin(vertexA.Y) * vertexA.Z)), vertexA.Y,
    (float)(-(Math.Sin(vertexA.Y) * vertexA.X) + (Math.Cos(vertexA.Y) *
    vertexA.Z)));

//Rotation about the Z-axis:
vertexNew = new Vector3((float)((Math.Cos(vertexA.Z) * vertexA.X)
    - (Math.Sin(vertexA.Z) * vertexA.Y)), (float)((Math.Sin(vertexA.Z) *
    vertexA.X) + (Math.Cos(vertexA.Z) * vertexA.Y)), vertexA.Z );
```

In this code fragment, we start with the vertex we want to rotate at position (2,1,1) and create a new vector to represent the amount of rotation, in degrees. In this case, we will rotate the vertex 30 degrees about the X-axis, 60 degrees about the Y-axis, and 90 degrees about the Z-axis. Next, the code rotates the vertex about each axis using trigonometry functions. Finally, we get the new vertex position at (0.2,2.2,1). It's worth noting that performing rotation calculations with vectors is unnecessarily complex. Rotation calculations are instead usually performed using matrices. Fortunately, we will not need to perform transformations manually or manipulate individual vertices. The Torque X 3D Framework provides more high-level methods that can fully transform shapes.

The Torque X 3D Framework

The Torque X 3D Framework is spread out across several classes, components, interfaces, and delegates. These framework elements can be organized into different categories, including: scene rendering, player input, scene reactions, and environmental elements. You have great flexibility in deciding what you want to render within a 3D scene and how to render it.

Rendering the Scene

Rendering a 3D shape to the scene works quite differently from rendering a 2D material to the scene. In the case of rendering a 2D material, all you need to do is create an object of type T2DSceneObject and register it with the TorqueObjectDatabase. With 3D shapes, you must first create an object of type TorqueObject, then add a 3D-rendering component, and then register it with the TorqueObjectDatabase. This gives you much more control over how 3D shapes appear onscreen and enables you to swap out rendering elements at runtime. The Torque X 3D Framework includes many powerful classes and components that help with creating a complete 3D scene.

T3DSceneGraph

The T3DSceneGraph class maintains a container of all objects within the 3D scene. Torque X supports the existence of multiple-scene graphs, which lets you create multiple views into your game. The AddObject() and RemoveObject() methods are used to add objects into a specific scene graph and remove them. Each scene graph has a camera attached to it that is used to render the scene based on a position and field of view. The scene graph also maintains a list of light positions.

T3DCameraComponent

The T3DCameraComponent class is the basic camera class for all 3D objects and is attached to a scene graph. All 3D scenes must have a camera attached. You can set fundamental camera properties, such as its transform (position and rotation), field-of-view, and the far visible distance. The camera also has the ability to attach to an object with an offset position and rotation. This lets you keep the camera focused on an object without having to constantly update the position of the camera manually.

T3DSceneComponent

The T3DSceneComponent class enables objects to become 3D scene objects. This class contains all of the properties that we recognize from the 2D scene objects, such as position, rotation, scale, object type, visibility level, scene graph, and so on. It also adds necessary 3D properties, such as a bounding box, a world box, and a 3D transform structure. This component must be added to an object in order for it to render onscreen.

T3DTSRenderComponent

The T3DTSRenderComponent class loads and renders a DTS shape to the scene. This component must be attached to an object in order to associate a 3D shape with it. Its properties include a file path to the DTS-model file and a reference to a Shape object. This class can also load DSQ animation-sequence files and create animation threads for playback.

TSAnimation

The TSAnimation class animates a DTS shape when you specify a DSQ animation sequence file and thread for animation playback. You can interact with this class to play, pause, stop, and get or set the current position within an animation.

T3DStaticTSRenderComponent

The T3DStaticTSRenderComponent class creates a DTS shape that doesn't move or animate. The best feature of this class is that it automatically sets up a polysoup collision mesh for the 3D model. This component is ideal for nonmoving structures, such as buildings or race tracks that have a 3D shape that never move and require a detailed collision surface.

Processing Player Input

Processing player input in a 3D scene is very similar to that of a 2D scene. The InputMap is still a fundamental element of capturing keyboard and controller events. However, the Torque X 3D Framework also offers a few additional components to make 3D movement even easier.

T3DInputComponent

The T3DInputComponent class provides a simple framework for providing controller or keyboard input for an object. This component simply manages player indexes and needs to be inherited by your own input controller class to add the specific input mapping. Your derived class should implement the input mappings within the _SetupInput() method and then process the input within the _UpdateInput() method.

Reacting to the Scene

The Torque X 3D Framework has an impressive built-in physics system. The physics system is able to process rigid collision reactions with a variety of collision materials and collision-mesh implementations.

T3DRigidComponent

The T3DRigidComponent class enables physics and collisions for an object. When an object adds a T3DRigidComponent, it can set properties such as mass, gravity scale, velocity, and rotation scale. It also can specify which objects it can collide with, identify a collision surface shape, and define collision materials. With collision materials you can turn a sphere into a solid rock or a rubber ball. This component can also set a RigidBody, which processes external forces, momentum, linear velocity, and angular velocity.

T3DRigidConstraintComponent

The T3DRigidConstraintComponent class sets up a constraint relationship between two objects. These two objects can be bound together by an anchor, ball joint, or contact constraint as determined by the RigidConstraint property. This component is useful for constraining two objects together, such as a swinging door connected to a wall.

T3DTriggerComponent

The T3DTriggerComponent class is a specialization of the T3DRigidComponent that essentially replaces its parent's OnCollision delegate with specialized delegates for OnEnter, OnStay, and OnLeave. This component can be used wherever a 3D trigger is needed. This is perfect for AI activation triggers or even creating specialized physics zones, where gravity and surface friction can be tweaked.

Adding Environmental Elements

It will probably not be long before you will want to create a more natural looking environment. Fortunately, the Torque X 3D Framework also includes a lot of environmental objects, such as terrain, sky, sun, and particle emitters.

XTerrain

The XTerrain class provides a 3D terrain object for a scene. It stores the height and opacity maps and calculates and stores the activation levels. Other attributes include position, repeat tiling, and designated scene graph. The specific height map and level of detail data is implemented in one of three attached terrain-data classes: TGETerrainData, RAWTerrainData, and GeneratedTerrainData.

The TGETerrainData class offers terrain data that is based on the Torque Game Engine's classic .ter file format. Its properties include a path to the .ter terrain file, a lightmap texture, and a detail texture. The RAWTerrainData class works with raw terrain data that can be imported from a variety of sources, including USGS data. Its properties are similar and include a path to the .raw terrain data file, a lightmap texture, and a detail texture. Lastly, the GeneratedTerrainData offers a procedurally generated terrain that is generated mathematically. Its properties include grid size, number of smoothing passes, and jitter.

Sky

The Sky class provides a basic skybox object for the 3D scene. With good enough textures for all interior sides of the skybox, you can create a convincingly endless 3D scene that reaches the horizon. The key properties of the Sky class include the scene graph, the transform (position) of the skybox, the distance at which the sky is rendered, and paths to the image files that make up each side of the skybox.

Sun

The Sun class provides an image of a sun for the 3D scene. It does not provide any actual light to the scene, but a LightComponent can be attached to it and a light-direction vector can be obtained from it to properly cast shadows. You can also specify two different materials to represent the animated sun flares. Other properties let you specify the size of the sun and the rotation speed of the sun flares.

Particle Effects

Particle effects within a 3D scene can be used in a variety of ways, ranging from fire, smoke, and explosions, to environmental elements, such as rain and floating ashes. The Torque X 3D Framework separates particle effects into two elements: the particle emitter and the individual particle.

The T3DParticleEmitter class creates the object within the 3D scene which emits particles. You can set this object's transform, velocity, wind velocity, and reference to a T3DParticleEmitterData. The T3DParticleEmitterData class defines more specific properties for the emitter, such as ejection period, ejection velocity, ejection angles, and particle counts, etc. It also keeps a reference to a T3DParticleData object. The T3DParticleData class defines the individual particle with properties, such as material, lifetime, size, speed, and rotation.

The DTS 3D Model Format

Although the Torque X Framework is able to work with all 3D-model formats supported by XNA, you will find that is optimized to work with the DTS-model format.

The DTS Shape

Unlike 3D-modeling packages or motion pictures, a game engine must be able to render huge amounts of geometry and effects in real time. In order to do this, many shortcuts are taken during the rendering process to ensure optimal frame rate. DTS is a model format designed to be both flexible and optimized for rendering with Torque X.

The DTS-model format is optimized for small, complex objects. These can range from rocks and trees to individual detail objects such as chairs and tables. They can be attached to player or vehicle models, in the case of weapons, packs, or flags. All DTS objects can be animated using bone structures. Animations can be blended to form complex motions from simple components. The DTS-model format identifies mount points, which is great for character and vehicles models.

Object Hierarchy

Different model formats have different ways of organizing the essential details of the 3D shape, such as meshes, bounding box, animation sequences, etc. Similarly, the DTS-model format has a very specific node hierarchy that must be followed to create a valid DTS-model file. The objects that matter most to the DTS format include a bounding box mesh, the 3D shape's actual mesh, nodes for collision and level-of-detail markers, and mesh groups.

Each object, including the actual mesh shape, has a name and the DTS-model format has a very specific expectation for what these names should be.

The object hierarchy, as shown in Figure 11.4, illustrates a hierarchy for a simple box shape. Although this example of hierarchy representation comes from 3D Studio Max, most modeling software has an equivalent way to represent a hierarchy of 3D objects.

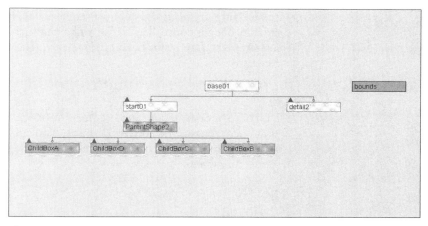

Figure 11.4. An example DTS object hierarchy.

The GarageGames website has many great online guides for modeling DTS shapes using 3D Studio Max and Maya.

Mesh Groups

The DTS-model format doesn't require a 3D shape to be composed of one single mesh or a single continuous collection of connected polygons. Instead, the DTS format enables multiple meshes to exist and be combined together to form a 3D shape. For example, the 3D box shown in Figure 11.1 could be created as a single mesh of 12 connected polygons or as 6 different planar meshes of 2 polygons that represent each side. In either case, you still end up with a total of 12 polygons.

It doesn't really make much difference when you're creating a simple box, but it does make a difference with a more complex shape, like a character. Typically, a 3D modeler creates a complex character by sculpting simpler primitive shapes, such as spheres, cylinders, and boxes. Since the DTS-model format supports multiple submeshes, the 3D modeler doesn't need to merge the polygons together.

Texture Mapping

The DTS-model format requires UV-texture mapping coordinates in order to be rendered within Torque X. The texture file must be a bitmap, such as PNG or JPG, and stored alongside the DTS-model file. Multiple subobject texture maps are supported as long as all subobjects are bitmap textures. Texture map dimensions must also be powers of two (32, 64, 128, 256, 512) with a maximum size of 512X512. Textures do not have to be square.

Translucent textures are supported. To make an object translucent, the texture on the object must have an alpha channel. The amount of translucency is controlled by the alpha channel. Also, double-sided materials are supported, which is useful for see-through objects, such as a chain-linked fence.

Bounding Box

The DTS-model format also requires a bounding box mesh named *bounds* that encompasses the entire 3D shape. You can programmatically show and hide this bounding box with your game code, which can be useful for in-game character selections.

Levels of Detail

The DTS-model format also has built-in support for variable levels of detail. This means that you can create multiple, lower-resolution mesh shapes for the same 3D shape. Then, when the 3D shape moves further from the camera, the game engine can swap out the higher-resolution 3D model with the lower-resolution model. And since lower resolution means fewer polygons to process, the game engine can maintain a snappy performance.

When done carefully, levels of detail are completely invisible to the user. The high-resolution model will be swapped to a lower-resolution model at such a distance that the details that are lost are too small to be seen. Which detail level is used is determined by the pixel height of the object onscreen. This prevents users with a high-resolution setting from noticing the reduction of detail while showing fewer polygons onscreen for users with lower resolutions.

Currently, the Torque X Framework does not swap levels of detail. So, for now, creating different resolution versions of your shapes aren't beneficial. It is discussed here because the rules of naming are still required in order to create the DTS model.

Collision Meshes

The DTS-model format also includes the ability to define custom collision meshes. These are very simple mesh shapes that represent custom collision geometry. This is perfect for a concave object, such as an arch, where a generic collision box wouldn't make sense. Instead, a few collision meshes can work together to offer a more realistic collision representation. However, there are some limitations with collision meshes. They must be convex and have as few polygons as possible because collision checks are performed per polygon.

There is no right way to create collision meshes. It really depends on how you want to implement collision detection in your game. Different collision schemes can also be used for different shapes. Some shapes might use simple sphere collision derived from the bounding box, while others might have custom-built collision meshes.

Custom collision meshes are created by assigning a negative detail number to the shape, such as Col-1, and then creating a corresponding detail marker, such as Collision-1. In Torque X, meshes with a negative number in the name will not render.

The Torque X Framework currently does not support the individual collision meshes that are defined within the DTS-model format. Instead, DTS shapes within a Torque X game make use of primitive shapes, such as cubes and spheres.

DTS Animation

The DTS-model format also supports mesh animation. There are two different ways to enable animation. You can either embed all animation sequences within the DTS file, or you can have every animation sequence stored within its own DSQ file. Keeping the base mesh and skeleton in the DTS file and storing each animation sequence in its own DSQ file is the preferred method since it gives more explicit control over the mesh. Having a separate copy of the mesh for each sequence will also prevent one animation's motion from altering another animation on the same node.

Animation Threads

To fully understand the animation system, you must realize that several animation threads can be played simultaneously on the same shape, at different speeds, in both directions, while controlling different parts of the object hierarchy. This allows you to blend many simple animation sequences to create very complex character motion. If two threads try to control the same node, the sequence priority will determine which thread controls a particular node.

In practice, the best way to go about doing things is to export different types of animation to control different parts of the character and then have them hooked up to different controls. In the game, you can look around while running. Instead of having a run-look-left, run-look-middle, and run-look-right animations, there is a run animation and a look animation that are being played at the same time. In this way, you can get a great deal of flexibility out of very few animations. You can play back the look animations with one animation thread, while the lower-body movement animations are played back on another animation thread.

Animation threads are typically advanced during the UpdateAnimation() callback method that is specified by the IAnimatedObject interface. In the next chapter, we'll use the UpdateAnimation() callback method to move an active animation forward.

```
public void UpdateAnimation(float dt)
{
    if (_currentAnimation != null)
    {
        _currentAnimation.Thread.AdvanceTime(dt);
    }
}
```

Blend Animations

There are special animation sequences that can be marked as blended that enable additive animation on the node structure of the shape. These sequences do not conflict with other animation threads and can be played on top of a node animation contained in other animation threads.

Blend animations are relative and only read the changes that occur over the course of the animation and not the absolute position of the nodes. This means that if a node is transformed by a blend animation, it includes only the transform information for that node, and it will add that transformation on top of the existing position in the base shape.

Effectively, blend animations add additional animation on top of other animations. If a sequence is a blend, the transforms will be added on top of the other animations already playing in the engine on a node-by-node basis. The animation values only are added.

A blend can be played as a normal sequence, or it can be played on top of other sequences. When another sequence is playing, it will alter the root position, and the blend will be applied on top of that.

If you try to do a blend sequence where the root position is different than the normal root (in the default root animation), you might expect that the blend will blend it to the new root (the position the character is positioned in during the blend animation). But it doesn't work this way. Since nothing would actually be animating, it doesn't move the bones to the new position. Only transform offsets from the blend sequence root position are contained in the blend sequence.

Sequence Objects

Sequence objects are necessary if animation is to be exported. The sequence object tells the exporter how to export animation data over a given range of time in 3D Studio Max and what to call the sequence. A sequence object can be created like any other helper object found within 3D Studio Max. In the Create tab, select the Helpers menu and then use the roll-out menu to choose General DTS Objects.

Sequence helpers that you place in the scene are unlinked objects that float in the world. They do not need to be linked to anything. Sequence helpers are used to define the beginning and end of an animated sequence. You can set these parameters by adding keyframes to the Sequence Begin/End track. This track is an on/off-type track. The animation information will export only when its value is set to On. By default, the first key you add will define the beginning of the animation, and the second will determine the end.

Animation Triggers

Animation triggers can be added to sequence helper objects. You can have up to 32 animation triggers. These triggers are turned on by adding a keyframe with the appropriate trigger number as a value and turned off by adding another keyframe with negative value on the trigger number that you assigned on the first trigger keyframe.

If you like, you can only turn them on and assume that other code will turn them off as they are read. As an example, the easiest way to deal with footsteps is to have one trigger for each foot (say, 1 = left, 2 = right). You may have an application where you want to know when the foot is supposed to be on the ground. In that case, you would turn on the Foot on Ground state when it first contacts the ground and turn it off when the foot leaves the ground. Thus each foot would have two trigger keys: a positive (e.g., +1) one when the left foot hits the ground and a negative (e.g., −1) one when it leaves the ground. Add the values and keyframes in the trigger track in the track view of the sequence helper.

If you want your character to leave footprints, all you have to do is go to the trigger track of the appropriate sequence and add a trigger key and a value. In the default Torque engine, 1 = left foot, 2 = right foot.

Adding a 3D Shape to Your Project

In order to add new models to your XNA game, you must first include them within XNA Game Studio.

- Open the Game project and select the Content folder.

- Select Project ➤ New Folder from the main menu and name the folder Shapes.

- Copy your DTS models and related texture graphics into the Shapes folder.

- After the shapes are copied, select the Shapes folder and select Project ➤ Add Existing Item to choose the new models to be included.

After the DTS-model files have been added to the Game project, you need to set their pipeline properties. You do not need to set the project properties for the texture files since they will automatically be set to compile.

- Select the new DTS files.

- Select View ➤ Properties Window from the main menu.

- Set the Build Action to Content and the Copy to Output Directory to Copy Always.

Now, every time your game is compiled, it will take the model files and add them to the output directory. The image files will be compiled into the optimized .xnb file format. It is very important to note that setting the Build Action to Content only applies to the DTS models because there is no native content processor for DTS shapes within XNA. If you plan to use other 3D-model formats, such as .x or .fbx, then you can set the Build Action to Compile and use the XNA content processor to build the model into a .xnb file.

Figure 11.5. A 3D shape added to a 2D game.

Adding a 3D Shape to a 2D Game

The simplest example of adding a 3D shape to a game is to add a shape to a 2D game. Torque X 2D games are capable of including 3D shapes with the help of the T2DShape3D class. With the help of this class, you can create 2D games that add a little more realism with the help of 3D shapes and lighting. It's also easier to create some games, such as isometric-view games, which routinely need to show the different sides of game elements.

Adding a 3D Player to a 2D Scene

To add a 3D shape to your 2D game, start by including the DTS-model file and related texture files to your game project. Next, add the code that renders it onscreen. In this example, we'll load the orange_player DTS model that is packaged with the Torque X FPS sample game.

```
public void CreatePlayer()
{
    T2DShape3D shape = new T2DShape3D();
    shape.Name = "Player";

    shape.SetShape(@"data\shapes\boombot\orange_player.dts");
    shape.ShapeScale = new Microsoft.Xna.Framework.Vector3(10);

    shape.Components.AddComponent(new MovementComponent());
    shape.Components.AddComponent(new T2DPhysicsComponent());

    TorqueObjectDatabase.Instance.Register(shape);
}
```

In this case, the model file player.dts is included with the project in XNA Game Studio. An instance of T2DShape3D is created and assigned the name Player for later reference. Next, the path is set that points to the model file. Then, add the MovementComponent and T2DPhysicsComponent so that we can move the shape around the screen using the arrow keys. Lastly, we register the object with the TorqueObjectDatabase so that the shape can appear onscreen. Next, let's try some basic 3D transforms, such as scaling, rotation, and translation.

Rotating the 3D Player

Rotating a 3D shape traditionally requires complex matrix transformations. However, in a Torque X 2D game, the process is significantly simpler. You can easily rotate a shape about any axis by creating a Vector3 object and setting the amount of rotation in degrees along each axis.

```
shape.Rotation2 = new Vector3(0, 90, 0);
```

This code fragment rotates the 3D shape 90 degrees about the Y-axis. You can program a continuous rotation in a ProcessTick() method. This would work well for a power-up item within the game or a vehicle-selection user interface.

```
T2DShape3D shape;
float angle = 0f;
```

```
public void ProcessTick(GarageGames.Torque.Sim.Move move, float dt)
{
    angle += 0.25F;
    shape.Rotation2 = new Vector3(0, angle, 0);
}
```

This method assumes that the shape's variable points to a stored reference in the created T2DShape3D object and a float variable named angle. On each tick, this method increments the angle variable and uses it to fill the Vector3 object that determines the rotation amount. A higher incremental value, such as 1, will make the rotation faster whereas a lower value, such as 0.01, will make the rotation slower.

Scaling the 3D Player

You can increase the size, or scale, of a 3D shape by setting the ShapeScale property. This property is also a Vector3 to allow you to set the scale along the X, Y, or Z axes.

```
shape.ShapeScale = new Microsoft.Xna.Framework.Vector3(10);
```

In this code fragment, the ShapeScale property is assigned to a new Vector3 object that is initialized to a value of 10 in all three directions. This is equivalent to initializing a vector as Vector3(10,10,10). You can also program a continuous increase in the scale of a 3D shape within a ProcessTick() method.

```
T2DShape3D shape;
float scale = 0f;

public void ProcessTick(GarageGames.Torque.Sim.Move move, float dt)
{
    if (scale < 20)
        scale += 0.25F;
    else
        scale = 0F;

    shape.ShapeScale = new Microsoft.Xna.Framework.Vector3(scale);
}
```

As the ProcessTick() method is called on every tick, the class variable scale is increased by 0.25 with a maximum value of 20. When the scale value reaches 20, the scale returns to zero. Next, the ShapeScale property is assigned to the new scale value, effectively growing the 3D shape over time.

Translating the 3D Player

A 3D shape can be translated, or moved, around a 2D scene with the help of the SetPosition() method and the Layer property. Both work exactly the same as any other 2D scene object.

```
shape.SetPosition(Vector2.Zero, true);
shape.Layer = 0;
```

In this code fragment, the shape's position is set to (0,0), which is the center of the 2D scene. You can also program a continuous translation across the 2D scene within a ProcessTick() method.

```
T2DShape3D shape;
float xPosition = 0f;

public void ProcessTick(GarageGames.Torque.Sim.Move move, float dt)
{
  if (xPosition < 20)
    xPosition += 0.25F;
  else
    xPosition = 0F;

  shape.SetPosition(new Vector2(xPosition,0), true);
}
```

Now, with every tick, the 3D shape is translated to the right since the position's X coordinate is increasing while the Y coordinate remains at zero. This is a very simple example of translation. In the next section, we will start working with 3D shapes within a 3D scene.

Creating a 3D-Game Project

Adding a 3D shape to a 2D game is a great way to become familiar with rendering and transforming 3D shapes. But it's not quite the same as creating a 3D game. So, let's move on to the exciting part—working with 3D scenes.

Creating a New 3D Game

Start by returning to XNA Game Studio and creating a new project. Select the Starter Game 3D project template as shown in Figure 11.6 and name it MyXnaFPS.

The template creates a new project for a 3D game that is similar to the 2D-game template. Like its 2D-game counterpart, the 3D project includes a

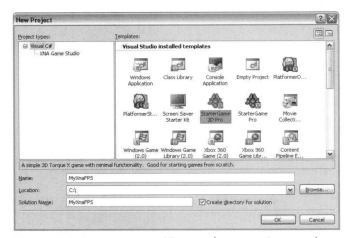

Figure 11.6. Creating a new 3D game from a project template.

Figure 11.7. Running your first 3D game project.

Game.cs file that represents the starting point for the game and a levelData.txscene file that contains a definition for a game level. But that's where the similarity ends. The contents of the level file reveal definitions for T3DScenegraph, Sun, Sky, and Terrain objects. When you compile and run the game, differences become obvious. You now have a real 3D game.

Even though this scene involves very little source code and a fairly small level file, it still bundles a lot of functionality. The scene illustrates a sky box with a seemingly endless horizon, a flaring sun in the sky, a vast desert setting with a detailed texture and lightmapped shadows, and a free-roaming camera bound to the keyboard or game controller. It's an impressive start but definitely needs some company. Let's make this game more interesting by adding our 3D player model.

Adding a Player 3D Model

After you add your DTS-model files and images added to your project, it's time to start rendering them in the game. Adding scene objects into a 3D game is very similar to adding scene objects into a 2D game. Essentially, create some sort of TorqueObject descendent, add components, and then register them with the TorqueObjectDatabase.

Rendering a shape onscreen minimally requires three elements, as shown in Figure 11.8. First, you need to have a TorqueObject-derived object. Then, you need to have a T3DTSRenderComponent that defines which shape to load and a T3DSceneComponent that defines how and where in the scene the shape will appear.

Let's create a CreatePlayer() method which will add our player to the Scene. Open your project's Game.cs file and add the following namespace references to the top. This will expose the Torque X 3D classes needed to create and render the player.

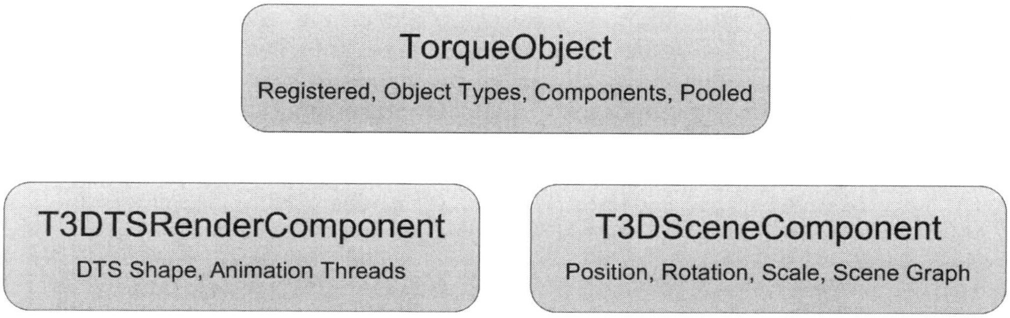

Figure 11.8. The essential classes needed to create a 3D shape.

using GarageGames.Torque.T3D;
using GarageGames.Torque.T3D.
    RigidCollision;
using Microsoft.Xna.Framework;

> If you plan to use another 3D-model format, for example a .x or .fbx file, you would replace the attached T3DTSRenderComponent with a T3DXNARenderComponent and set its filename property to point to the mesh file.

Next, find the BeginRun() method and add a call to the CreatePlayer() method at the end. Just as with the 2D games, everything begins with the BeginRun() method. In this case, the levelData.txscene file is loaded. Then, a GUISceneView object reference is created along with a reference to a 3D camera. This is a great place to create other scene elements, such as our player.

```
protected override void BeginRun()
{
    base.BeginRun();

    SceneLoader.Load(@"data\levels\levelData.txscene");

    GUISceneview sceneView =
        TorqueObjectDatabase.Instance.FindObject<GUISceneview>
        ("DefaultSceneView");

    T3DCameraComponent camera = TorqueObjectDatabase.
        Instance.FindObject<T3DCameraComponent>
        "CameraComponent");

    sceneView.Camera = camera;
    CreatePlayer();
}
```

Now, let's add the CreatePlayer() method to this file. First, we create a new TorqueObject instance, named objPlayer. Next, we add the necessary components to render the player model. An instance of the T3DTSRenderComponent is created and its ShapeName property is set to point to the DTS-model file. An instance of the T3DSceneComponent is also created and its position within the 3D world is set. Next, both of these components are added to the objPlayer object. Finally, the player object is registered with the TorqueObjectDatabase and appears in the scene.

```
public void CreatePlayer()
{
    TorqueObject objPlayer = new TorqueObject();
    objPlayer.Name = "PlayerObject";

    T3DSceneComponent componentScene = new
    T3DSceneComponent();
    componentScene.Position = new Vector3(1024, 1036, 300);
    componentScene.SceneGroup = "PlayerObject";
    objPlayer.Components.AddComponent(componentScene);

    T3DTSRenderComponent componentRender = new
        T3DTSRenderComponent();
    componentRender.ShapeName = @"data\shapes\boombot\orange_
        player.dts";
```

Figure 11.9. Rendering the player model in the 3D scene.

```
componentRender.SceneGroupName = "PlayerObject";
objPlayer.Components.AddComponent(componentRender);

//register the player object
TorqueObjectDatabase.Instance.Register(objPlayer);
}
```

This is the bare minimum code required to add your player model to the scene. When the game runs, the player model will be created and positioned within the scene at (1024,1036,300).

You can use the WASD and arrow keys to fly around the scene and view your player from different angles. In the next chapter, we'll transform this static model into an interactive player.

Summary

In this chapter, we covered the fundamentals of 3D programming with a review of the most common concepts. We also took a closer look at the core components of 3D games, the 3D model, and what requirements exist to bring a 3D model into a Torque X game. Next, we reviewed the Torque X 3D Framework and all of the classes it encompasses and then used these elements to create a simple 3D scene that renders our player model. In the next chapter, we'll bring our player model to life with animation, physics, collisions, and interaction with other game elements.

3D Player Object

12

In the last chapter, you were introduced to some basic 3D-game concepts and the Torque X 3D Framework. The chapter ended by creating a simple 3D scene and adding a player model to it. In this chapter, you will take that player starting point and add additional functionality to make it an interactive player within a 3D game.

We'll begin with our existing player object and add device input that moves the player model around the 3D scene. Next, we'll add some physics to the player model to let gravity bring him to the ground and set up an animation framework that responds to the player input. Finally, we'll conclude the chapter by adding some detail to the player, such as a simple blob shadow.

Components Are Everywhere

In the Torque X 2D Framework, we worked with a lot of different object classes while building out a game. Some of these classes included T2DSceneObject, T2DStaticSprite, T2DAnimatedSprite, T2DScroller, and so on. The Torque X 3D Framework has far fewer classes that implement game objects than the 2D Framework. Instead, all 3D game objects are defined by the collection of components that are attached to a single generic TorqueObject. The more components you add to an object, the more functionality it gets.

Creating Complex Objects with Components

Consider a 3D camera. In the Torque X 2D Framework, you simply work with a single object, such as the T2DSceneCamera. In the Torque

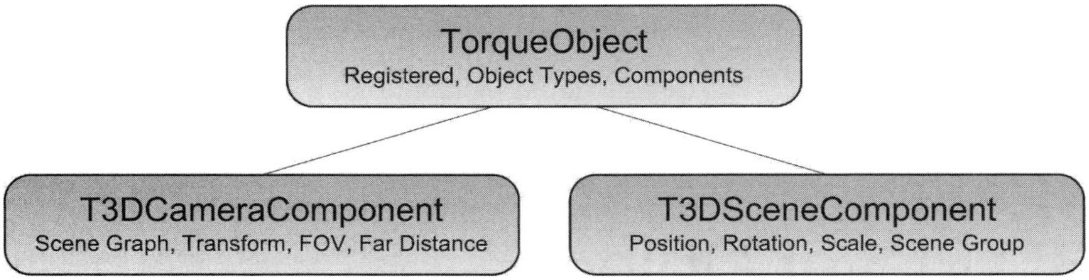

Figure 12.1. The 3D Camera composition.

X 3D Framework, however, you create a 3D camera by first creating a TorqueObject and then attaching a T3DCameraComponent as well as a T3DSceneComponent as shown in Figure 12.1. The one step of creating a T2DSceneCamera is broken out into four basic tasks within the 3D Framework. You'll notice that it's very similar to how we created the 3D player at the end of the last chapter.

- Create the parent TorqueObject.

- Create the scene component to give a position and rotation within the scene.

- Create the camera component to offer a view into the scene.

- Register the assembled TorqueObject.

As always, you can either create a new camera component from code or within the XML level data. In code, these four tasks can be packaged within a CreateCamera() method and added to your project.

```
public void CreateCamera()
{
    TorqueObject objCamera = new TorqueObject();
    objCamera.Name = "Camera";

    T3DSceneComponent componentScene = new
    T3DSceneComponent();
    componentScene.SceneGroup = "Camera";
    componentScene.Position = new Vector3(1024, 1024, 300);
    objCamera.Components.AddComponent(componentScene);

    T3DCameraComponent componentCamera = new
        T3DCameraComponent();
```

```
      componentCamera.SceneGroupName = "Camera";
      objCamera.Components.AddComponent(componentCamera);

      TorqueObjectDatabase.Instance.Register(objCamera);
}
```

Scene groups are containers that are organized into a tree and sorted according to where they are positioned in the world. The purpose of scene groups is to improve the rendering performance by skipping hidden objects when it is time to render. For many game objects, such as the player and camera, there will be a top-level scene group that contains all the renderable components attached to it. The scene group itself holds the properties that describe position, rotation, scale, visibility, and so on. Components that are attached to the game object must get a reference to the scene group so that they can also access these scene properties.

Components need to be connected together by a SceneGroupName property. It's not enough that each component shares the same parent TorqueObject. You *must* explicitly connect each component with this property. If you do not, it's very likely that your object will fail to register and then not appear within the game.

You can probably guess what it's going to take to create a 3D spawn point. You simply start with a basic TorqueObject and then attach a T3DSpawnPointComponent and a T3DSceneComponent. The following code demonstrates how.

```
   public void CreateSpawnPoint()
   {
      TorqueObject objSpawnPoint = new TorqueObject();
      objSpawnPoint.Name = "SpawnPoint";

      T3DSceneComponent componentScene = new
         T3DSceneComponent();
      componentScene.SceneGroup = "SpawnPoint";
      componentScene.Position = new Vector3(1024, 1024, 300);
      objSpawnPoint.Components.AddComponent(componentScene);

      T3DSpawnPointComponent componentSpawnPoint =
         new T3DSpawnPointComponent();
      componentSpawnPoint.SceneGroupName = "SpawnPoint";
      objSpawnPoint.Components.AddComponent
         (componentSpawnPoint);

      TorqueObjectDatabase.Instance.Register(objSpawnPoint);
   }
```

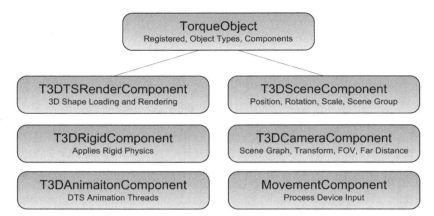

Figure 12.2. The components that make up a player object.

It should be clear to see that any combination of components can be assembled to create unique entities within a game. You can also imagine what kind of components are going to be required in order to create a useful 3D player object. And in many cases, you're going to need to create your own components to get the job done.

Creating a Player Object

Now that you have a sense of how components are assembled to create complex objects, you can start to imagine what it's going to take to create a more useful and interactive 3D player object. At the end of the last chapter, we started with the very basic components of a player. As Figure 12.2 shows, we will need to add several more components to a TorqueObject in order to create a more interesting player object.

Many of these components are stock components that are already packaged with the Torque X 3D Framework. However, there is one that is oddly missing, a movement component. Let's start off by adding the physics component, and then we can create a new movement component and add it to the player.

Adding Player Physics

At the end of the last chapter, we created a 3D model to represent the game player. Although it was great to finally see a 3D representation of the player onscreen, you might notice that he simply hovers motionless in the air. We'll need to add a physics component in order to have the player fall to the ground.

Gravity and the RigidCollisionManager

The RigidCollisionManager accommodates all of the physics work within Torque X. Anything that needs to respond to the effects of the physics system needs to be registered with the RigidCollisionManager. Typically, a RigidCollisionManager is defined for the entire scene. It is usually defined within the level data file within the <SceneData> group as follows:

```
<RigidManager type="GarageGames.Torque.T3D.RigidCollision.
    RigidCollisionManager" name="RigidManager" />
```

Since the terrain needs to process physics, a T3DRigidComponent needs to be attached to it. This is also typically done within the level data file.

```
<RigidComponent type="GarageGames.Torque.T3D.
    T3DRigidComponent">
  <RenderCollisionBounds>false</RenderCollisionBounds>
  <CollisionShapes>
      <CollisionShape>
      <Shape type="GarageGames.Torque.T3D.RigidCollision.
          CollisionXTerrainShape" />
      </CollisionShape>
  </CollisionShapes>
  <GravityScale>0.0</GravityScale>
  <Immovable>true</Immovable>
  <RigidManager nameRef="RigidManager" />
  <RigidMaterial type="GarageGames.Torque.T3D.RigidCollision.
 RigidMaterial">
      <Restitution>0.0</Restitution>
      <KineticFriction>1.0</KineticFriction>
      <StaticFriction>1.0</StaticFriction>
  </RigidMaterial>
</RigidComponent>
```

If we want any sort of rigid physics capability added to our player, then we also need to modify the CreatePlayer() method to also include a T3DrigidComponent. First, we need to find the RigidCollisionManager object. Next, we add a T3DRigidComponent to the player object with its GravityScale and Mass properties set, along with a reference to the RigidCollisionManger. The following code shows the changes to our CreatePlayer() method.

```
public void CreatePlayer()
{
    //find the physics resolver
    RigidCollisionManager rigidManager = TorqueObjectDatabase.
        Instance.FindObject<RigidCollisionManager>("RigidManager");

    TorqueObject objPlayer = new TorqueObject();
    objPlayer.Name = "PlayerObject";

    //give the player a shape
    T3DTSRenderComponent componentRender = new
        T3DTSRenderComponent();
    componentRender.SceneGroupName = "PlayerObject";
    componentRender.ShapeName = @"data\shapes\boombot\blue_player.
        dts";
    objPlayer.Components.AddComponent(componentRender);

    //give the player a presence within the scene
    T3DSceneComponent componentScene = new
        T3DSceneComponent();
    componentScene.SceneGroup = "PlayerObject";
    componentScene.Position = new Vector3(1024, 1036, 300);
    objPlayer.Components.AddComponent(componentScene);

    //give the player some physics attributes, like gravity and collision
    T3DRigidComponent componentPhysics = new
        T3DRigidComponent();
    componentPhysics.SceneGroupName = "PlayerObject";
    componentPhysics.GravityScale = 1.5f;
    componentPhysics.Mass = 10.0f;
    componentPhysics.RigidManager = rigidManager;
    componentPhysics.CollisionBody.AddCollisionShape(new
        CollisionBoxShape());
    objPlayer.Components.AddComponent(componentPhysics);

    TorqueObjectDatabase.Instance.Register(objPlayer);
}
```

Now, when the player is created, it falls towards the ground and stands firmly on the visible terrain. You can adjust many properties that change how fast the player falls and how much bounce results with a collision against the terrain. We will continue to use the physics system to move the player around the 3D scene. As the player moves, we can also trigger different animations to present the illusion of walking or jumping.

Animating the 3D Player

The Torque X 3D Framework has several classes to work with in order to control animations. These classes offer a lot of flexibility for different methods of animation playback.

The **Animation** class is a base class that defines the interface through which animations are played, paused, updated, etc. Instances of derived classes can be added to a T3DAnimationComponent to be handled automatically, or used alone and handled explicitly.

The **TSAnimation** class animates a DTS sequence in a specified thread. The thread will be created if it doesn't exist, and it must be added to an animation component that is on the same object as the TSRenderComponent that is being animated.

The **AnimationState** class serves as the base state for animations added to the AnimationFSM. Update is automatically called on the animation associated with the state when it is the current state. Derived classes must implement the Execute method to determine what state, if any, animations should be switched to.

The **AnimationFSM** class is a finite state machine that animates based on the current state. State-based animations are useful for things like player objects, since they often have different states depending on input and physics. States can be added dynamically before registration (when Setup is called) or in XML.

The **AnimationSet** class stores a list of animations and dispatches all method calls to each one. This is useful for having multiple animations that all need to be played, updated, etc. at the same time.

The **TrackAnimation** class represents an animation whose position tracks the value of an interface. This is great for connecting a frame of animation to a variable and is often used for "looking-up" and "looking-down" animations.

The **TSTrackAnimation** class sets the position of a DTS animation based on an interface value. This must be added to an animation component that is on the same object as the T3DTSRenderComponent that is being animated.

The **T3DAnimationComponent** component manages animations. There are several different types of animations included by default, and new types can be created by inheriting from the Animation class. Animations themselves manage playing, pausing, time scale, etc. This class just holds a list of animations and calls Update on each one every time the scene is rendered. Each animation has a reference back to the manager it is in. Therefore, if animations need any special information about the object they are animating, they can get it from the manager.

Creating a Player Movement Component

The new player-movement component will perform the task of capturing player input, triggering the desired player animation, and then moving the player in the direction indicated by the input. Actual player movement within the 3D world will be achieved through the use of physics forces while triggering the appropriate animations.

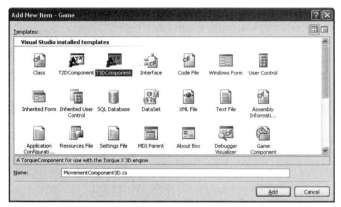

Figure 12.3. Creating a new player-movement component.

Creating the MovementComponent3D

Creating a 3D component requires exactly the same steps as creating 2D components, only now we can use the T3DComponent template. Create a new component, MovementComponent3D, as shown in Figure 12.3.

Next, change the class declaration so that the new component inherits from the T3DInputComponent abstract class instead of the TorqueComponent class. Also, include namespace references to XNA's Input packages at the top.

using Microsoft.Xna.Framework.Input;

public class MovementComponent3D : **T3DInputComponent,
IAnimatedObject**
{
}

That should do it for the class declaration. Next, add the private fields to the class. There are a number of different types of fields we need to keep track of:

- the current player index,

- player movement speeds,

- camera properties,

- references to attached player components,

- animation properties.

We will need to store the player index in case there is more than one player within the game. This value will be fed into the InputMap that is created.

We also need to store configurable values that determine the player's turning and movement speeds. These fields will be exposed as properties that can be set within Torque X Builder 3D to easily adjust the game play.

The same holds true for some of the camera properties. We can let the designer or even the game player decide if the camera controls should be inverted and with what offset from the player the camera should be positioned.

Holding a local reference to the other player components is a performance optimization. We could certainly search for the other components every time we need them but performing such a search every couple of milliseconds is a waste. So, we'll just find the other components at one time when this component is registered.

Lastly, the animation fields keep track of the currently playing animation. It's helpful for us to track this, especially on each update when we might want to change the current animation. Add the following private fields to the MovementComponent3D.cs file.

```
//input control
int _playerIndex = 0;

//player motion properties
float _turnSpeed = 2.5f;
float _moveSpeed = 4.5f;
float _playerAngle = 0.0f;

//camera properties
bool _invertedCamera = false;
Vector3 _cameraEuler = Vector3.Zero;
T3DCameraComponent _camera;
Vector3 _cameraOffset = new Vector3(0.0f, -15.0f, 8.0f);

//player components
T3DRigidComponent _rigidComponent;
T3DAnimationComponent componentAnimation;
T3DSceneComponent _playerSceneComponent;

//animation properties
TSAnimation _currentAnimation;
CurrentAnimationPlaying _currentAnimationPlaying;

enum CurrentAnimationPlaying
{
    Idle,
    Forward,
```

```
    Back,
    Fall,
    Left,
    Right,
    Land,
    Dead
}
```

Now that we have our private fields set, let's expose them as public properties. Creating MoveSpeed, TurnSpeed, InvertedCamera, and InputMap properties will be helpful when it's time to fine-tune the game later on.

```
public float MoveSpeed
{
   get { return _moveSpeed; }
   set { _moveSpeed = value; }
}

public float TurnSpeed
{
   get { return _turnSpeed; }
   set { _turnSpeed = value; }
}

public bool InvertedCamera
{
   get { return _invertedCamera; }
   set { _invertedCamera = value; }
}

public InputMap InputMap
{
   get { return _inputMap; }
}
```

Next, let's handle the methods which deal with component registration. First, we need to find the T3DRigidComponent that is already attached to the player. We can use the built-in Owner property to find this among all the components attached to the owning TorqueObject. With this owner in hand, we can query its list of components with a call to the FindComponent() method.

```
protected override bool _OnRegister(TorqueObject owner)
{
      if (!base._OnRegister(owner))
            return false;
```

```
_rigidComponent = this.Owner.Components.FindComponent
    <T3DRigidComponent>();

_playerSceneComponent = this.Owner.Components.
    FindComponent<T3DSceneComponent>();

return true;
}
```

We'll use our reference to the T3DRigidComponent to set the velocity of the player. The player's T3DSceneComponent will be used to tell our component where the player is at any given moment. And the reference to the T3DCameraComponent will let us update the position of the camera to follow. But more about that later. We should also add some cleanup to the _OnUnRegister() method to clear out the ControlObject property when the component shuts down.

```
protected override void _OnUnregister()
{
    base._OnUnregister();

    PlayerManager.Instance.GetPlayer(_playerIndex).ControlObject =
        null;
}
```

Our next task will be to set up the InputMap object and map specific input to movement actions that drive our player around the scene.

Set up the InputMap Object

Capturing input in a 3D game is essentially the same as it is in a 2D game. You need to create an InputMap object and bind events to methods that take action. The Torque X 3D Framework makes the process a little more intuitive by providing an abstract base class, named T3DInputComponent. An abstract class is useless until it is inherited by a nonabstract class that implements its methods. In this case, a derived class is required to implement the _SetupInput() and _UpdateInput() methods. Let's start with the _SetupInput() method.

```
protected override void _SetupInput(InputMap inputMap, int gamepad,
    int keyboard)
{
    // wasd
    inputMap.BindMove(keyboard, (int)Keys.D, MoveMapTypes.
        StickDigitalRight, 0);
    inputMap.BindMove(keyboard, (int)Keys.A, MoveMapTypes.
        StickDigitalLeft, 0);
```

```
inputMap.BindMove(keyboard, (int)Keys.W, MoveMapTypes.
    StickDigitalUp, 0);
inputMap.BindMove(keyboard, (int)Keys.S, MoveMapTypes.
    StickDigitalDown, 0);

// arrows
inputMap.BindMove(keyboard, (int)Keys.Right, MoveMapTypes.
    StickDigitalRight, 1);
inputMap.BindMove(keyboard, (int)Keys.Left, MoveMapTypes.
    StickDigitalLeft, 1);
inputMap.BindMove(keyboard, (int)Keys.Up, MoveMapTypes.
    StickDigitalUp, 1);
inputMap.BindMove(keyboard, (int)Keys.Down, MoveMapTypes.
    StickDigitalDown, 1);


//get the player object and his animation component
TorqueObject player = TorqueObjectDatabase.Instance.FindObject
    <TorqueObject>("PlayerObject");

componentAnimation = player.Components.FindComponent
    <T3DAnimationComponent>();

//set up the animtions
SetupAnimations();

ProcessList.Instance.AddAnimationCallback(Owner, this);
}
```

The T3DInputComponent abstract class conveniently offers an InputMap object for us to work with. So, all we need to do is set the input bindings we want. In this case, we map the WASD keys to move index 0 and the Arrow keys to move index 1. Later, we'll reference these move indexes and update the player accordingly. For now, we also take the opportunity to get a hold of the player object and save a local reference to its T3DAnimationComponent. We'll use this reference to trigger the animations we want in response to the player input. We'll also call the SetupAnimations() method which initializes all of the animation threads and then start requesting animation ticks with a call to AddAnimationCallback().

Processing Input Updates

The other method our class is required to implement, as a descendent of the T3DInputComponent abstract class, is the _UpdateInput() method. This is much like the ProcessTick() method that we have been implementing for all of our other components. We'll use this method to see what buttons are being pressed and translate those input commands into movement instructions for our player. Later, we'll use the translation to animate the player as it moves around the scene.

As far as player movement goes, the _UpdateInput() method needs to accomplish two specific tasks: rotate the player as it turns and move the player around the scene. Turning the player is a little complicated in that it deals with a tricky math construct, known as the quaternion, to deal with 3D rotations.

As you might recall, we used the BindMove() method to map the left and right arrow keys to the stick index 1, as indicated by the last parameter to BindMove(). We'll use this binding to rotate the player left or right. We start by getting the stick input value, which will be a value between -1.0 and 1.0, and assign it to a float variable named rotX. Next, we'll perform some logarithmic scaling to determine how much to rotate the player. The results are passed into the a CreateFromYawPitchRoll() method to return a quaternion value that can be set for the scene group's rotation. The same rotation calculations can also be applied pitch (rotY) and roll (rotZ) values for games that might want to rotate on all axes, such as an airplane or spaceflight simulator.

Moving the player around the scene is much simpler than rotating it. We start by getting the matrix transform for the player. We can extract the right and forward vectors from the matrix using the MatrixUtil helper class. These vectors can then be multiplied by the amount of stick input in the X and Y directions and then scaled by a _moveSpeed multiplier. The resulting vector is assigned as a velocity value for the player's rigid physics component.

```
protected override void _UpdateInput(Move move, float dt)
{
    if (move.Sticks.Count < 2)
        return;

    //
    // Move the player object within the scene
    //
    //process rotations
    float rotX = move.Sticks[1].X;
    rotX = (float)Math.Pow(Math.Abs(rotX), Math.E) * (rotX > 0.0f ?
        1.0f : -1.0f);

    float rotY = _invertedCamera ? move.Sticks[1].Y : -move.Sticks[1].Y;
    rotY = (float)Math.Pow(Math.Abs(rotY), Math.E) * (rotY > 0.0f ?
        1.0f : -1.0f);
    _playerAngle = (_playerAngle - (_turnSpeed * dt * rotX)) % (2.0f *
        (float)Math.PI);
```

```
SceneGroup.Rotation = Quaternion.CreateFromYawPitchRoll(0.0f,
    0.0f, _playerAngle);

//process movement
Matrix playerTranslationMatrix = _playerSceneComponent.
    Transform;
Vector3 right = MatrixUtil.MatrixGetRow(0, ref
    playerTranslationMatrix);
Vector3 forward = MatrixUtil.MatrixGetRow(1, ref
    playerTranslationMatrix);
Vector3 vel = ((forward * move.Sticks[0].Y) + (right * move.
    Sticks[0].X)) * _moveSpeed;
_rigidComponent.Velocity = vel;


//
// Animate the player object as it moves within the scene
//
if (move != null)
{
    //side stepping
    if (move.Sticks[0].X > 0)
    {
        if (_currentAnimationPlaying != CurrentAnimationPlaying.Left)
        {
            _currentAnimationPlaying = CurrentAnimationPlaying.Left;
            _currentAnimation = (TSAnimation)componentAnimation.
                GetAnimation("Left");
            _currentAnimation.Play();
        }
        return;
    }
    else if (move.Sticks[0].X < 0)
    {
        if (_currentAnimationPlaying != CurrentAnimationPlaying.
            Right)
        {
            _currentAnimationPlaying = CurrentAnimationPlaying.Right;
            _currentAnimation = (TSAnimation)componentAnimation.
                GetAnimation("Right");
            _currentAnimation.Play();
        }
        return;
    }
```

```
    //forward/backward
    if (move.Sticks[0].Y > 0)
    {
        if (_currentAnimationPlaying != CurrentAnimationPlaying.
            Forward)
        {
            _currentAnimationPlaying = CurrentAnimationPlaying.
                Forward;
            _currentAnimation = (TSAnimation)componentAnimation.
                GetAnimation("Forward");
            _currentAnimation.Play();
        }
        return;
    }
    else if (move.Sticks[0].Y < 0)
    {
        if (_currentAnimationPlaying != CurrentAnimationPlaying.Back)
        {
            _currentAnimationPlaying = CurrentAnimationPlaying.Back;
            _currentAnimation = (TSAnimation)componentAnimation.
                GetAnimation("Back");
            _currentAnimation.Play();
        }
        return;
    }

    if (_currentAnimationPlaying != CurrentAnimationPlaying.Idle)
    {
        _currentAnimationPlaying = CurrentAnimationPlaying.Idle;
        _currentAnimation = (TSAnimation)componentAnimation.
            GetAnimation("Idle");
        _currentAnimation.Play();
    }
}

}
```

The important lesson here is that we do not manually position the player object. Instead, we apply a velocity to the player object and let the physics component set the position of the player. The reason for this is that we want the player shape to react to collisions within the scene, such as remaining above the terrain and colliding with other shapes. If we arbitrarily set the player's position, these collisions are not automatically processed.

If you want your player to continue moving, even after the forward key is released, you can make the velocity additive instead of absolute. Change: _rigidComponent.Velocity = vel; to _rigidComponent.Velocity += vel; This might be useful for the coasting of a wheeled vehicle or the drift of a spacecraft.

Animating the Player

The _UpdateInput() method is also responsible for animating the player. It triggers an appropriate animation by first validating that input was actually received, which is indicated by a nonnull Move structure. Next, the method evaluates which stick input axis was pressed to determine if the player is moving forward, backward, or to the side.

This method next checks to see if the animation that should be playing is already the currently playing animation. This way, we can just let the current animation thread continue playing instead of restarting the same animation on every tick update. If the desired animation is not playing, then the current animation is set to the desired animation by setting the current TSAnimation object to an animation that is returned by the T3DAnimationComponent. Lastly, the TSAnimation's Play() method can be called to start the animation thread's playback.

The only problem to be aware of is that the Play() method just starts an animation; in order to continue it, you need to advance the time yourself. This is where the UpdateAnimation() method comes in. This method is also specified by the IAnimatedObject interface and is called on every tick so that animation components can advance the animation-playback thread. All you need to do here is check to see that there is a current animation playback in progress. If there is, then advance the playback thread. The _currentAnimation object will hold a different animation depending upon the current action of the player.

```
public void UpdateAnimation(float dt)
{
    if (_currentAnimation != null)
    {
        _currentAnimation.Thread.AdvanceTime(dt);
    }
}
```

Rounding out the Public Methods

This component is going to need a couple more public methods. The CopyTo() method is should be very familiar by now and we still need it to properly clone this component.

```
public override void CopyTo(TorqueComponent obj)
{
    base.CopyTo(obj);
```

```
      MovementComponent3D obj2 = (MovementComponent3D)obj;
      obj2.InvertedCamera = InvertedCamera;
      obj2.PlayerIndex = PlayerIndex;
      obj2.MoveSpeed = MoveSpeed;
      obj2.TurnSpeed = TurnSpeed;
   }
```

The SetupAnimations() method goes through the process of defining all of the animation threads that exist for the 3D shape. In this case, there are six animations defined within the DTS model. Their sequence names are root, run, fall, back, side, and land. Note that sometimes animations can be reused by playing them in reverse, as done with the left animation. Just set the animationLeft.TimeScale property to a negative value to playback in reverse.

```
   public void SetupAnimations()
   {
      //Idle Animation
      TSAnimation animationIdle = new TSAnimation();
      animationIdle.ThreadName = "ActionThread";
      animationIdle.SequenceName = "root";
      animationIdle.Name = "Idle";
      componentAnimation.AddAnimation(animationIdle);

      //Forward Animation
      TSAnimation animationForward = new TSAnimation();
      animationForward.ThreadName = "ActionThread";
      animationForward.SequenceName = "run";
      animationForward.Name = "Forward";
      componentAnimation.AddAnimation(animationForward);

      //Fall Animation
      TSAnimation animationFall = new TSAnimation();
      animationFall.ThreadName = "ActionThread";
      animationFall.SequenceName = "fall";
      animationFall.Name = "Fall";
      componentAnimation.AddAnimation(animationFall);

      //Back Animation
      TSAnimation animationBack = new TSAnimation();
      animationBack.ThreadName = "ActionThread";
      animationBack.SequenceName = "back";
      animationBack.Name = "Back";
      componentAnimation.AddAnimation(animationBack);
```

```
//Left Animation
TSAnimation animationLeft = new TSAnimation();
animationLeft.ThreadName = "ActionThread";
animationLeft.SequenceName = "side";
animationLeft.Name = "Left";
animationLeft.TimeScale = -1.0F;
componentAnimation.AddAnimation(animationLeft);

//Right Animation
TSAnimation animationRight = new TSAnimation();
animationRight.ThreadName = "ActionThread";
animationRight.SequenceName = "side";
animationRight.Name = "Right";
componentAnimation.AddAnimation(animationRight);

//Land Animation
TSAnimation animationLand = new TSAnimation();
animationLand.ThreadName = "ActionThread";
animationLand.SequenceName = "land";
animationLand.Name = "Land";
componentAnimation.AddAnimation(animationLand);

//Dead Animation
TSAnimation animationDead = new TSAnimation();
animationDead.ThreadName = "ActionThread";
animationDead.SequenceName = "land";
animationDead.Name = "Dead";
componentAnimation.AddAnimation(animationDead);

    _currentAnimation = animationIdle;
}
```

It is worth mentioning that the SetupAnimations() method only defines the animations that can be played back; it does not actually play them.

Attaching the MovementComponent3D to the Player

Now that we have a solid player movement component, we can add it to our 3D player just like any other component. Remember to set the SceneGroupName to properly link this component with the parent object. A T3DAnimationComponent will also need to be attached to the player object.

```
public void CreatePlayer()
{
```

```
//find the physics resolver
RigidCollisionManager rigidManager = TorqueObjectDatabase.
    Instance.FindObject<RigidCollisionManager>("RigidManager");

TorqueObject objPlayer = new TorqueObject();
objPlayer.Name = "PlayerObject";

T3DSceneComponent componentScene = new
    T3DSceneComponent();
componentScene.Position = new Vector3(1024, 1036, 300);
componentScene.SceneGroup = "PlayerObject";
objPlayer.Components.AddComponent(componentScene);

T3DTSRenderComponent componentRender = new
    T3DTSRenderComponent();
componentRender.ShapeName = @"data\shapes\boombot\orange_
    player.dts";
componentRender.SceneGroupName = "PlayerObject";
objPlayer.Components.AddComponent(componentRender);

//give the player some physics attributes, like gravity and collision
T3DRigidComponent componentPhysics = new
    T3DRigidComponent();
componentPhysics.SceneGroupName = "PlayerObject";
componentPhysics.GravityScale = 1.5f;
componentPhysics.Mass = 10.0f;
componentPhysics.RigidManager = rigidManager;
componentPhysics.CollisionBody.AddCollisionShape(new
    CollisionBoxShape());
objPlayer.Components.AddComponent(componentPhysics);

//add the animation component
T3DAnimationComponent componentAnimation = new
    T3DAnimationComponent();
componentAnimation.SceneGroupName = "PlayerObject";
objPlayer.Components.AddComponent(componentAnimation);

//add the player-movement component
MovementComponent3D componentMovement = new
    MovementComponent3D();
componentMovement.SceneGroupName = "PlayerObject";
objPlayer.Components.AddComponent(componentMovement);

TorqueObjectDatabase.Instance.Register(objPlayer);
}
```

After you compile and run your game, your player should be moving and animating in response to device input. You might also notice that we no longer have control over the camera. We'll fix that next, but if you want to see your player animation working, you can stop the player from falling by temporarily setting the GravityScale property on the componentPhysics object to zero.

Moving the Camera with the Player

The role of the 3D camera is to specify a viewpoint into the 3D scene. It works with the scene graph to determine what is rendered. The camera requires a position and rotation, known as a transform, a near distance, a far distance, and a field-of-view. These properties work together to define what scene elements are rendered.

A camera object is added to the scene, just like any other scene object, and is registered with the TorqueObjectDatabase. It also can have components attached to it. The default levelData.txscene file that is created by the StarterGame 3D project template defines a camera with a T3DSceneComponent to identify its position and a FreeCameraComponent to enable the camera to fly around the scene in response to player input.

```
<CameraComponent type="GarageGames.Torque.T3D.
    FreeCameraComponent" name="CameraComponent"/>
```

Unfortunately, the FreeCameraComponent creates an InputMap object that will conflict with our movement component's Input map. To resolve this conflict, let's change the FreeCameraComponent into a T3DCameraComponent by changing the camera definition within the levelData.txscene file to the following.

```
<CameraComponent type="GarageGames.Torque.T3D.
    T3DCameraComponent" name="CameraComponent"/>
```

Since we want to update the position of the camera with the player, it makes sense to handle the camera updates within the MovementComponent3D class. We can start by updating the _OnRegister() method to get a hold of the registered camera.

```
protected override bool _OnRegister(TorqueObject owner)
{
    if (!base._OnRegister(owner))
        return false;

    _rigidComponent = this.Owner.Components.FindComponent
        <T3DRigidComponent>();
```

```
_playerSceneComponent = this.Owner.Components.
   FindComponent<T3DSceneComponent>();

_camera = TorqueObjectDatabase.Instance.
   FindComponent<T3DCameraComponent>("CameraComponent");

return true;
}
```

Next, we can change the UpdateInput() method to position the camera along with the player object. After the rigid component's velocity is added, include the following code fragment.

```
if (_camera != null)
{
   Vector3 cameraPosition = Vector3.Add(SceneGroup.Position,
      _cameraOffset);
   _camera.SetTransform( Matrix.CreateTranslation(cameraPosition),
      false );
}
```

This code fragment first checks to ensure that the component has a valid reference to the camera component. Next, the position of the camera is calculated with some vector math that adds the scene-group position of the movement component with the offset vector defined earlier within the movement component. Since the camera's position, or transform, is defined by a translation matrix, we need to convert the Vector3 into a matrix. Fortunately, the Matrix class provides a CreateTranslation() method to do just that.

Adding a Player Shadow

Throughout this chapter, we have been adding a number of components to the player object in order to add more functionality. One more component worth adding is the T3DBlobShadowCasterComponent. This component projects a representation of a shadow below the player, as shown in Figure 12.4. This component can be added to the end of our CreatePlayer() method.

```
public void CreatePlayer()
{
   //find the physics resolver
   RigidCollisionManager rigidManager = TorqueObjectDatabase.
      Instance.FindObject<RigidCollisionManager>("RigidManager");
```

Figure 12.4. Adding a shadow component to the player object.

```
TorqueObject objPlayer = new TorqueObject();
objPlayer.Name = "PlayerObject";

T3DSceneComponent componentScene = new
    T3DSceneComponent();
componentScene.Position = new Vector3(1024, 1036, 300);
componentScene.SceneGroup = "PlayerObject";
objPlayer.Components.AddComponent(componentScene);

T3DTSRenderComponent componentRender = new
    T3DTSRenderComponent();
componentRender.ShapeName = @"data\shapes\boombot\orange_
    player.dts";
componentRender.SceneGroupName = "PlayerObject";
objPlayer.Components.AddComponent(componentRender);

//give the player some physics attributes, like gravity and collision
T3DRigidComponent componentPhysics = new
```

```
        T3DRigidComponent();
    componentPhysics.SceneGroupName = "PlayerObject";
    componentPhysics.GravityScale = 1.5f;
    componentPhysics.Mass = 10.0f;
    componentPhysics.RigidManager = rigidManager;
    componentPhysics.CollisionBody.AddCollisionShape(new
        CollisionBoxShape());
    objPlayer.Components.AddComponent(componentPhysics);

    //add the animation component
    T3DAnimationComponent componentAnimation = new
        T3DAnimationComponent();
    componentAnimation.SceneGroupName = "PlayerObject";
    objPlayer.Components.AddComponent(componentAnimation);

    //add the player movement conmponent
    MovementComponent3D componentMovement = new
        MovementComponent3D();
    componentMovement.SceneGroupName = "PlayerObject";
    objPlayer.Components.AddComponent(componentMovement);

    //add a simple shadow component
    T3DBlobShadowCasterComponent componentShadow = new
        T3DBlobShadowCasterComponent();
    componentShadow.SceneGroupName = "PlayerObject";
    objPlayer.Components.AddComponent(componentShadow);

    TorqueObjectDatabase.Instance.Register(objPlayer);
}
```

The T3DBlobShadowCasterComponent projects the shadow based on the direction of the sun. This requires having a Sun object within the scene that has an attached T3DLightComponent with a directional light source. Shadows are cast upon any surface that has a collision mesh, including terrains and static meshes.

Summary

In this chapter, we put our new knowledge of the Torque X 3D Framework to work by applying it to a common player object. We started with physics properties, such as gravity and collisions. Then, we explored player input and model animation. Now that we have a lonely player wandering through the desert, it's time to add some more game objects to the scene to fill it up and make it more interesting. In the next chapter, we'll populate our 3D scene with some structures and particle effects and look into methods for changing the terrain into something more specific to your own game. We'll also add some game elements, such as power-ups and triggers that help to complete a game setting.

3D Game Objects

13

There are many 3D objects that can be added to enhance your game. These can be environmental objects, such as a sky box, terrain, and fog, or these can be game objects, such as power-ups and triggers. Together, they can help you define your game mechanic.

Adding a Sky to the Scene

Most 3D games that are set outdoors make use of a sky box. A sky box is really not much more than a giant cube that surrounds your scene with inward facing textures and moves with the camera. It's a powerful way to set the mood for the game. You can easily change the mood of your game from a bright and cheerful spring day to a dark and mysterious night. As Figure 13.1 illustrates, you can have a sky box that presents the illusion of a horizon or fill the sky box with a star-field texture and remove the terrain to create an environment for space battles.

The Torque X 3D Framework provides the Sky object to create and manage your game's sky box. As a complete game object, it doesn't require a scene component in order to appear within the game.

The sky box is normally defined in your game's level-data file. But you can also create the Sky object in code. The following code demonstrates how to create a Sky object, set its textures, and define a distance. The SkyDistance property helps improve rendering performance by not keeping the engine guessing how far out it needs to render.

```
public void CreateSky()
{
    //create the sky
```

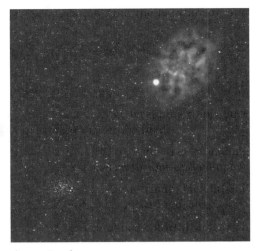

Figure 13.1. Different sky boxes can easily change the setting for your game.

```
Sky objSky = new Sky();
objSky.Name = "Sky";
objSky.Sides[0] = "data/skies/front";
objSky.Sides[1] = "data/skies/right";
objSky.Sides[2] = "data/skies/back";
objSky.Sides[3] = "data/skies/left";
objSky.Sides[4] = "data/skies/top";
objSky.Sides[5] = "data/skies/bottom";
objSky.RenderBottom = true;
objSky.SkyDistance = 5;

//register the sky object
TorqueObjectDatabase.Instance.Register( objSky );
_currentlySelectedObject = objSky;

return;
}
```

Although you don't need to attach any components, the Sky object is still a TorqueObject (by inheritance) and must be registered with the TorqueObjectDatabase. Since you can specify the texture file for each inward-facing side of the sky box, you can also change them on demand. This is helpful for games that might want to change the sky box dynamically or procedurally without loading a new scene.

Adding a Sun to the Scene

Another useful game object, for both terrestrial and space games, is the Sun. This object performs a couple of useful tasks. For starters, it renders an animated corona, or sun flare, for added realism in the game. But it also provides a directional light source. This is extremely useful for some of the shader effects, such as the shadow caster for the player's shadow and the normal map shader to reveal surface detail on the player's skin texture.

The Sun object is also typically defined within the level-data file, but can be created in code as well.

Figure 13.2. A Sun object added to the 3D scene.

It also inherits from TorqueObject and must be registered before it can be added to the scene. The Sun also requires a little more set-up in that it needs one or two texture materials to represent the visible corona, or sun flare. It also needs to have a directional light source added.

```
public void CreateSun()
{
    //create the Sun
    Sun objSun = new Sun();
    objSun.Name = "Sun";

    T3DSceneComponent componentScene = new
        T3DSceneComponent();
    objSun.Components.AddComponent(componentScene);

    DirectionalLight lightSun = new DirectionalLight();
    lightSun.DiffuseColor = new Vector3(0.9f, 0.9f, 0.63f);
    lightSun.AmbientColor = new Vector3(0.4f, 0.5f, 0.65f);
    lightSun.Direction = new Vector3(0f, -0.8191521f, -0.5735765f);
    lightSun.ConstantAttenuation = 1;
```

```
//create the corona materials
SimpleMaterial coronaMaterial1 = new SimpleMaterial();
coronaMaterial1.TextureFilename = "data/skies/corona01";

SimpleMaterial coronaMaterial2 = new SimpleMaterial();
coronaMaterial2.TextureFilename = "data/skies/corona02";

T3DLightComponent componentLight = new T3DLightComponent();
componentLight.LightList.Add(lightSun);

//set the Sun's visible materials
objSun.Material1 = coronaMaterial1;
objSun.Material2 = coronaMaterial2;

//register the Sun
TorqueObjectDatabase.Instance.Register(objSun);
}
```

The Sun doesn't necessarily need to represent a sun in the sky. Several Sun objects can be added to the scene and placed in different positions to cast light and create shadows.

Adding Some Fog to the Scene

Fog helps to gently fade 3D objects out of a scene based on a designated distance. This prevents an unexpected disappearance of the 3D shape when it is finally removed from the scene and ultimately helps to improve performance while keeping the 3D scene attractive.

A fog material is set on the scene graph and rendered with every pass to slowly fade them to a solid color as they get farther away. Properties include the fog color, the near distance to start the fog rendering, and the far distance at which the fog is fully rendered.

```
public void CreateFog()
{
    //create the fog material
    DistanceFog materialFog = new
        DistanceFog();
    materialFog.FogColorAsVector3 =
```

Figure 13.3. A 3D scene without fog (left) and with fog (right).

```
        new Vector3(0.941f, 0.859f, 0.612f);
    materialFog.FogNearDistance = 100;
    materialFog.FogFarDistance = 900;

    //set the fog material
    T3DCameraComponent camera =
        TorqueObjectDatabase.Instance.
        FindObject<T3DCameraComponent>
        ("CameraComponent");

    ((T3DSceneGraph)camera.SceneGraph).FogMaterial = materialFog;
}
```

Setting the FogNearDistance value lower brings the fog closer to the camera. The difference between the FogNearDistance and FogFarDistance determines how quickly 3D objects will fade from the camera view.

Fog works really well when it's color-matched with the sky box. You can pick a point in your sky-box texture where the horizon is drawn and sample the color. Then, set the DistanceFog material color to this color for a nice blend.

Creating a Terrain

Another important 3D element for any outdoor game is a terrain for the player to traverse. Torque X is very flexible when it comes to terrains. The XTerrain class supports the creation of three different types of terrains:

- A Torque Game Engine legacy terrain.

- A RAW chunked geometry terrain.

- A procedurally generated terrain.

All terrains are implemented using the XTerrain class. Each different terrain type is implemented by creating a data object derived from the TerrainData class, setting its appropriate values, and then setting it to the Data property of the XTerrain class.

Creating the Terrain

Regardless of which type of terrain you plan to create, you always need to start with the XTerrain class. The XTerrain class inherits from TorqueObject, so it must be registered with the TorqueObjectDatabase and can have components. In fact, the most important component attached to the XTerrain is the T3DRigidComponent, without which everything would fall through the terrain.

We begin creating a terrain by getting a local reference to the scene's rigid physics manager. Next, we create the XTerrain object and set its public properties. Then, we need to attach a T3DSceneComponent to the XTerrain to give it a presence within the 3D scene. The only other component we need to add is a T3DRigidComponent so that it is processed with all other rigid physics reactions within the scene. This component needs a RigidMaterial to define the collision surface and a collision shape provided by the CollisionXTerrainShape class. Lastly, we need to specify a TerrainData object that contains the details about the terrain's shape. All that remains is to register with the TorqueObjectDatabase.

```
public void CreateTerrain()
{
    //find the physics resolver
    RigidCollisionManager rigidManager = TorqueObjectDatabase.
        Instance.FindObject<RigidCollisionManager>("RigidManager");

    //create the terrain
    XTerrain objTerrain = new XTerrain();
    objTerrain.Name = "Terrain";
    objTerrain.HorizontalScale = 8;
    objTerrain.VerticalScale = 1;
    objTerrain.LevelZeroError = 0;
    objTerrain.ViewError = 2;
    objTerrain.LODLevels = 4;
    objTerrain.LODError = 0.5f;
    objTerrain.Repeat = true;
    objTerrain.Visible = true;

    //give the terrain presence in the scene
    T3DSceneComponent componentScene = new
        T3DSceneComponent();
    componentScene.Position = new Vector3(0, 0, 0);
    componentScene.SceneGroup = "Terrain";
    objTerrain.Components.AddComponent(componentScene);

    RigidMaterial materialRigid = new RigidMaterial();
    materialRigid.Restitution = 0f;
    materialRigid.KineticFriction = 1f;
    materialRigid.StaticFriction = 1f;

    //give the terrain some physics attributes
    T3DRigidComponent componentPhysics = new
        T3DRigidComponent();
```

```
componentPhysics.SceneGroupName = "Terrain";
componentPhysics.GravityScale = 0f;
componentPhysics.RigidManager = rigidManager;
componentPhysics.RigidMaterial = materialRigid;
componentPhysics.Immovable = true;
//componentPhysics.CollisionBody.AddCollisionShape(new
//CollisionXTerrainShape());
objTerrain.Components.AddComponent(componentPhysics);

// ------  SPECIFY A TERRAIN DATA TYPE  ------
TGETerrainData terrainData = new TGETerrainData();
terrainData.TerrainFilename = "data/terrains/terrain.ter";
terrainData.LightMapFilename = "data/terrains/lightmap.png";
terrainData.TexturePathSubstitution = "data/terrains";
terrainData.DetailMaterial = "TerrainDetailMaterial";
objTerrain.Data = terrainData;

//register the terrain
TorqueObjectDatabase.Instance.Register(objTerrain);
}
```

At this point, we still have an incomplete terrain object. We need to attach a TerrainData with one of the preferred data formats in order to have it appear within the scene. Typically, the terrain format you choose depends upon the toolset and function of the terrain.

Using Legacy Terrain Data

The legacy terrain data format dates back to the original Torque Game Engine and uses a heightmap to determine the terrain's shape. The terrain data is stored in a .ter file and can really only be edited with the Torque Game Engine's Terrain Editor. The purpose for including support for format is to facilitate the migration of games into the Torque X Framework.

To use the legacy terrain format, copy the following code fragment to the end of your CreateTerrain() method. This fragment creates an instance of the TGETerrainData class and specifies paths to the .ter terrain file and the lightmap texture file.

```
//specify terrain data
TGETerrainData terrainData = new TGETerrainData();
terrainData.TerrainFilename = "data/terrains/terrain.ter";
terrainData.LightMapFilename = "data/terrains/lightmap.png";
terrainData.TexturePathSubstitution = "data/terrains";
terrainData.DetailMaterial = "TerrainDetailMaterial";
objTerrain.Data = terrainData;
```

Using Raw Terrain Data

To use the Raw terrain format, copy the following code fragment to the end of your CreateTerrain method. This fragment creates an instance of the RAWTerrainData class and specifies a path to the .raw terrain file and the lightmap texture file.

```
RAWTerrainData terrainData = new RAWTerrainData();
terrainData.TerrainFilename = "data/terrains/l3dt_generated.raw";
terrainData.LightMapFilename = "data/terrains/l3dt_generated_
    LM.jpg";
terrainData.UniqueTextureFilename = "data/terrains/l3dt_generated_
    TX.jpg";
terrainData.DetailMaterial = "TerrainDetailMaterial";
objTerrain.Data = terrainData;
```

At present, the most popular tool for creating Atlas terrains is called Large 3D Terrain Creator (L3DT) by Bundysoft (www.bundysoft.com/L3DT). This reasonably priced software guides you through the creation of large RAW terrain files. When working with L3DT, try the following guidelines. Start by selecting File ➢ New Project from the main menu and then selecting the Design/Inflate algorithm.

- Set a map size of 16 for the X and Y values.

- Set the horizontal scale to 10.

- Do not enable disk paging for mosaic maps.

- Enable edge wrapping to produce a terrain that can be tiled.

- Experiment with the remaining settings, such as elevations and climates.

- Create a Design map, Heightfield, Terrain normals, and a Light map.

L3DT presents a colorful show as it produces all of the related terrain files. When it completes, you can browse through the collection of detailed texture maps as shown in Figure 13.4.

You can save the project and all maps directly to your game project's data/terrains folder as l3dt_generated. Next, you can export the files that the RAWTerrainData class needs.

Figure 13.4. Interacting with L3DT generated texture maps.

- Select File ➤ Export ➤ Export map...

- Select the Heightfield map.

- Set the file format to Raw.

- Browse to the data/terrains folder and set the file name to l3dt_generated.raw.

- Do not resize the file by one or flip the heightmap as formerly done with TGEA.

After the terrain maps have been exported, return to XNA Game Studio and add the l3dt_generated.raw, l3dt_generated_LM.jpg, and l3dt_generated_TX.jpg files into your game project. Remember to set the properties for the .raw file. The Build Action property should be set to Content and the Copy to Output directory property should be set to Copy if Newer.

Using Procedural Terrain Data

The procedural terrain dynamically creates a terrain landscape at runtime based upon parameters you set in code. It's a great solution for games that do not require a specific terrain shape because it renders quickly and does not need to include any extra terrain data files. This works well for a flight simulator, where you can see a terrain but not really interact with it. However, it may not work well for land-based games, where the specific placement of ground structures is required.

To use the procedural terrain format, copy the following code fragment to the end of the CreateTerrain method. This fragment creates an instance of the GeneratedTerrainData class and specifies several computational properties as well as a lightmap texture file.

```
//specify terrain data
GeneratedTerrainData terrainData = new GeneratedTerrainData();
terrainData.Size = 1025;
terrainData.SmoothingPasses = 2;
terrainData.Jitter = 3;
terrainData.TerrainFilename = "data/terrains/terrain.ter";
terrainData.LightMapFilename = "data/terrains/lightmap.png";
terrainData.TexturePathSubstitution = "data/terrains";
objTerrain.Data = terrainData;
```

Particle Effects

Creating particle effects using the Torque X 3D Framework is very similar to the 2D Framework. You still need to provide the particle material,

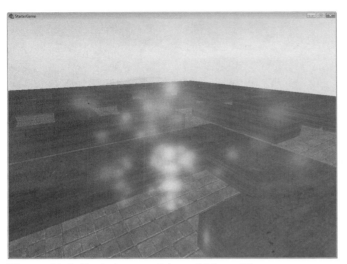

Figure 13.5. Emitting particles within a 3D scene.

define the properties of the effect, and create a particle emitter. The greatest difference is that in the 2D Framework, you work with a single T2DParticleEmitter class, whereas in the 3D Framework, you must create a TorqueObject and add components, such as T3DParticleEffectComponent.

In both frameworks, creating particle effects involves creating a material for the individual particle, creating a particle-effect definition, and then creating a particle emitter to produce the particles. The following CreateParticleEffect() method accomplishes all three of these tasks.

```
public void CreateParticleEffect()
{
    //create a scene object to hold the particle effect
    TorqueObject objParticleEffect = new TorqueObject();

    SimpleMaterial particleMaterial = new SimpleMaterial();
    particleMaterial.Name = "SparkleParticleMaterial";
    particleMaterial.TextureFilename = "data/skies/corona01.png";
    particleMaterial.IsTranslucent = true;
    particleMaterial.IsColorBlended = true;

    //set up the particle data
    T3DParticleData particleData = new T3DParticleData();
    particleData.Material = particleMaterial;
    particleData.UseInvAlpha = false;
    particleData.DragCoefficient = 0;
    particleData.GravityCoefficient = -0.05f;
    particleData.WindCoefficient = 0.5f;
    particleData.SpinRandomMin = -30.0f;
    particleData.SpinRandomMax = 30.0f;
    particleData.LifeTimeMS = 4000;
    particleData.LifeTimeVarianceMS = 250;
    particleData.Times = new float[3] { 0.0f, 0.5f, 1.0f };
    particleData.Sizes = new float[3] { 0.5f, 0.75f, 1.5f };
    particleData.Colors = new Vector4[] {
        new Vector4(0.9f, 0.9f, 0.9f, 0.2f),
        new Vector4(0.9f, 0.9f, 0.9f, 0.9f),
        new Vector4(0.9f, 0.9f, 0.9f, 0.0f) };
```

```
//set up the emitter data
T3DParticleEmitterData emitterData = new
    T3DParticleEmitterData();
emitterData.EjectionPeriodMS = 25;
emitterData.EjectionVelocity = 0.5f;
emitterData.VelocityVariance = 0.5f;
emitterData.EjectionOffset = 0;
emitterData.ThetaMin = 0;
emitterData.ThetaMax = 90;
emitterData.OrientParticles = true;
emitterData.ParticleData = particleData;

//set up the emitter
T3DParticleEmitter emitter = new T3DParticleEmitter();
emitter.UseLocalTransform = true;
emitter.ParticleEmitterData = emitterData;

//set up the particle effect
T3DParticleEffectComponent componentEffect = new
    T3DParticleEffectComponent();
componentEffect.SceneGroupName = "ParticleEffectObject";
componentEffect.PlayOnRegister = true;
componentEffect.DeleteWhenFinished = false;
componentEffect.Emitters.Add(emitter);
objParticleEffect.Components.AddComponent(componentEffect);

T3DSceneComponent componentScene = new
    T3DSceneComponent();
componentScene.SceneGroup = "ParticleEffectObject";
componentScene.Position = new Vector3(1024,1028,285);
objParticleEffect.Components.AddComponent(componentScene);

//register the particle emitter
TorqueObjectDatabase.Instance.Register(objParticleEffect);

return;
}
```

As expected by now, this method begins by creating a TorqueObject. Next, it creates a SimpleMaterial instance and points it to a .png file. The material is set to translucent so the edges of this particle softly fade.

Next, this method defines the style for each particle being emitted by defining a T3DParticleData object. First, the particle material is selected, then a series of physics and rotation-related properties are specified to define the particle's motion. Next, the particle's lifetime is specified as well as the particle's size and color changes as time progresses.

Now that the particle is well defined, this method defines the behavior of the particle emitter. The T3DParticleEmitterData object first specifies some timing, such as how often and how fast a particle is emitted. Next, the emitter specifies the direction of emission and then points to the T3DParticleData object instance that defines each particle. With the emitter data specified, this method can create a T3DParticleEmitter object that points to the emitter data.

Finally, we can start working with a T3DParticleEffectComponent that indicates if particle emission should start immediately and if it should run continuously versus deleting itself after a cycle (like an explosion effect). This component can then be attached to the parent TorqueObject, along with a scene component to specify a position, and then be registered with the TorqueObjectDatabase.

Now, the newly created particle object can be placed anywhere or mounted to anything with a T3DMountComponent.

Adding 3D Primitive Shapes

Torque X has some basic primitive shapes that can be created, such as a cube, sphere, and plane. These primitive shapes can be a lot more useful than you might first think. These shapes are great for "white-boxing" scenes for experimental game play. Instead of creating an experimental game by first building elaborate 3D models, you can simulate the game mechanic with these basic primitives. You can use a sphere shape to represent the player, plane shapes to represent platforms or walls, and differently shaped cubes to represent other game elements. Once you have your basic game mechanic working, you can dedicate time to improving the artwork with better 3D models.

Creating a Cube

Adding a 3D cube to the scene is just as easy as adding a complex 3D mesh. It still requires a TorqueObject with a T3DSceneComponent attached to it. But instead of a DTS or XNA mesh-render component, you simply add a T3DBox to it. T3DBox is a component that renders the cube shape. You can also paint the cube with a texture by specifying a material.

The following method creates a 3D cube that hovers within a 3D scene. It begins with a TorqueObject. Next, a scene component is added to specify a position within the scene. Next, a SimpleMaterial object is created and points to a texture file. Lastly, the T3DBox component is created and points to the new material. After the cube is registered, it appears within the 3D scene.

Figure 13.6. Rendering 3D primitives, such as a cube (left), sphere, or plane (right).

```
public void CreateBox()
{
   TorqueObject objBox = new TorqueObject();
   objBox.Name = "Box";

   T3DSceneComponent componentScene = new
      T3DSceneComponent();
   componentScene.SceneGroup = "Box";
   componentScene.Position = new Vector3(1080, 1080, 300);
   objBox.Components.AddComponent(componentScene);

   SimpleMaterial material = new SimpleMaterial();
   material.TextureFilename = "data/shapes/maze/stone.jpg";

   T3DBox boxComponent = new T3DBox();
   boxComponent.SceneGroupName = "Box";
   boxComponent.Material = material;
   objBox.Components.AddComponent(boxComponent);

   TorqueObjectDatabase.Instance.Register(objBox);
}
```

Again, there are countless uses for this simple primitive shape. The most common use is for populating a 3D scene with a lot of placeholder entities, ranging from tall buildings scattered around a scene for a mech battle game to walls that make up a test level in a first-person shooter game. These cubes do not need to be perfectly square either. You can change the Size property and set the X, Y, Z dimensions of the box to fit into a test level. For example, a vertical wall could be shaped by adding the following property.

```
boxComponent.Size = new Vector3(5,1,5);
```

Creating a Sphere

Creating a sphere primitive is very similar to creating the box primitive. It also has just as many uses within a test level. It is often even used to represent a placeholder shape for the player object or the hordes of attacking AI objects.

```
public void CreateSphere()
{
    TorqueObject objSphere = new TorqueObject();
    objSphere.Name = "Sphere";

    T3DSceneComponent componentScene = new
        T3DSceneComponent();
    componentScene.SceneGroup = "Sphere";
    componentScene.Position = new Vector3(1080, 1100, 300);
    objSphere.Components.AddComponent(componentScene);

    SimpleMaterial material = new SimpleMaterial();
    material.TextureFilename = "data/shapes/maze/stone.jpg";

    T3DSphere sphereComponent = new T3DSphere();
    sphereComponent.SceneGroupName = "Sphere";
    sphereComponent.Material = material;
    sphereComponent.Radius = 2.0f;
    objSphere.Components.AddComponent(sphereComponent);

    TorqueObjectDatabase.Instance.Register(objSphere);
}
```

The CreateSphere() method is effectively the same as the CreateBox() method. The T3DSphere component sets a Radius property instead of a Size property to determine its size .

Creating a Plane

The last mesh primitive is the plane and is useful for tabletops, roofs, or floating platforms. The CreatePlane() method goes through the same steps as the other primitive examples but instead attaches a T3DPlane component to the TorqueObject.

```
public void CreatePlane()
{
    TorqueObject objPlane = new TorqueObject();
    objPlane.Name = "Plane";

    T3DSceneComponent componentScene = new
        T3DSceneComponent();
    componentScene.SceneGroup = "Plane";
    componentScene.Position = new Vector3(1080, 1120, 300);
    objPlane.Components.AddComponent(componentScene);

    SimpleMaterial material = new SimpleMaterial();
    material.TextureFilename = "data/shapes/maze/stone.jpg";

    T3DPlane boxComponent = new T3DPlane();
    boxComponent.SceneGroupName = "Plane";
    boxComponent.Material = material;
    objPlane.Components.AddComponent(boxComponent);

    TorqueObjectDatabase.Instance.Register(objPlane);
}
```

You can set its dimensions by setting the Height and Width properties. There is also a Tesselation property that increases the number of triangles used to create the plane from two. Although any number of triangles used will still result in a plane, the tessellation will improve the appearance of larger planes that receive vertex lighting or use a clip-mapped texture.

Adding Static 3D Models

Earlier, we used T3DTSRenderComponent to render the player model to the scene. We also had to add a physics component to the player to keep him from falling through the terrain and into oblivion. Fortunately, we don't have to go through such an extensive set-up when it comes to buildings and other structures that will not move.

The Torque X Framework provides the T3DStaticTSRenderComponent, which will render a model as an immovable shape, complete with polysoup collision support. The greatest benefit of polysoup is that every renderable triangle becomes a collision surface. For structures, such as the maze shown in Figure 13.7, you do not need to create a separate collision mesh in addition

Figure 13.7. A 3D scene with a static mesh maze.

to your model. Instead, just bring your model into the scene and every turn and curve becomes collidable.

The following CreateMaze() method takes a 3D mesh representation of a maze that was exported into the DTS-model format and adds it into the 3D scene as a static shape. Our player object will be able to wander around within this maze and collide into solid walls, even though no collision shape was explicitly defined.

```
public void CreateMaze()
{
    //find the physics resolver
    RigidCollisionManager rigidManager
    = TorqueObjectDatabase.Instance.
    FindObject<RigidCollisionManager>
    ("RigidManager");

    TorqueObject objMaze = new TorqueObject();
    objMaze.Name = "Maze";

    //create this object as a static mesh
    T3DStaticGeometryComponent componentStatic =
        new T3DStaticGeometryComponent();
    componentStatic.SceneGroup = "MazeGroup";
    componentStatic.Position = new Vector3(1024, 1024, 275);
    objMaze.Components.AddComponent(componentStatic);

    //give the object a shape
    T3DStaticTSRenderComponent componentStaticRender =
        new T3DStaticTSRenderComponent();
    componentStaticRender.SceneGroupName = "MazeGroup";
    componentStaticRender.ShapeName = "data/shapes/maze/maze.dts";
    objMaze.Components.AddComponent(componentStaticRender);

    //specify the physics resolver
    T3DRigidComponent componentRigid = new T3DRigidComponent();
    componentRigid.SceneGroupName = "MazeGroup";
    componentRigid.RigidManager = rigidManager;
    componentRigid.Immovable = true;
    objMaze.Components.AddComponent(componentRigid);
```

TorqueObjectDatabase.Instance.Register(objMaze);
}

At first glance, the CreateMaze() method looks like several of the other create methods we have covered. Since it does involve physics, we need to get a reference to the RigidCollisionManager in order to process collisions. After the TorqueObject is created, we start by adding the T3DStaticGeometryComponent. This is a specialized form of the T3DSceneComponent, so we don't need to include that as usual. Like its scene component parent, it does have properties for position and rotation within the scene. Next, we add a T3DStaticTSRenderComponent to render the DTS shape and create the polysoup mesh. Lastly, a T3DRigidComponent is added so that the RigidManager is aware of this shape and can process it along with all other calculations. Once the object is registered with the TorqueObjectDatabase, it's ready for use within the game.

Triggers

Triggers are a very common form of player interaction within modern games. They are invisible regions within a scene that perform an action when an object enters or leaves them. You can use triggers in your game to perform a variety of options, from activating alarms to detecting a car crossing the finish line to marking a progressive save point within a game.

Since we want a trigger to react to the presence of our player, let's create a new TorqueObjectType that identifies our player. Add the following code fragment to the bottom of the CreatePlayer() method.

```
//attach an object type to the player
TorqueObjectType typePlayer = TorqueObjectDatabase.Instance.
    GetObjectType("Player");
objPlayer.ObjectType += typePlayer;
```

Next, let's add a method that creates the trigger and places it somewhere within our 3D scene. Triggers are essentially collision events that invoke a callback to a delegate method you specify. We need to get a local reference to the RigidCollisionManager. We also need to get a reference to the Player object type so that we can instruct this trigger to only process collisions with the player.

Next, we create a TorqueObject and start adding components. The scene component indicates where in the scene the trigger will be placed. The CreateTrigger() method also defines a CollisionBoxShape object that specifies the size of the trigger's collision box. Lastly, we add the T3DTriggerComponent to the object. This component identifies the collision body, identifies the colliding object type, and specifies which call back delegates will receive the collision notification. We also set a reference to the rigid manager and mark the trigger immovable. Now the trigger can be registered and added into the scene.

```
public void CreateTrigger()
{
    //find the physics resolver
    RigidCollisionManager rigidManager = TorqueObjectDatabase.
        Instance.FindObject<RigidCollisionManager>("RigidManager");

    //get the Player object type
    TorqueObjectType typePlayer = TorqueObjectDatabase.Instance.
        GetObjectType("Player");

    TorqueObject objTrigger = new TorqueObject();
    objTrigger.Name = "Trigger";

    //add the scene component
    T3DSceneComponent componentScene = new
        T3DSceneComponent();
    componentScene.SceneGroup = "Trigger";
    componentScene.Position = new Vector3(1024, 1035, 280);
    objTrigger.Components.AddComponent(componentScene);

    //create the trigger collision box
    CollisionBoxShape boxCollision = new CollisionBoxShape();
    boxCollision.Size = new Vector3(2.0f);

    //add the trigger component
    T3DTriggerComponent componentTrigger = new
        T3DTriggerComponent();
    componentTrigger.SceneGroupName = "Trigger";
    componentTrigger.CollisionBody.AddCollisionShape(boxCollision);
    componentTrigger.CollidesWith = typePlayer;
    componentTrigger.OnEnter = ProcessEnter;
    componentTrigger.OnLeave = ProcessLeave;
    componentTrigger.RigidManager = rigidManager;
    componentTrigger.Immovable = true;
    objTrigger.Components.AddComponent(componentTrigger);

    TorqueObjectDatabase.Instance.Register(objTrigger);
}
```

With a trigger created, all that's left is to implement the reaction code. When any object that has a Player object type enters the trigger region, the

ProcessEnter() delegate method is called. This is where you can add your custom game code. The ProcessLeave() method is called once the player object leaves the trigger region.

```
public static void ProcessEnter(T3DTriggerComponent trigger,
    T3DRigidComponent obj)
{
    //perform enter trigger code here
}

public static void ProcessLeave(T3DTriggerComponent trigger,
    T3DRigidComponent obj)
{
    //perform leave trigger code here
}
```

Power-Up Objects

One very common use for a trigger is a power-up, or collectible object. This is often an object that exists within the game that the player collects by running into it to gain points or more power. Its implementation is essentially the same as the basic trigger. The main difference is that the object also displays a 3D shape instead of being completely invisible.

On the surface, the CreatePowerup() method looks a lot like the CreateTrigger() method. The biggest difference is the addition of a T3DTSRenderComponent, which will load and render the 3D jewel shape that represents the power-up. Otherwise, much of its functionality remains the same in that it has a presence within the scene, it collides with the player, and it calls a delegate method to process the collision.

```
public void CreatePowerup()
{
    //find the physics resolver
    RigidCollisionManager rigidManager = TorqueObjectDatabase.
        Instance.FindObject<RigidCollisionManager>("RigidManager");

    //get the Player object type
    TorqueObjectType typePlayer = TorqueObjectDatabase.Instance.
        GetObjectType("Player");

    TorqueObject objPowerup = new TorqueObject();
    objPowerup.Name = "Powerup";

    //add the scene component
    T3DSceneComponent componentScene = new
```

```
        T3DSceneComponent();
componentScene.SceneGroup = "Powerup";
componentScene.Position = new Vector3(1024, 1035, 280);
objPowerup.Components.AddComponent(componentScene);

T3DTSRenderComponent componentRender = new
    T3DTSRenderComponent();
componentRender.ShapeName = @"data\shapes\maze\jewel.dts";
componentRender.SceneGroupName = "Powerup";
objPowerup.Components.AddComponent(componentRender);

//create the trigger collision box
CollisionBoxShape boxCollision = new CollisionBoxShape();
boxCollision.Size = componentRender.Shape.Bounds.Max;

//add the trigger component
T3DTriggerComponent componentTrigger = new
    T3DTriggerComponent();
componentTrigger.SceneGroupName = "Powerup";
componentTrigger.CollisionBody.AddCollisionShape(boxCollision);
componentTrigger.CollidesWith = typePlayer;
componentTrigger.OnCollision = ProcessCollision;
componentTrigger.RigidManager = rigidManager;
componentTrigger.Immovable = true;
objPowerup.Components.AddComponent(componentTrigger);

TorqueObjectDatabase.Instance.Register(objPowerup);
}
```

Once the power-up object is registered with the object database, it's ready to start processing collisions with the player. Unlike the OnEnter and OnLeave properties, the power-up uses the OnCollision property, which supplies much more information to the delegate method. In this case, the ProcessCollision() method applies the health increase of the power-up and then deletes the power-up object from existence.

```
public static void ProcessCollision(T3DRigidComponent us,
    T3DRigidComponent them,
    RigidContactConstraint.Contact[] contacts, int contactCount,
    float dt)
{
    //get the current health level
    float currentHealth;
    PlayerManager.Instance.GetPlayer(0).GetData("HealthLevel", out
        currentHealth);
```

```
    //increase and store the new health level
    currentHealth += 15;
    PlayerManager.Instance.GetPlayer(0).SetData("HealthLevel",
        currentHealth);

    //remove the power-up shape
    them.Owner.MarkForDelete = true;
}
```

Another interesting detail about this power-up implementation is that it makes use of the PlayerManager object. In the past, we've used the PlayerManager object to get the control object and input map for the game player. This class also provides services for reading and writing data that is specific to a player. As such, it's another great place to store values such as score, health level, etc.

Creating a 3D Weapon

It's common for 3D games to have some sort of weapon to interact with other game entities. Creating the weapon is usually separated into two separate steps: creating the 3D shape and writing the code to enable the weapon.

The 3D shape for the weapon can be anything you imagine. If you plan to mount the weapon to a player, then you should specify a node where the weapon attaches and a node where projectiles are fired from. The DTS model format is probably best for weapons since you can easily access the shape's node data in code. If your weapon is going to send off a visible projectile, then you might also want some sort of 3D shape for that too. Projectile shapes aren't required, though, and you never actually see a bullet flying through the air. However, slower moving projectiles, such as missiles, can be visible and might require a 3D shape to represent them.

Writing the code for a weapon falls into two categories: the weapon component and the projectile template. The weapon component will be attached to the player object and expose a trigger that spawns and sends off each projectile. Those projectiles will be TorqueObject instances that are spawned from a template.

Creating the Weapon Component

The main purpose of the weapon component is to spawn projectiles. This component can either be attached to a weapon object or directly to the player object. The weapon component will find a specific node within the 3D shape where projectiles will be emitted from. This way, you can reuse this component, whether the weapon is a handgun attached to a soldier

Figure 13.8. Weapons can be attached to a player or float independently.

or a turret attached to a heavy tank. You can later extend this component to add properties that track the amount of ammunition that is available and set a rate of fire.

Let's start by creating a new component using the 3D Component new item template and naming it WeaponComponent3D. You can remove the ITickObject interface from the class declaration since we don't need to process ticks.

We need to add only one private field, a TorqueObject that points to the 3D projectile object template. Each time the weapon is fired, an instance of this projectile template will be created and sent on its way. For accessibility, this private field is exposed by a public get/set property.

```
private TorqueObject _projectileTemplate;

public TorqueObject ProjectileTemplate
{
    set { _projectileTemplate = value; }
    get { return _projectileTemplate; }
}
```

The default private methods that are generated by the T3DComponent template are fine as they are. We only need to update the CopyTo() method and implement the FireWeapon() method. Like all previous components, the CopyTo() method needs to fully copy over all properties to ensure accurate component cloning.

```
public override void CopyTo(TorqueComponent obj)
{
    base.CopyTo(obj);

    WeaponComponent3D obj2 = (WeaponComponent3D)obj;
    obj2.ProjectileTemplate = obj2.ProjectileTemplate;
}
```

Finally, the most important method of this component is the FireWeapon() method. This method clones an instance of the stored projectile template. Next, it gets the position of the component's parent by pulling the position information from another sibling component. Since the center of this component is located at the base of the player mesh, the Vector3.Add() method is used to adjust the particle-emission point. Since your 3D shape will likely be different, you'll need to adjust this offset value to match your player.

With the emission point set, it's time to send off the projectile. The FireWeapon() method gets a local reference to the projectile template's rigid component. Next, to send off the projectile in the right direction, a translation matrix is created and set to the scene component's transform. With the matrix in hand, this method gets the current rotation of the forward-facing vector and multiplies it by the projectile velocity passed into the method. With its velocity set, the projectile is sent on its way once. All that remains is to add the spawned projectile to the object database.

```
public void FireWeapon(float projectileSpeed)
{
    //spawn the projectile
    TorqueObject objProjectile = (TorqueObject)_projectileTemplate.
    Clone();

    //set the initial position of the projectile
    Vector3 vPosition = Owner.Components.FindComponent
        <T3DSceneComponent>().Position;
    vPosition = Vector3.Add(vPosition, new Vector3(0, 0, 2));
    objProjectile.Components.FindComponent<T3DSceneComponent>().
        Position = vPosition;


    //set the projectile's forward velocity
    T3DRigidComponent rigidComponent = objProjectile.Components.
        FindComponent<T3DRigidComponent>();
    Matrix playerTranslationMatrix = Owner.Components.
        FindComponent<T3DSceneComponent>().Transform;
    Vector3 forward = MatrixUtil.MatrixGetRow(1, ref
        playerTranslationMatrix);
    Vector3 vel = (forward * projectileSpeed);
    rigidComponent.Velocity += vel;

    //register the projectile with the object database
    TorqueObjectDatabase.Instance.Register(objProjectile);
}
```

Now that we have a component that can spawn projectiles and fire them off, we now need a projectile template.

Creating the Projectile Template

The projectile object does the bulk of the work for the weapon. It's the object that has to travel the distance from the player to the enemy, collide with it, and then apply the damage. The projectile template is created and spawned just like the enemy player template. This can be done within a new method, CreateProjectileTemplate().

The CreateProjectileTemplate() method starts by getting a local reference to the rigid manager. Next, the TorqueObject is created and its IsTemplate property is set to true. A scene component is added to the projectile to give it a location within the 3D scene. Next, a simple material is created and assigned to a new 3D sphere shape that will represent the projectile. Instead of a T3DSphere component, you could use a T3DTSShapeComponent and specify your own 3D shape instead. Next, an invisible collision shape is created for the projectile and a T3DRigidComponent is added that points to the collision shape.

With the template object defined, the last step is to add the template to the object database. Remember, templates are not registered like TorqueObjects. Templates are only added into the database and their cloned instances are registered.

```
public TorqueObject CreateProjectileTemplate()
{
    //find the physics resolver
    RigidCollisionManager rigidManager = TorqueObjectDatabase.
        Instance.FindObject<RigidCollisionManager>("RigidManager");

    TorqueObject objProjectile = new TorqueObject();
    objProjectile.Name = "ProjectileTemplate";
    objProjectile.IsTemplate = true;

    T3DSceneComponent componentScene = new
        T3DSceneComponent();
    componentScene.SceneGroup = "ProjectileTemplate";
    objProjectile.Components.AddComponent(componentScene);

    SimpleMaterial material = new SimpleMaterial();
    material.TextureFilename = "data/shapes/maze/stone.jpg";

    T3DSphere sphereComponent = new T3DSphere();
    sphereComponent.SceneGroupName = "ProjectileTemplate";
    sphereComponent.Material = material;
    sphereComponent.Radius = 0.05f;
    objProjectile.Components.AddComponent(sphereComponent);

    //define a proper collision shape
    CollisionSphereShape collisionShape = new CollisionSphereShape();
    collisionShape.Radius = 0.65f;
    collisionShape.Center = new Vector3(0.0f, -0.2f, 0.65f);
```

```
//give the player some physics attributes, like gravity and collision
T3DRigidComponent componentPhysics = new
    T3DRigidComponent();
componentPhysics.SceneGroupName = "ProjectileTemplate";
componentPhysics.OnCollision = ProcessProjectileCollision;
componentPhysics.RigidManager = rigidManager;
componentPhysics.CollisionBody.AddCollisionShape(collisionShape);
objProjectile.Components.AddComponent(componentPhysics);

//add a new template to the TorqueObjectDatabase dictionary
TorqueObjectDatabase.Instance.Dictionary.SetValue<TorqueObject>
    (objProjectile, objProjectile.Name, null);

return objProjectile;
}
```

Now, a projectile can be instanced at any time using the ProjectileTemplate template. The WeaponComponent3D will create this cloned instance and give it some velocity. Now we just need to specify what happens when the projectile collides with something. At the end of the CreateProjectileTemplate() method, we pointed the rigid physics component to a method named ProcessProjectileCollision(). This delegate method is called anytime the component collides with an object.

The ProcessProjectileCollision() method will test to see what type of object the projectile collided with and remove the collided object if it's an enemy. You can also add other activities, such as play explosion sound and particle effects. As is, this method simply gets a local reference to the Enemy object type. If the "them" object, which identifies the other party to the collision, is identified by the Enemy object type, then its MarkForDelete property is set.

```
public static void ProcessProjectileCollision(T3DRigidComponent us,
    T3DRigidComponent them,
    RigidContactConstraint.Contact[] contacts, int contactCount,
    float dt)
{
    //produce an impact effect

    //get the enemy object type
    TorqueObjectType typeEnemy = TorqueObjectDatabase.Instance.
        GetObjectType("Enemy");

    if (them.Owner.TestObjectType(typeEnemy))
    {
```

```
    //remove the enemy shape
    them.Owner.MarkForDelete = true;
  }
}
```

By now, we have a projectile template that can be cloned and a weapon component that spawns and moves projectiles. The last step in implementing a weapon is connecting the trigger. This requires a new key binding in player's InputMap. You can update the _SetupInput() method that belongs to the MovementComponent3D class with the following line.

```
inputMap.BindCommand(keyboard, (int)Keys.Space, FireWeapon, null);
```

The BindCommand() method connects the Space key to a method named FireWeapon(), which simply finds the WeaponComponent3D and calls its FireWeapon() method with a velocity parameter.

```
public void FireWeapon()
{
  Owner.Components.FindComponent<WeaponComponent3D>().
    FireWeapon(30);
}
```

There's a lot that you can do to build upon this simple weapon framework. For example, you can add a number of properties that track the amount of ammunition remaining and the different types of ammunition a player has. You can also experiment with the physics properties for each projectile for shooting bouncy rubber balls instead of bullets. You can add ballistics into the projectile's behavior to simulate the arc of cannon fire or arrows instead of the perfect line of a laser. In addition, you can make the projectile template more involved by attaching a streaming particle emitter for a tracer or an explosion particle effect to play upon impact.

Mounting Objects

The Torque X 3D Framework includes support for DTS shapes to be mounted to each other. Mounting one shape to another requires two important tasks. First, both 3D shapes must have node markers embedded within the mesh to indicate the mounting points. Unlike the 2D Framework, which can set an arbitrary mount point in code, the 3D Framework requires a mesh node to identify the mount point. The second task is to add a T3DMountComponent to the parent 3D object to be mounted.

The following code fragment can be added to the CreatePlayer() method to enable shape mounting. The only required property is the SceneGroupName.

```
T3DMountComponent componentMount = new
   T3DMountComponent();
componentMount.SceneGroupName = "PlayerObject";
objPlayer.Components.AddComponent(componentMount);
```

Now, any TorqueObject can be mounted to the parent object, including particle emitters, a camera, or other 3D shapes. The following method demonstrates object mounting. It begins by getting a local reference to the player object to be mounted and a child object that will be mounted, named Gun. The T3DMountComponent attached to the player is found and a call to its MountObject() method is made. The scene component for the Gun is passed as a parameter along with the name of the mount node for the parent and the mount node for the child.

```
public void MountSomethingToPlayer()
{
   TorqueObject objPlayer = TorqueObjectDatabase.Instance.FindObject
      <TorqueObject>("Player");
   TorqueObject objSomething = TorqueObjectDatabase.Instance.
      FindObject<TorqueObject>("Gun");

   if (objPlayer != null && objSomething != null)
   {
      T3DMountComponent componentMount = objPlayer.
         Components.FindComponent<T3DMountComponent>();
      T3DSceneComponent componentSceneChild = objSomething.
         Components.FindComponent<T3DSceneComponent>();

      componentMount.MountObject(componentSceneChild,
         "parentMountPoint0", "gunMountPoint0");
   }
}
```

Each 3D shape can have multiple mount nodes embedded within it, and multiple child shapes can be mounted to a single node.

Summary

In this chapter, we covered the foundations of building out a 3D scene. We started with environmental objects, such as Sky, Sun, Fog, and Terrain. Changing these elements make strong impacts to the game's theme and mood. Interestingly, these are also the only entities within the Torque X 3D Framework that can be created and rendered without components. For everything else in a 3D scene, we need to create a TorqueObject first and then add components to give them a purpose. This is clearly illustrated with entities, such as particle-effect emitters.

We also discovered that there are a few great 3D primitive shapes built in the Torque X 3D Framework. You can create cubes, spheres, and planes as objects that are placed into your scene. This is a great way to start creating a basic 3D scene with placeholder art instead of waiting for better quality 3D models to become available.

With some of this foundational work out of the way, this chapter also covered the makings of a basic game. We started with a static mesh shape with polysoup collision enabled to serve as our game's maze. Then, we added some triggers and a power-up object to interact with the player. Finally, we ended up creating a 3D weapon for the player that could be mounted and used to shoot projectiles at enemies. Now, we just need something to shoot at. In the next chapter, we'll explore the basics of adding AI functionality to some enemy units.

Adding 3D Artificial Intelligence

14

Adding Artificial Intelligence to any game is a difficult task. It's not easy to get the computer to reason the same way that people do. Although AI implementation is very game specific, there is some common ground that this chapter can cover. Many 3D games need some way for a simulated player to follow a path and either chase or avoid the player. This chapter outlines these common forms of AI as starting points for you to expand upon.

Adding an Enemy into the Game

Creating an enemy AI unit is similar to creating other scene objects for a game. We start with a basic TorqueObject and add all the components necessary, such as the scene and render components, to bring the enemy AI unit into the game. But we also need to create and add a new AI component to make it move and interact with our player.

Let's begin by creating a very simple AI object, such as a sphere, that follows the player around the scene. Let's also create this as a template, so that we can spawn as many of these spheres as we want.

Creating the Enemy Template

As the last chapter demonstrated, creating a template object is a little different from creating a scene object. The main difference is that we add the template to the TorqueObjectDatabase but do not actually register it. The CreateEnemyTemplate() method will create an enemy template and associate an Enemy object type. We will be able to clone as many as we like and have them interact with the player.

The CreateEnemyTemplate() method begins by getting a local reference to the RigidCollisionManager object, so that the enemy can interact with the physical world. Next, a TorqueObject is created and its IsTemplate property is set to true. After the TorqueObject is created, the T3DSceneComponent is created and attached. Next, a simple material for the sphere's texture is created.

Since our enemy AI unit is conceptual, we can just represent it with a 3D sphere shape using the T3DSphere component. Later, this can be replaced with a 3D mesh shape using a T3DTSRenderComponent. With the shape defined, this method sets the physics properties next. A CollisionSphereShape is created with a collision radius that matches the sphere's shape radius. A T3DRigidComponent is also created and set with mass and gravity values along with a reference to the rigid collision manager. We can also add a T3DBlobShadowCasterComponent to render a simple shadow below the object. Lastly, an object type, Enemy, is attached to the enemy template. Note that the object type is different from the actual template name, which is EnemyTemplate.

Again, since this is a template and not actually a scene object, we only add this object to the TorqueObjectDatabase's data dictionary. We do not call the Register() method as we would with any other scene object that appears in the game.

```
public void CreateEnemyTemplate()
{
    //find the physics resolver
    RigidCollisionManager rigidManager = TorqueObjectDatabase.
        Instance.FindObject<RigidCollisionManager>("RigidManager");


    TorqueObject objEnemyTemplate = new TorqueObject();
    objEnemyTemplate.Name = "EnemyTemplate";
    objEnemyTemplate.IsTemplate = true;

    T3DSceneComponent componentScene = new
        T3DSceneComponent();
    componentScene.Position = new Vector3(1035, 1035, 300);
    componentScene.SceneGroup = "EnemyTemplate";
    objEnemyTemplate.Components.AddComponent(componentScene);

    SimpleMaterial material = new SimpleMaterial();
    material.TextureFilename = "data/images/sphereskin.jpg";
    T3DSphere sphereComponent = new T3DSphere();
```

```
sphereComponent.SceneGroupName = "EnemyTemplate";
sphereComponent.Material = material;
sphereComponent.Radius = 0.5f;
objEnemyTemplate.Components.AddComponent(sphereComponent);

//define a proper collision shape
CollisionSphereShape collisionShape = new CollisionSphereShape();
collisionShape.Radius = 0.5f;

//give the enemy some physics attributes, like gravity and collision
T3DRigidComponent componentPhysics = new
    T3DRigidComponent();
componentPhysics.SceneGroupName = "EnemyTemplate";
componentPhysics.GravityScale = 5f;
componentPhysics.Mass = 30.0f;
componentPhysics.RigidManager = rigidManager;
componentPhysics.CollisionBody.AddCollisionShape(collisionShape);
objEnemyTemplate.Components.AddComponent(componentPhysics);

T3DBlobShadowCasterComponent componentShadow = new
    T3DBlobShadowCasterComponent();
componentShadow.SceneGroupName = "EnemyTemplate";
objEnemyTemplate.Components.AddComponent(componentShadow);

//attach an object type to the enemy
TorqueObjectType typeEnemy = TorqueObjectDatabase.Instance.
    GetObjectType("Enemy");
objEnemyTemplate.ObjectType += typeEnemy;

//add a new template to the TorqueObjectDatabase dictionary
TorqueObjectDatabase.Instance.Dictionary.SetValue<TorqueObject>
    (objEnemyTemplate, objEnemyTemplate.Name, null);
}
```

This method adds the EnemyTemplate to the object database. Now, we can spawn as many of them as we want to.

Spawning the EnemyTemplate

The SpawnEnemy() method clones a new enemy object from the EnemyTemplate and sets its location to match the position parameter passed into it. This method simply queries the TorqueObjectDatabase for the EnemyTemplate and then invokes the Clone() method to return a new TorqueObject. Next, we find the scene component for the new object and set its Position property to match the method's parameter. All that's left is to register the object to bring it into the scene.

```
public void SpawnEnemy( Vector3 position )
{
    TorqueObject _enemyTemplate = TorqueObjectDatabase.
        Instance.FindObject<TorqueObject>("EnemyTemplate");

    TorqueObject objEnemy = (TorqueObject)_enemyTemplate.Clone();

    objEnemy.Components.FindComponent<T3DSceneComponent>().
        Position = position;

    TorqueObjectDatabase.Instance.Register(objEnemy);
}
```

Now that we have a way to spawn instances of an enemy anytime we want, it's time to give them some smarts with a new AI component.

Proximity Attack

Probably the easiest AI unit to create is the proximity-attack unit. This form of enemy AI sits stationary in one spot until a player enters its firing range. Then, the AI unit jumps into action to face the player and unleash its attack. This simple form of AI is commonly found in turrets and is fairly easy to implement as a component.

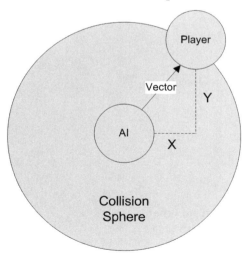

There are a couple different valid ways to implement a proximity attack component. One way is to actively search on every ProcessTick() update for a player and then calculate the distance from the AI unit. Although this works, this active searching can hurt game performance. Another way is to take a reactive approach and surround the AI with a spherical trigger. When anything enters the trigger region, the AI determines if it is the player and opens attack as necessary.

The CreateTurret() method works much like power-up object described in the last chapter. We begin with a reference to the rigid physics manager and query the object database for the Player object type. Next, we create the parent TorqueObject and then attach a scene component for positioning within the scene. Next, a DTS render component is added to render the shape of the turret.

For the collision shape, a sphere works well. Setting the Radius property will determine how far out the attack

Figure 14.1. Creating a proximity trigger for an AI turret.

range extends. This collision sphere is then added to a T3DTriggerComponent. This component also sets the Player object type as its target of choice and specifies a delegate method, AttackPlayer, to invoke when a collision occurs. The final step is to register this object with the object database.

```
public void CreateTurret()
{
    //find the physics resolver
    RigidCollisionManager rigidManager = TorqueObjectDatabase.
        Instance.FindObject<RigidCollisionManager>("RigidManager");

    //get the Player object type
    TorqueObjectType typePlayer = TorqueObjectDatabase.Instance.
        GetObjectType("Player");

    TorqueObject objTurret = new TorqueObject();
    objTurret.Name = "AiTurret";

    //add the scene component
    T3DSceneComponent componentScene = new
        T3DSceneComponent();
    componentScene.SceneGroup = "AiTurret";
    componentScene.Position = new Vector3(1024, 1035, 280);
    objTurret.Components.AddComponent(componentScene);

    T3DTSRenderComponent componentRender = new
        T3DTSRenderComponent();
    componentRender.ShapeName = @"data\shapes\turret\turret.dts";
    componentRender.SceneGroupName = "AiTurret";
    objTurret.Components.AddComponent(componentRender);

    //create the trigger collision sphere
    CollisionSphereShape sphereCollision = new CollisionSphereShape();
    sphereCollision.Radius = 5.0f;

    //add the trigger component
    T3DTriggerComponent componentTrigger = new
        T3DTriggerComponent();
    componentTrigger.SceneGroupName = "AiTurret";
    componentTrigger.CollisionBody.AddCollisionShape(sphereCollision);
    componentTrigger.CollidesWith = typePlayer;
    componentTrigger.OnCollision = AttackPlayer;
    componentTrigger.RigidManager = rigidManager;
    componentTrigger.Immovable = true;
```

```
    objTurret.Components.AddComponent(componentTrigger);

    TorqueObjectDatabase.Instance.Register(objTurret);
}
```

When the player, or any object marked with the Player object type passes through the collision sphere, the AttackPlayer delegate method is called to deliver the goods.

```
public static void AttackPlayer(T3DRigidComponent us,
    T3DRigidComponent them,
    RigidContactConstraint.Contact[] contacts, int contactCount,
    float dt)
{
    //get the player object type
    TorqueObjectType typePlayer = TorqueObjectDatabase.Instance.
        GetObjectType("Player");

    if (them.Owner.TestObjectType(typePlayer))
    {
        //perform the attack
    }
}
```

The AttackPlayer() method is called in response to the collision between the player and the turret's firing trigger. This is where your game code jumps in to implement the actual attack. It's a good spot for firing a weapon component attached to the turret, playing some sounds, and tracking player hits.

Creating a Universal AI Component

Now that we have an enemy unit that can be quickly spawned to attack players that wander into its firing range, the remainder of this chapter can be dedicated to building out a universal AI component that has a few basic objectives:

- chasing a player throughout the scene,
- avoiding contact with a player,
- following a pre-determined path.

To accomplish all of this, we can create a new 3D component. Return to XNA Game Studio and create a new 3D component, AiComponent.

Creating the AI Component

Since we know our AI component will operate in different states, such as chase, follow, follow path, etc., we need to have an easy way to identify those states. Create an enumeration within the AiComponent class declaration. The AiMode enumeration should be pretty self-explanatory.

```
public enum AiMode
{
    Idle,
    Chase,
    Avoid,
    FollowPath
}
```

Next, we need to define some private fields for the AI component to work with. First, we need to locally store a reference to the target TorqueObject. This is the object that the AI is completely focused on. For designer convenience, we can even make this an array of targets with a separate variable that identifies which target in the array is the current victim. If we have multiple players in the game, the AI can then be aware of both of them and attack the one specified.

The AI component also needs to keep a local reference to its own scene component and rigid physics component. This way, it can quickly figure out where it is and set a velocity to move around. The last fields define how often the AI computation should be performed. You can improve the game's performance if the AI can perform computations over longer periods. The last fields determine if the AI component is enabled and in what mode of operation it is.

```
private List<TorqueObject> _arrayTargets = new List<TorqueObject>();
private int _currentIndex;

private T3DRigidComponent _rigidComponent;
private T3DSceneComponent _mySceneComponent;

private float _tickInterval = 10;
private float _tickPeriod = 0;
private bool _enabled = true;
private AiMode _aiMode = AiMode.Chase;
```

Since this will certainly be a component that level designers will be adjusting, we should expose the private fields with public properties that can be read by Torque X Builder.

```
public AiMode AiControlMode
{
```

```
    set { _aiMode = value; }
    get { return _aiMode; }
}

public bool Enabled
{
    get { return _enabled; }
    set { _enabled = value; }
}

public List<TorqueObject> Targets
{
    get { return _arrayTargets; }
    set { _arrayTargets = value; }
}

public int CurrentTargetIndex
{
    get { return _currentIndex; }
    set { _currentIndex = value; }
}

public float TickInterval
{
    get { return _tickInterval; }
    set { _tickInterval = value; }
}
```

The _OnRegister() method is the best place to perform one-time start-up tasks, like obtaining a local reference to the object's scene and rigid components. Also, since this component requires a regular heartbeat, we need to call the AddTickCallback() method.

```
protected override bool _OnRegister(TorqueObject owner)
{
    if (!base._OnRegister(owner) )
        return false;
    _rigidComponent = this.Owner.Components.FindComponent
        <T3DRigidComponent>();
    _mySceneComponent = this.Owner.Components.FindComponent
        <T3DSceneComponent>();

    ProcessList.Instance.AddTickCallback(this.Owner, this);

        return true;
}
```

The last overhead task remaining is to update the CopyTo() method to make sure all fields properly copy over when the component is cloned.

```
public override void CopyTo(TorqueComponent obj)
{
    base.CopyTo(obj);
    AiComponent obj2 = (AiComponent)obj;
    obj2._arrayTargets = _arrayTargets;
    obj2._tickPeriod = _tickPeriod;
    obj2._enabled = _enabled;
    obj2._currentIndex = _currentIndex;
    obj2._aiMode = _aiMode;
}
```

With all of the component overhead out of the way, it's time to start adding the specific AI functionality.

Chasing the Player

By now, it should be no surprise that the bulk of the AI work will reside within the ProcessTick() method. This method first checks to see if the component is enabled. If not, it's a waste of precious CPU ticks to continue processing. Next, this method checks to see if it is time to perform an AI update. By introducing the concept of a processing interval, we can let the game designer make some decisions about how often the component should update the AI balance against overall game performance.

After resetting the process timer and checking to ensure the current target is valid, the ProcessTick() method gets a reference to the target object's scene component. The position of the scene component is stored to a working variable. Next, a calculation is performed to measure the vector distance between the AI object and the target object.

A switch statement is added to control the flow of processing based on the current AI state. In this case, the AiMode.Chase state is implemented. The AI's velocity component is set to the distance vector to drive it in the direction of the target.

```
public virtual void ProcessTick(Move move, float dt)
{
    if (_enabled)
    {
        //don't need to process every tick
        if (_tickPeriod <= _tickInterval)
        {
```

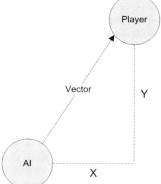

Figure 14.2. Following a vector between the AI and the player.

```
        _tickPeriod++;
        return;
    }

    _tickPeriod = 0;

    Vector3 distanceVector;

    if (_arrayTargets[_currentIndex] != null)
    {
        T3DSceneComponent componentScene =
            _arrayTargets[_currentIndex].Components.FindComponent
                <T3DSceneComponent>();

        //get the position of the target
        Vector3 position = componentScene.Position;

        //calculate distance between component and target
        distanceVector = Vector3.Subtract(componentScene.Position,
            _mySceneComponent.Position);

        switch( _aiMode )
        {
            case AiMode.Chase:
                //convert the distance vector into a force vector
                _rigidComponent.Velocity = distanceVector;
                break;
        }
    }
}
```

That's it for now. The AI component can be added to the enemy template definition within the CreateEnemyTemplate() method. The following code finds the player object and sets it as a target for the AiComponent. Then, the AiComponent is added to the enemy template.

```
TorqueObject objPlayer = TorqueObjectDatabase.
    Instance.FindObject<TorqueObject>("PlayerObject");

AiComponent componentAI = new AiComponent();
componentAI.Targets.Add(objPlayer);
objEnemyTemplate.Components.AddComponent(componentAI);
```

Now each spawned enemy object will chase the player. It does this by searching for the player object, computing a vector that stretches between the enemy and the player, and setting a velocity along the same vector.

Avoiding the Player

Creating a component that avoids the player is essentially the same work as creating one that chases the player. Since we compute a vector that stretches from the AI component to the player, all we need to do is reverse, or negate, that vector. Let's add another case to the switch statement in the ProcessTick() method that handles this.

```
case AiMode.Avoid:
    //reverse the direction of motion
    distanceVector = Vector3.Negate(distanceVector);

    //convert the distance vector into a force vector
    _rigidComponent.Velocity = distanceVector;
    break;
```

The Negate() method reverses any vector passed into it and will always return a vector that points away from the target. Once the velocity is set, the AI object will always move away from the player.

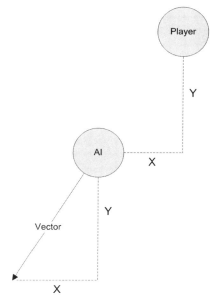

Figure 14.3. Following an escape vector from the AI to the player.

Following a Path

Now that we have the ability to have an AI object locate a player and chase it, it isn't much more work to have it chase another and another in succession. Essentially, we end up with a path-following AI. All we need to do is create markers to define the path. Each marker is simply a TorqueObject that has an attached scene component with a position specified as shown in Figure 14.4.

Let's add an additional case to the switch statement within the ProcessTick() method. This time, we check to see if the distance between the AI component and the target is less than one unit. If it is, then the target index is increased to point to the next target in the array. If there are no more targets remaining in the array, then point back to the first target in the array. If the component is farther than one unit away, then set the velocity along the direction of the vector that points to the next path marker.

```
case AiMode.FollowPath:
```

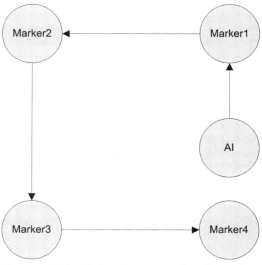

Figure 14.4. Following a path of marker targets.

```
if (distanceVector.Length() < 1)
{
    //advance to the next target point
    if (_currentIndex + 1 >= _arrayTargets.Count)
        _currentIndex = 0;
    else
        _currentIndex++;
}
else
{
    distanceVector.Z = 0;
    _rigidComponent.Velocity = distanceVector;
}

break;
```

The end result is that the component moves towards each path marker until it is reached and then turns to the next path marker. At the end of the list, it returns to the first path marker. Ideally, the path markers would be arranged within the scene to form a patrol route for the enemy AI. A simple method can be created to produce a series of patrol markers.

```
public void CreatePatrolPath(string Name, Vector3 position)
{
    TorqueObject objPathMarker = new TorqueObject();
    objPathMarker.Name = Name;

    T3DSceneComponent componentScene = new
        T3DSceneComponent();
    componentScene.SceneGroup = Name;
    componentScene.Position = position;
    objPathMarker.Components.AddComponent(componentScene);

    TorqueObjectDatabase.Instance.Register(objPathMarker);
}
```

Now, when attaching the AiComponent to the EnemyTemplate, it can create a list of path markers and add them to the component's target array.

```
TorqueObject objPlayer = TorqueObjectDatabase.
    Instance.FindObject<TorqueObject>("PlayerObject");
AiComponent componentAI = new AiComponent();
componentAI.Targets.Add(CreatePatrolPath("Marker1",
    new Vector3(1024, 1024, 200)));
componentAI.Targets.Add(CreatePatrolPath("Marker2",
```

```
                   new Vector3(1044, 1024, 200)));
    componentAI.Targets.Add(CreatePatrolPath("Marker3",
                   new Vector3(1044, 1044, 200)));
    componentAI.Targets.Add(CreatePatrolPath("Marker4",
                   new Vector3(1044, 1024, 200)));
    objEnemyTemplate.Components.
    AddComponent(componentAI);
```

Changing the AI's Mind

By now, we have a versatile AI component that operates differently in each mode. It makes sense that game code can programmatically change that operating mode based on some decisions. For example, the component could be set to the FollowPath mode to patrol the scene. If its proximity-alert code kicks in, as in the case of the turret example, then the component can switch to Chase mode as it attacks the player. Additional code can test to see if the AI object's weapon is out of ammunition or has a low health level. If so, the component could change its operating mode to Avoid to retreat from the player or set a new target for the nearest power-up object and switch back to Chase mode.

There's a lot of room for growth in the AiComponent to really personalize the AI logic for your game. Try experimenting with different ways to challenge the player. You can also add some randomness to the logic to help break the predictability. Perhaps some AI units could move slower or faster than others.

Summary

In this chapter, we added some basic artificial intelligence to enemy scene objects within a game. The AI isn't very sophisticated, but it is enough to provide the player with some interactive entertainment. The first example of AI we implemented was a proximity-based solution that remains stationary and only attacks players that pass into range. The next example of AI we implemented was one that moves the enemy unit around the scene to either chase or avoid the player. We also concluded that chasing a player was essentially the same thing as chasing way-points and evolved our AI component to include basic path-following capability. We concluded this chapter by introducing the concept of a state-dependent brain that dynamically changes the mode of the AI unit from stationary or patrol to chase or avoid. This provides you with a solid starting point to build upon and implement AI behaviors that are more specific to your game.

Finishing the Game   V

Working with Audio

15

Great audio can really enhance a game. Sounds ranging from ambient music loops to action effects to user interface cues help to round out the complete game experience. Adding audio to a game for XNA is much more restrictive than a game for the PC. The restriction comes with the fact that XNA is managed code and the use of unmanaged code required to directly access video and audio hardware is prohibited. In this chapter, we will dive into the audio tools used for a Torque X game.

Creating Game Audio with Audacity

Game audio typically consists of sound effects, background music, and voices. You can either search or license existing audio, or create your own audio files with sound-editing tools. A great solution for capturing and editing audio is an open-source application, named Audacity. You can visit http://audacity. sourceforge.net and download Audacity 1.2.6 for Windows. Audacity can record sounds from an attached microphone and apply filters to modify the sound. Figure 15.1 shows Audacity with a recorded waveform ready for editing.

Game creators familiar with the existing Torque Game Engines are probably already familiar with the rich

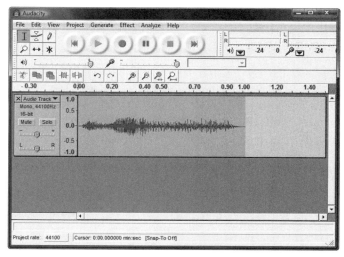

Figure 15.1. Using Audacity to create original sound files.

features of Audacity. Newcomers might be pleasantly surprised with the powerful sound-editing capability that comes packaged within this free utility, including multi-track editing, analysis tools, and a collection of sound filters. To demonstrate, let's create a fun character voice that resembles the popular Goa'uld character from the television series *Stargate SG-1*.

Creating a Character Voice

The work of creating character voices can vary from simple voice recordings on a PC microphone to a complete studio sound booth with expensive recording equipment. We'll stick with the less costly approach.

- Connect a PC microphone to your computer and start Audacity.

- Press the red Record button and record your greeting, such as, "Prepare to meet your maker." Press the brown Stop button to end the recording.

- Select the entire track by choosing Edit ≻ Select ≻ All from the main menu.

- Copy the sound into a new track by choosing Edit ≻ Duplicate from the main menu.

- Click into the first track and select the entire track by dragging the cursor from the beginning of the waveform to the end.

- Amplify the first track by selecting Effect ≻ Amplify from the main menu.

- Click into the second track and select it from beginning to end.

- Select Effect ≻ Change Pitch and lower the pitch by entering a percent change of –25.

- With the same track selected, select Effect ≻ Base Boost with a Frequency of 300Hz and a Boost of 24 dB.

This a decent starting point and you can easily spend a lot of time experimenting with techniques to distort the voice. You can add more tracks and vary their pitches to get the right sound. When you have a sound you like, be sure to note the steps it takes to repeat the effect. When you create more character dialogue, you will need to apply the same distortions to make them sound consistent.

When the sound is ready, save the project to a .wav file by selecting File ≻ Export as WAV from the main menu. Save all wave files to your Torque X game's project folder under \data\sounds. You can even further subdivide your sounds into more folders, such as voices, background, effects, etc. For now, export your sound to a file named greeting.wav.

Working with Microsoft's XACT Tool

To help overcome the different audio requirements between Windows and the Xbox 360, Microsoft has provided the Cross-Platform Audio Toolkit, or XACT. The XACT tool is installed with XNA Game Studio. To open it, select Start ➢ All Programs ➢ Microsoft XNA Game Studio Express ➢ Tools ➢ Microsoft Cross-Platform Audio Creation Tool (XACT). We will use this tool to import audio files and convert them into a format that XNA games can work with.

An XACT project contains many working elements, including wave banks, sound banks, and cues. We'll become more familiar with these elements soon, so let's start by creating a new XACT project by selecting File ➢ New Project from the main menu and designating a new file, named Game-Sounds.xap, into a folder with your game project, named \data\sounds.

Creating a Wave Bank

XACT organizes audio files into a collection, known as a wave bank. A game may have several wave banks with similarly grouped sounds. You might want to keep frequently played sound effects in the memory of one

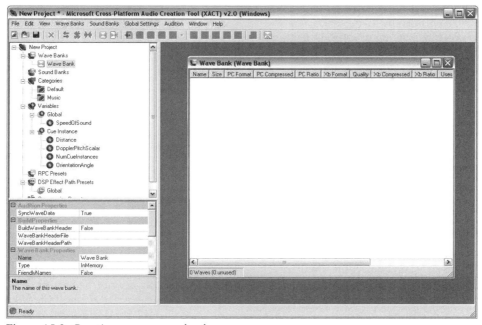

Figure 15.2. Creating a new wave bank.

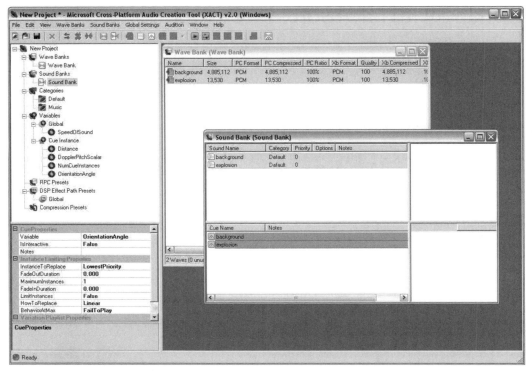

Figure 15.3. Adding audio files to a wave bank.

wave bank and read and larger sounds, such as background music, from disk as it is played back.

Only .wav files can be added to a wave bank. Select the Wave Banks ➢ New Wave Bank command from the main menu, as shown in Figure 15.2, to create a new wave bank. The wave bank is initially empty, so the next task is to start importing audio files.

Select the Wave Banks ➢ Insert Wave File(s) command from the main menu or use the related pop-up menu as shown in Figure 15.3. Browse to the recently created greeting.wav file.

Newly added audio files will appear italicized in red to indicate that they are not assigned to a sound bank. When a sound is in use by a sound bank, the label will turn to normal text. This is helpful in keeping the size of your final game smaller. Often, the file size of a game is determined by the amount of audio content it contains. So, if a big sound file is packaged with a game that is never used, it would be a big waste. Any sound file that is still red when the sound project is finished should be removed to reduce the game's footprint.

Creating a Sound Bank

A sound bank is where individual sounds are assembled by mixing and merging original sound files stored within the wave bank. The purpose of the sound bank is to make efficient use of sound files already stored within the project. Suppose you have three sound files within the wave bank. You can blend and mix these different sounds together without physically creating a new sound that takes up more space. You can easily modify a sound by changing its volume and pitch or create categories of sounds. Select the Sound Banks ➢ New Sound Bank command from the main menu. This will create an additional horizontally split window to hold the sound bank.

To add a sound to the sound bank, drag the audio files from the wave bank to the sound bank. You can drag the same file multiple times if you wish. The advantage of this is that you will be able to adjust the volume, pitch, and other settings without having a completely different audio file. Also note that now that the audio files are in use, the wave bank changes from italicized red text to normal green text.

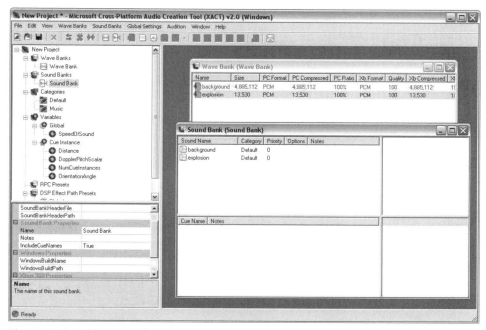

Figure 15.4. Adding sounds into the sound bank.

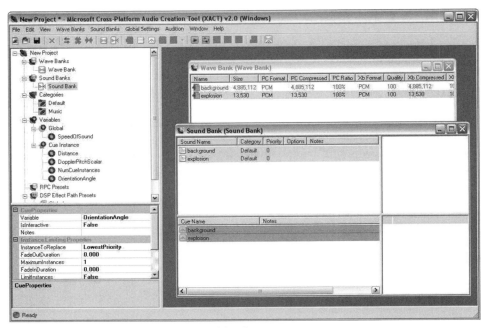

Figure 15.5. Adding cues from the sound bank.

Creating a Sound Cue

Sound cues are used to actually play the sounds. The Cue Name is the identifier that we will reference in our code later. For now, you can rename this to whatever you wish. At this point, drag you audio files from the sound bank (top) to the sound cue list (bottom). The results should resemble Figure 15.5.

Next, we can save and build the project. Save the project as XactProject. xap in a new directory, sounds, under your game's data directory. You can always make additional changes later by opening the .xap project file. Selecting File ➤ Build from the main menu and browse to your game's new data/sounds directory. When you build the project, XACT creates several output files. The output files are separated into two directories, named Win and Xbox, and contain the audio packages for both Windows and Xbox 360 games, respectively. These output files include the binary forms of the wave bank, sound bank, and cue. The next step is to get them into Game Studio Express.

Pulling Audio into XNA Game Studio

From within XNA Game Studio, select the project node and right-click the mouse. Select Add ➤ Existing Item. Browse to the new data/sounds directory and select the XactProject.xap file. Set its Build Action property to Content and its Copy to Output Directory to Copy if Newer. Only the .xap file needs to be added to the game project, not the individual .wav audio files.

After you add the GameSounds.xap file to your project, the content pipeline will use this as a reference to your audio files and will automatically build your wave and sound banks in your project when the game project is built.

Ensure that all .wav files that are included in your XACT project have been copied to your Game's data/sounds directory. If you do not do this, the content pipeline will not be able to find the .wav files to build. Now you are ready to go ahead and rebuild the game project. The next step will be to update the Torque X game code to play back the audio.

Bringing Sound to Torque X

Now that we have audio files in the format XNA is happy with, we can update the Torque X game code to playback the sounds within the game. Fortunately, starting audio playback is much easier than pulling audio files through XACT.

The first step is to update the torqueSettings.xml file attached to the game project. By default, the EnableAudio property is set to false. Change the EnableAudio property to true and add an additional line that points to the GameSounds.xgs file named after your XACT project.

```
<EnableAudio>true</EnableAudio>
<AudioGlobalSettingsFile>data\sounds\GameSounds.xgs
    </AudioGlobalSettingsFile>
```

These properties initialize the Torque X sound manager. With the Torque X settings file updated, we're ready to add the audio capability to a game. The first step is to update the namespace references to include the XNA audio support. This provides our code with access to the WaveBank, SoundBank, and Cue classes.

```
using Microsoft.Xna.Framework.Audio;
```

Next, we need a few private fields to hold local references to the wave bank, sound bank, and cue. By scoping these fields to the class, we can check the state of an existing playback. Also, as you develop your game further, it is likely that you will have multiple wave banks, sound banks, and cues.

```
WaveBank _waveBank;
SoundBank _soundBank;
Cue _greetingCue;
```

These fields can be initialized and pointed in the right direction. The wave bank and sound bank takes a reference to an XNA AudioEngine object. In this case, we are providing the AudioEngine object that is managed by the TorqueEngineComponent class. The .xwb and .xsb files are the compiled wave bank and sound bank files produced by XACT during the compile process. You can either build these files manually within XACT using the File ➤ Build menu command or let XNA Game Studio compile your .xap file automatically. Add the following assignments to the wave bank and sound bank fields.

```
//load the sounds
_waveBank = new WaveBank(Engine.SFXDevice, @"data\sounds\Wave
    Bank.xwb");
_soundBank = new SoundBank(Engine.SFXDevice, @"data\sounds\
    Sound Bank.xsb");
_greetingCue = _soundBank.GetCue("greeting");
```

The last step is to perform the actual playback. Where this occurs depends upon your use of the sounds. For ambient background music, we can start playback in the game's BeginRun() method or a component's _OnRegister() method.

```
if (!_greetingCue.IsPlaying)
    _greetingCue.Play();
```

It's usually a good idea to check if the cue is already playing first, especially if the playback is triggered automatically by a ProcessTick() method or player input.

Creating a Game Audio Component

As you can see, adding audio to your game is not too difficult, but it does require some work to set up. You can pull these elements together to create a basic sound component for your game. This component will playback in two modes: a normal mode in which playback is interrupted and a fixed mode in which a playback is not interrupted. This way you can have some sounds, such as machinegun fire, that interrupt the previous playback. Alternatively, you can playback other sounds, such as voice dialogue, that are not cutoff before they're finished.

Start by creating a new T2DComponent or T3DComponent, named SoundComponent, and add the following private fields. The first three fields should look familiar. The _playFixedSound field identifies the current playback sound as uninterruptable. The _soundName field specifies which Cue name to play.

```
WaveBank _waveBank;
SoundBank _soundBank;
Cue _cueFixed;
bool _playFixedSound;
string _soundName;
```

Next, create the accessor properties to expose the sound name and the fixed length attribute. This way, sounds can be specified by the designer using Torque X Builder.

```
public bool PlayFixedSound
{
  get { return _playFixedSound; }
  set { _playFixedSound = value; }
}

public string FixedSoundName
{
  get { return _soundName; }
  set { _soundName = value; }
}
```

Next, update the CopyTo() method for a clean clone. This is always an important step for all TorqueComponents. In this case, the sound name and fixed length property are explicitly copied over.

```
public override void CopyTo(TorqueComponent obj)
{
  base.CopyTo(obj);

  SoundComponent obj2 = (SoundComponent)obj;
  obj2.PlayFixedSound = PlayFixedSound;
  obj2.FixedSoundName = FixedSoundName;
}
```

The _OnRegister() method initializes the wave bank and sound bank. Both objects are passed the XNA AudioEngine object that is maintained by the TorqueEngineComponent. The .xwb and .xsb filenames match the wave bank and sound bank tree nodes specified within XACT. If your project contains multiple wave banks and sound banks, you will need additional code that loads them. The _OnRegister() method finishes off by calling AddTickCallback() to start processing ticks.

```
protected override bool _OnRegister(TorqueObject owner)
{
    if (!base._OnRegister(owner) || !(owner is T2DSceneObject))
            return false;

    _waveBank = new WaveBank(Game.Instance.Engine.SFXDevice,
        "data/sounds/Wave Bank.xwb");

    _soundBank = new SoundBank(Game.Instance.Engine.SFXDevice,
        "data/sounds/Sound Bank.xsb");

    ProcessList.Instance.AddTickCallback(Owner, this);

    return true;
}
```

The ProcessTick method() checks to see if a fixed length sound is being played back. If so, it continues that playback thread.

```
public virtual void ProcessTick(Move move, float dt)
{
    if (_playFixedSound)
    {
        PlaybackFixedSound(_soundName);
    }
}
```

The final methods perform the actual sound playback. The PlaybackFixedSound() method first checks to ensure there is a valid sound bank. Next, it checks to see if the cue is not null and not already playing back. The cue is initialized with a name passed into the GetCue() method and then played.

```
public void PlaybackFixedSound(string SoundName)
{
    //check if wave/sound banks are initialized
    if (_soundBank != null)
    {
        //playback the requested sound
        if (_cueFixed == null || !_cueFixed.IsPlaying)
        {
            _cueFixed = _soundBank.GetCue(SoundName);
            _cueFixed.Play();
        }
    }
}
```

The PlaySound() is even simpler in that it doesn't bother to check if there is a playback already in progress. This method only checks that the sound bank is valid. If so, it creates a new cue object with a supplied cue name and then begins playback.

```
public void PlaySound(string SoundName)
{
    //check if wave/sound banks are initialized
    if (_soundBank != null)
    {
        //playback the requested sound
        Cue cueSound = _soundBank.GetCue(SoundName);
        cueSound.Play();
    }
}
```

Now the component can be compiled and pulled into Torque X Builder. From Torque X Builder, add the SoundComponent to any scene object. Click the PlayFixedSound checkbox and then enter a name for a valid Cue within your XACT project. When the level is loaded, the selected sound plays in an endless loop.

Figure 15.6. The Sound-Component in Torque X Builder.

From your game code, you can also attach this component to any object within the scene and then later call upon this component to playback any sound by providing a valid Cue name.

```
SoundComponent _sound;
_sound = Owner.Components.FindComponent<SoundComponent>();
_sound.PlaySound("MachineGun");
```

You can expand upon the SoundComponent by creating different sound groups that are specific to your game. Try creating different types of wave banks that are loaded from memory versus streamed from disk. Try experimenting with pitches, pans, and volumes of sounds within the sound bank.

Summary

In this chapter we learned about Microsoft's Cross-Platform Audio Toolkit and used it to convert standard .wav audio files into wave banks and sound banks that the XNA Framework can work with. Next, we jumped back into Torque X code and added the ability to play back the newly added audio files with a custom sound component that can be attached to any scene object. In the next chapter, we will take a look at the user interface elements of the Torque X Framework to build game set-up screens and in-game HUD components.

Adding the Game GUI

The Graphical User Interface, or GUI for short, encapsulates all controls that are used to interact with a game. GUI controls are found in all games and take many different forms, from game set-up screens to popup messages to in-game Heads-Up Display. The Torque X Framework GUI is based on the GUI methodologies of previous Torque engines, so it has had plenty of time to evolve into a robust and well-structured framework. In this chapter, you will learn the fundamentals of GUI building with Torque X. Then you will apply those fundamentals to create some game set-up screens and HUD controls.

User Interface Elements

User interfaces are necessary for nearly every type of game. Their function ranges from simple game set-up screens to information elements displayed during game play. Images should be created in the TorqueX-accepted file formats, including .png, .jpg, and .bmp. All image files will be ultimately converted into XNA's universal file format, .xnb.

Game Set-Up Screens

Game set-up screens guide the game player from the initial start-up of the game to the actual game-play screen. This usually includes a title screen for the game, an options screen to configure the game-play settings, a help screen, and the credits screen. In many games, a navigation map can be created that shows the path of set-up screens from start-up to playing the game. Your game might include significantly more game set-up screens or only one.

HUD Graphics

HUD, or Heads-Up Display, Graphics appear on screen during game play. The purpose of HUD graphics is to communicate important game-related information to the player while the game is in progress. Common examples of HUD graphics include score, remaining lives, crosshair, compass, and ammunition levels.

It is worth noting that prolonged display of high-contrast HUD elements on certain televisions may cause permanent damage in the form of burning into the inner coating of the television sets. This effect can be seen in classic arcades where coin-op machines with rear-projection monitors have caused burn-in damage. Players who pause their games for long periods, especially on high-definition televisions, are at greater risk of causing damage.

The Torque X User Interface Framework

Torque X does not include a GUI Editor and is not persisted to an xml file. So, the entire user interface for your game must be programmed in C#. You will need to become familiar with the different GUI classes to effectively create and manage user interfaces in your game (Figure 16.1).

Organizing the Canvas

Every Torque X game that uses the TorqueEngineComponent will have a GUICanvas automatically created. If your game is created from the

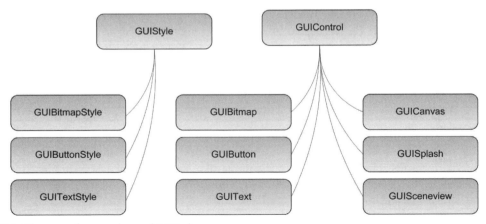

Figure 16.1. The most frequently used GUI classes.

StarterGame template or another TorqueGame feature, you do not have to create a canvas. GUICanvas is a singleton, meaning that only one is present at any time.

Think of the canvas like a painter's canvas on which all rendering occurs. The first thing that must exist before a game can be seen is the GUICanvas. The canvas provides the drawing area for all the GUIControls and, in turn, the game itself. Additionally, the canvas is responsible for processing and dispatching input events.

Adding Content Controls

When a game's user interface is created, GUICon-trols join into a GUI hierarchy. Several buttons and a background image could join together to become the starting screen for a game. The GUICanvas will always be the root of the currently active GUI hierarchy, because the canvas is responsible for keeping track of the stack of content controls. Seperate hierarchies of GUIControls always render from bottom to top. Figure 16.2 illustrates the control hierarchy as it might appear for a game's main menu screen.

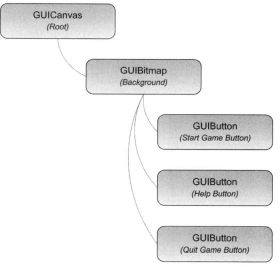

Only one content stack can be attached to the GUICanvas hierarchy at any time, with the exception of dialog boxes. Only the content stack that is part of this hierarchy is rendered, and when it is removed from that hierarchy, the GUIs in that stack will stop rendering until that stack is added again. Content can be added to the canvas in one of two ways. If you know the name of the main content control, you can pass the name of the control to the SetContentControl() method.

Figure 16.2. An example hierarchy for a game set-up screen.

```
// my content control is named "MainScreen"
GUICanvas.Instance.SetContentControl("MainScreen");
```

If you have a reference to the content control object, you can pass that object reference to the SetContentControl() method.

```
// assuming myContent is correctly set up
GUIControl myContent;
GUICanvas.Instance.SetContentControl(myContent);
```

When a control is set as the content control on the canvas, the current content control is automatically removed. When content is added and removed from the canvas, all the controls in that content stack go through a process called awakening and sleeping. When content is added, all the controls that belong to that content are considered awake, whether or not the control is currently visible or active. When content is removed, all of the controls that belong to that content are considered asleep. Only controls that are both awake and visible are rendered.

Displaying Information in Dialog Boxes

Dialog boxes are like content controls in that they can be made up of several child controls with one main control acting as the content control. When pushing a dialog to the canvas, you assign a layer to the dialog. Layers help control the order of rendering, so a dialog assigned layer one would render in front of a dialog of layer zero, regardless of the order in which the dialogs were pushed to the canvas. Typically you will want to add dialogs to layer zero. Unlike content controls, dialogs are not automatically resized to the extents of the canvas. This allows dialogs to be any size and anywhere on the screen. Also, unlike content controls, they are not limited to having only one on the screen at a time. However, when a content control is changed, all dialogs on layer zero are automatically closed. Just like content controls, dialogs can be added to and removed from the canvas in one of two ways.

You can pass the name of the dialog control to the PushDialogControl() method.

```
// my dialog control is named "OptionsDialog"
GUICanvas.Instance.PushDialogControl("OptionsDialog", 0);

// remove the dialog
GUICanvas.Instance.PopDialogControl("OptionsDialog");
```

Or, you can pass an object reference to the PushDialogControl() method.

```
// assuming myDialog is correctly set up
GUIControl myDialog;
GUICanvas.Instance.PushDialogControl(myDialog, 0);

// remove the dialog
GUICanvas.Instance.PopDialogControl(myDialog);
```

Rendering the Canvas

If you are using the GUICanvas object provided by the TorqueGame class, then the canvas will automatically receive draw calls from the XNA framework. If not, however, then you will have to manually tell the canvas to render itself.

```
// this call should be placed in a render loop
GUICanvas.Instance.RenderFrame();
```

Before rendering the content, the canvas size automatically adjusts to the back buffer size allowing the full width and height of the display to be used. The canvas will then prerender all bottom-level content controls (the main content controls, not their children). This gives the main content controls a chance to resize themselves with the canvas and, depending on the options, preserve or override their aspect ratio before actual rendering occurs. If the canvas detects that a content control's aspect ratio differs from the aspect ratio of the canvas, it will then proceed to render a letterbox. After the letterbox has been rendered, the canvas will again loop through all bottom-level content controls and render them. The canvas only renders the content controls and dialog controls but not the children, so it is the responsibility of each control to render its own children.

```
// render the control
// ...
// render this control's children
_RenderChildControls(offset, updateRect);
```

Optionally, after the render phase, the canvas can render safe zone regions to the screen, which can be used to adjust the content to be compliant with NTSC standards.

Processing the User Input

The canvas is responsible for dispatching Torque input events to the current stack of content controls. The canvas is automatically wired into the InputManager. However, this does not mean the canvas will receive all input events. The InputManager dispatches events in three stages, and if it is determined that a previous stage has handled the input event, it will skip the other stages. The canvas is second in line after the global InputMap. This means that if the global InputMap handles the input event, the canvas will not receive it.

When the canvas receives the input event, it will first try and dispatch the event to the focus control. A focus control is a control that responds to input, such as a button. If there is a focus control, and it handles the input, no further controls in the content stack will receive the input event. If the focus control doesn't handle the input, it will be passed to the control's parent. Again, if the next control to receive the input doesn't process the input event, it will be passed down the content stack until it finally reaches the canvas again. If there was no focus control when the canvas initially received the input event, it will pass the event to the bottom content control.

GUI controls can handle input events in two different ways. The first way is to provide the control with an InputMap with device and function bindings. The second way is to override GUIControl::OnInputEvent, which is the method that receives the input events from the canvas or any child controls. Typically you would do this when the control requires special input handling that a normal InputMap cannot provide. The two methods are not exclusive, so it is possible to employ both for maximum flexibility. Here, an InputMap processes input for a GUIControl.

```
// create the GUIControl
GUIControl ctrl = new GUIControl();

// find the gamepad device
int gamepadID = InputManager.Instance.FindDevice("gamepad0");

// bind an input to a particular action
ctrl.InputMap.BindCommand(gamepadID, (int)XGamePadDevice.
    GamePadObjects.A, null, SomeFunction);
//Overriding ::OnInputEvent to handle the TAB keyboard event:
// inside the class definition
public override bool OnInputEvent(ref TorqueInputDevice.
    InputEventData data)
{
  // look for events from the keyboard
  if (data.DeviceTypeId == TorqueInputDevice.KeyboardId)
  {
    // look for TAB input events
    if (data.ObjectId == (int)Microsoft.Xna.Framework.Input.Keys.
      Tab)
    {
      // process the TAB keyboard event
    }
  }
  else
    base.OnInputEvent(data);
}
```

Applying Control Styles

A GUIStyle is used by every GUIControl that provides static data about the GUIControl with which it becomes associated. This data helps define the look and/or behavior of that GUIControl. Specialized GUIControls may require specialized GUIStyles designed to work with the unique additions to the GUIControl. A control will not function properly without an associated style, therefore it will fail to be awakened if a style does not exist when being added to the canvas. By using different styles, a single control can look and behave completely differently from one style to the next. This is a powerful and flexible way to provide a rich and unique experience to your game.

It should be noted that Styles differ from GUIControlProfiles of previous Torque engines. In previous engines, only one class held all of the various properties. Although the goal is the same, the approach we use in Torque X is an attempt to help clean up the process. Here, we use a specialized style to customize an opening splash ad screen.

```
// create the Style for our splash ad
GUISplashStyle splashStyle = new GUISplashStyle();

// fade from a black screen to an image in 2 seconds
splashStyle.FadeInSec = 2;

// display the image for 4 seconds before fading to black
splashStyle.FadeWaitSec = 4;

// fade from the image to a black screen in 2 seconds
splashStyle.FadeOutSec = 2;

// use this image
splashStyle.Bitmap = @"data\images\GarageGames.png";
//Associating the specialized style with the splash GUI:
// create the splash gui
GUISplash ctrl = new GUISplash();

// tell the control what style it will use
ctrl.Style = splashStyle;
```

Initializing Controls

The GUIControl class is the root class for all GUI controls in Torque X. It is derived from TorqueFolder and can contain any number of child controls. Each GUIControl maintains a bounding rectangle in the coordinate system of its parent control. A GUIControl must associate with a GUIStyle before it can be properly used. The GUIControl class is designed to be as flexible as possible when extending the class with specialized controls.

Because a game is bound to have many different objects that form the entire game's user interface, it can be almost impractical to manually create them. Fortunately, you can automatically create and initialize your game shell, but it does require some initial set-up work to function correctly, so let's look over those requirements.

The various screens comprising your game interface should preferably be placed in their own namespace. For example, if your game is in the namespace StarterGame, you could place your UI classes in StarterGame.UI.

The classes designed for your game's user interface must implement the interface IGUIScreen. IGUIScreen is essentially a dummy interface that is used by C# Reflection to search for and create instances of the classes implementing it.

Creating a Splash Screen

Figure 16.3. Example of a splash screen.

It's time to put this new knowledge to work by adding some new user interface screens into a game. We'll implement each new screen in its own class that can be displayed (Figure 16.3).

Create the Class

Begin by creating a new class for the splash screen, named GuiSplashScreen. From within XNA Game Studio, select Project ➢ Add Class, and then enter the filename, as shown in Figure 16.4.

The generic class created will need to have a few additions. First, add the assembly references to the following namespaces.

```
using Microsoft.Xna.Framework;
using Microsoft.Xna.Framework.Graphics;
using GarageGames.Torque.Platform;
using GarageGames.Torque.Core;
using GarageGames.Torque.Sim;
using GarageGames.Torque.GUI;
using GarageGames.Torque.MathUtil;
using GarageGames.Torque.T2D;
```

Next, change the class declaration so that GuiSplashScreen inherits from GUISplash and IGUIScreen.

```
public class GuiSplashScreen :
GUISplash, IGUIScreen
{
}
```

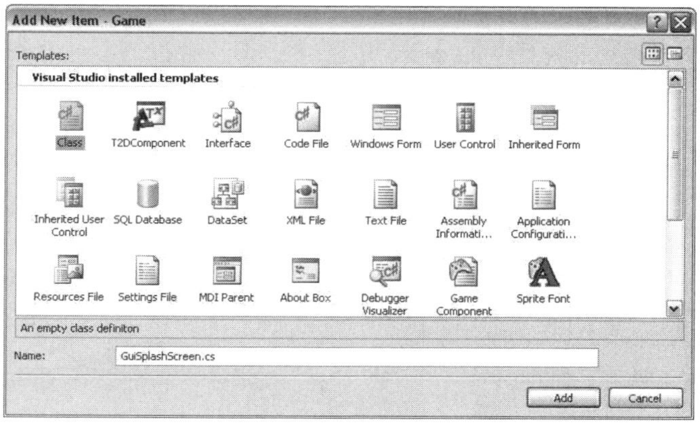

Set Up the Splash Screen Parameters

Next, fill in the class constructor code.

```
public GuiSplashScreen()
{
    // create the Style for our splash ad
    GUISplashStyle splashStyle = new GUISplashStyle();
    splashStyle.FadeInSec = 2;     // black to image 2 seconds
    splashStyle.FadeOutSec = 2;    // image to black 2 seconds
    splashStyle.FadeWaitSec = 4;   // still image for 4 seconds
    splashStyle.Bitmap = @"data\images\splashscreen";
    splashStyle.PreserveAspectRatio = true;

    // set some info for this control
    Name = "GuiSplashScreen";
    Style = splashStyle;
    Size = new SizeF(800, 600);
    OnFadeFinished = OnSplashFinished;
}
```

Figure 16.4. Creating a new splash screen class.

The good news is that the GuiSplash class, from which GuiSplashScreen inherits, does all the hard work for us, so all we have to do is set up our constructor with our own splash screen parameters. We start by creating a new style for this screen of type GUISplashStyle. This style type already has properties to capture the fade-in, display, and fade-out time periods. It also has a bitmap property that points to the image that will be displayed—in this case, splashscreen.jpg. Be sure that your splash screen bitmap is registered with your game project by either dropping it into Torque X Builder or selecting Project ➢ Add Existing Item from within Game Studio Express. This way, the bitmap can be properly compiled into a image format that XNA can consume.

Next, some properties specific to our GuiSplashScreen class are set, such as the name, the style object recently set up, the dimensions of the splash

When creating games for Xbox 360, remember that the game will most likely be displayed on a widescreen. To avoid distortion, you can letterbox screens to maintain a clear 4:3 aspect ration. In the splash screen example, add the following to the constructor.

```
// create a black letterbox
// only visible on widescreen displays
GUIStyle lbStyle = new GUIStyle();
lbStyle.IsOpaque = true;
lbStyle.FillColor = Color.Black;
GUIControl letterbox = new
    GUIControl();
letterbox.Style = lbStyle;
GUICanvas.Instance.LetterBoxControl =
    letterbox;
```

}

screen, and a reference to a method serving as the event handler for the OnFadeFinished event.

After the Splash Screen

The GuiSplash class has a callback method, OnSplashFinished(), that is called when the splash screen finishes its fade-out step. You can use this method to either load a game level or transition to another game set-up screen. To jump right into the game, add the following method implementation to the GuiSplashScreen class.

```
public void OnSplashFinished()
{
    //Load the txscene level file
    StarterGame.Game.Instance.SceneLoader.
        Load(@"data\levels\levelData.txscene");
}
```

Instead of jumping right into the game with a level load, change the OnSplashFinished() method to display the main menu screen, which will be created in the next section.

```
public void OnSplashFinished()
{
    //Load the main menu
    GUICanvas.Instance.SetContentControl("GuiMainMenu");
}
```

In either case, we still need to load the splash screen when the game engine starts. Open the Game.cs file, and edit the BeginRun() method to load the splash screen.

```
protected override void BeginRun()
{
    base.BeginRun();

    // show the splash screen
    GUIUtil.InitGUIScreens("StarterGame");
    GUICanvas.Instance.SetContentControl("GuiSplashScreen");
}
```

This method first calls the BeginRun() method belonging to the base class. Then, this method initializes all GUI screens that belong to the

StarterGame namespace, including our GuiSplashScreen. If you have changed your project's namespace to something other than the default StarterGame, then you'll need to change the InitGUIScreens() method to match. After initializing the GUI screens, the BeginRun() method selects the GuiSplashScreen class as the active display. At this point, the splash screen steps in performs its fade-in and fade-out tasks.

Creating a Game Menu Screen

Creating a splash screen was fairly easy because all we had to do was inherit from an existing GuiSplash class, make some minor changes, and then set the canvas to point to it. It will require a few extra steps to create an interactive screen, such as a game menu screen. Ultimately, a game set-up screen can be as complicated as you want it to be, with any combination of bitmaps, text labels, buttons, and other controls (Figure 16.5).

Figure 16.5. Example of a main menu.

Creating the Class

Let's start by adding a new class to the project, named GuiMainMenu. Add the following namespace references at the top of the file.

```
using Microsoft.Xna.Framework;
using Microsoft.Xna.Framework.Graphics;
using GarageGames.Torque.Platform;
using GarageGames.Torque.Core;
using GarageGames.Torque.Sim;
using GarageGames.Torque.GUI;
using GarageGames.Torque.MathUtil;
using GarageGames.Torque.T2D;
```

Next, modify the class declaration so that it inherits from the GuiBitmap class and implements the IGUIScreen interface. By inheriting from the GuiBitmap class, we're effectively turning our GuiMainMenu into a fancy bitmap class. By implementing the IGUIScreen interface, we enable the Torque X Framework to initialize our new class using .NET Reflection.

```
class GuiMainMenu : GUIBitmap, IGUIScreen
{
}
```

Next, we need to flesh out the class constructor. This is where most of the work for our screen will happen.

```
public GuiMainMenu()
{
    // create the Style for the main menu backdrop
    GUIBitmapStyle bitmapStyle = new GUIBitmapStyle();
    bitmapStyle.SizeToBitmap = false;
    bitmapStyle.PreserveAspectRatio = true;

    Name = "GuiMainMenu";
    Style = bitmapStyle;
    Bitmap = @"data\images\mainmenu";
    Size = new SizeF(800, 600);

    OnGUIWake = OnMainScreenWake;
}
```

Since a class constructor is always automatically called when an object is created, it's the perfect place to put our set-up code. Since we can't render a control without an attached style, that's where we'll start. First we create the GUIBitmapStyle object and disable its autosizing ability, as well as lock the aspect ratio. This should prevent the bitmap from stretching on widescreen displays. Next, we implement some important properties. The Name property identifies this screen so that we can reference it by name when we're ready to display it. The Style property points back to the style just defined. The Bitmap property points to the graphic that will represent this screen, and Size indicates its dimensions. The OnGUIWake property points to the delegate method—in this case, OnMainScreenWake()—which will be called when the splash screen becomes active. All that remains is to implement the OnMainScreenWake() method to perform any desired tasks that should occur when the screen becomes active.

```
public void OnMainScreenWake(GUIControl mainGUI)
{
    // perform your custom screen-activation tasks
}
```

Transitioning between Canvas States

In this example, we have a very simple menu screen with two options: load the game level or quit the game entirely. If the game is started, we need to load the game level and play it. Add the following method to the GuiMainMenu class to carry out this task.

```
public void LoadLevel()
{
    SceneLoader.Load(@"data\levels\levelData.txscene");
}
```

When the game ends, we'll probably want to go back to the main menu, so let's add a counterpart to this function that will unload the scene. In this case, we'll just request a garbage collection clean-up. This just requests that any unused, allocated memory be freed up. There's no guarantee that the .NET Framework will actually clear out any objects, but this method call does indicate our request. This will help reduce the chances that automatic garbage collection will begin during game play.

```
public void UnloadLevel()
{
    SceneLoader.UnloadLastScene();

    // try and cleanup some garbage
    System.GC.Collect();
}
```

To move between the play screen and the main menu screen, we can simply listen for changes to the scene's state from the Torque X Framework. In the next section, we'll create the GuiPlay class as the game-play screen.

```
public void OnSceneLoaded(string sceneFile, TorqueSceneData scene)
{
    GUICanvas.Instance.SetContentControl("GuiPlay");
}

public void OnSceneUnloaded(string sceneFile, TorqueSceneData scene)
{
    GUICanvas.Instance.SetContentControl("GuiMainMenu");
}
```

The OnSceneLoaded() method will switch the GUICanvas over to display the GuiPlay screen. Likewise, the OnSceneUnloaded() method will switch the GUICanvas back to the GuiMainMenu screen. Both methods use the SetContentControl to accomplish this, referencing the screen by name. However, for these methods to be called by the Torque X Framework, they must first be registered as event delegates. Edit the BeginRun() method to attach these two methods as event handlers, hooked into the SceneLoader object.

```
// install scene load callbacks into the scene loader
SceneLoader.OnSceneLoaded = this.OnSceneLoaded;
SceneLoader.OnSceneUnloaded = this.OnSceneUnloaded;
```

Now our event delegates should be called by the framework as the game's scene is loaded and unloaded.

Processing User Input

Now that we have a main menu screen that automatically loads after the splash screen finishes its cycle, we need to have some way for players to choose the menu options. This sounds like the perfect job for another InputMap object. Add the following code to the GuiMainMenu constructor to capture the player's keyboard or gamepad input.

```
public GuiMainMenu()
{
        // bind the first gamepad's A and B buttons to start and exit the
        // game accordingly
        int gamepadId = InputManager.Instance.FindDevice("gamepad0");

        InputMap.BindCommand(gamepadId, (int)XGamePadDevice.
            GamePadObjects.A, null, Game.Instance.LoadLevel);

        InputMap.BindCommand(gamepadId, (int)XGamePadDevice.
            GamePadObjects.B, null, Game.Instance.Exit);

        InputMap.BindCommand(gamepadId, (int)XGamePadDevice.
            GamePadObjects.Back, null, Game.Instance.Exit);


        // bind the keyboards enter and escape keys to start and exit
        // the game accordingly
        int keyboardId = InputManager.Instance.
            FindDevice("keyboard");

        InputMap.BindCommand(keyboardId, (int)Microsoft.Xna.
            Framework.Input.Keys.A, null, Game.Instance.LoadLevel);

        InputMap.BindCommand(keyboardId, (int)Microsoft.Xna.
            Framework.Input.Keys.Enter, null, Game.Instance.LoadLevel);

        InputMap.BindCommand(keyboardId, (int)Microsoft.Xna.
            Framework.Input.Keys.Escape, null, Game.Instance.Exit);

        InputMap.BindCommand(keyboardId, (int)Microsoft.Xna.
            Framework.Input.Keys.B, null, Game.Instance.Exit);
}
```

Now the main menu screen can process the keyboard and gamepad inputs and either load the game level or quit the game entirely. When the gamepad's A button is pressed, the LoadLevel() method we added earlier is called to load the game, using the SceneLoader object. When the gamepad's B button is pressed, the Exit() method is called, and the engine begins to shut down. The next step is to create the GuiPlay screen, where the actual game play can occur.

Creating the Game Play Screen

When you create a new game with the StarterGame project template, the Torque X Framework creates a default canvas that renders the game. However, once we start pointing Torque X to other GUI screens, the original canvas is lost. Therefore, we need to either save a reference to the original canvas or create and load a new one. There are a lot of good reasons to create a new one, including the ability to fully customize the play screen.

Creating the Class

Let's start by creating another empty class file, named GuiPlay, and add it to our project. Be sure to add the necessary namespaces at the top of the file.

```
using Microsoft.Xna.Framework;
using Microsoft.Xna.Framework.Graphics;
using GarageGames.Torque.Platform;
using GarageGames.Torque.Core;
using GarageGames.Torque.Sim;
using GarageGames.Torque.GUI;
using GarageGames.Torque.MathUtil;
using GarageGames.Torque.T2D;
```

Next, change the GuiPlay class declaration to inherit from the GUISceneview class and implement the IGUIScreen interface. The purpose of the GUISceneview class is to render a scene graph. Therefore, any class that is derived from GUISceneview inherits the ability to render a scene. We've also seen that implementing the IGUIScreen interface enables the Torque X Framework to initialize this screen.

```
public class GuiPlay : GUISceneview, IGUIScreen
{
}
```

Next, fill out the constructor code to complete the screen set-up.

```
public GuiPlay()
{
```

```
// create the Style for our play screen
GUIStyle playStyle = new GUIStyle();
playStyle.Anchor = AnchorFlags.All;

// set some info for this control
Name = "GuiPlay";
Style = playStyle;
Size = new SizeF(800, 600);
}
```

The constructor method creates a style for this screen. Then, the screen properties are set, including the reference name of the screen, the style definition, and the dimensions of the screen.

That's all there is to it! The GuiPlay screen will be called when a game level is loaded and the OnSceneLoaded() event handler is triggered. Now that we have our own custom game-play screen, it's easy to add other GUI controls, such as a GUIText control to display the player's score.

Adding Text to the Game Play Screen

There are many cases for adding text into the scene, ranging from presenting score and player names to displaying text captions that accompany dialog. We'll add some text to our own GuiPlay class. First, add a new private field, named _playerScore, to the class.

```
public class GuiPlay : GUISceneview, IGUIScreen
{
    public GuiPlay()
    {
        ...
    }

            GUIText _playerScore;
}
```

Now that we have a GUIText control available, we need to attach a style and set some properties. Add the following to the bottom of the GuiPlay class constructor method.

```
//add controls directly into the playing gui
GUITextStyle textStyle = new GUITextStyle();
textStyle.FontType = "arial16";
textStyle.TextColor = Color.White;
textStyle.SizeToText = true;

_playerScore = new GUIText();
_playerScore.Style = textStyle;
```

```
_playerScore.Text = "Hello, Torque X !";
_playerScore.Position = new Vector2(60f, 10);
_playerScore.Visible = true;
_playerScore.Folder = this;
```

We start by creating a GUITextStyle object and setting its properties to format the text, using the 16-point Arial font with white text and automatically sized to fit the contained text. Next, the GUIText control is initialized and has the GUITextStyle attached. The text to be displayed on screen can now be set. Finally, the position and visibility is set, and then the Folder is specified. After rebuilding the code, the text should appear on the screen.

We're not limited to adding the Torque X Framework's stock GUI controls. We can also create our own custom HUD controls and then add them into the GuiPlay screen as well. In the next section, we'll do just that by adding a functional radar control.

Creating a Game HUD Element

You can create a lot of function user interface elements by simply combining the stock GUI controls. But, there are many other occasions when you'll want to create your own custom control with its own custom rendering. A great example of such a control is a radar scope that indicates the player's position as well as the positions of other nearby objects. Figure 16.6 illustrates the use of a radar control in a sample game.

Create the Class

The first step to creating a custom control is creating a new class, GuiRadarControl, and adding it to the project. Be sure to add the necessary namespace references at the top.

```
using Microsoft.Xna.
    Framework;
using Microsoft.Xna.
    Framework.Graphics;
using GarageGames.
```

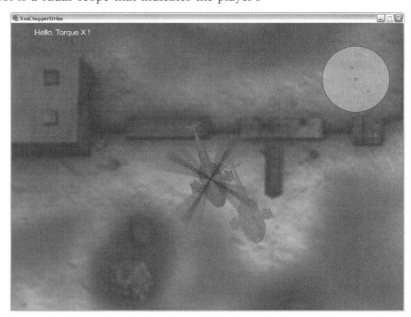

Figure 16.6. Tracking AI movement with a custom radar control.

```
    Torque.Platform;
using GarageGames.Torque.Core;
using GarageGames.Torque.Sim;
using GarageGames.Torque.GUI;
using GarageGames.Torque.MathUtil;
using GarageGames.Torque.T2D;
using GarageGames.Torque.Util;
using GarageGames.Torque.SceneGraph;
```

Next, change the class declaration to inherit from the GUIControl class and to implement the ITickObject interface. If your custom control had more in common with a GUIText or GUIButton class, then you could also inherit from either of them. We also implement the ITickObject interface, since a radar control must be updated on a regular basis.

```
class GuiRadarControl : GUIControl, ITickObject
{
}
```

Private Fields

Our radar control is going to need a handful of private fields to function properly. The _interval field will indicate how frequently the radar control is updated. Although it is possible to update the radar control on every tick, there's no need. Updating the radar several times per second will only slow down the game's processing. The _distance field indicates how far away the radar will scan for objects.

The _bitmapRadar field will hold a reference to the graphic that represents the background of the radar control. The style that formats that graphic will be stored in the _bitmapStyle field.

Next, we need a few fields to track various positions. The _player field will hold a reference to the player object, so we can quickly find the player. The _playerPosition vector will track the player's position in the world. The _radarCenter field indicates where the center of the radar console is on the screen. Finally, we have a list collection called _listEnemies. This will store all the enemy objects we find in the area.

```
private float _interval;
float _distance = 300.0F;

public GUIBitmap _bitmapRadar;
private GUIBitmapStyle _bitmapStyle;

private T2DSceneObject _player;
```

```
private Vector2 _playerPosition;
private Vector2 _radarCenter;

private List<ISceneContainerObject> _listEnemies = new
    List<ISceneContainerObject>();
```

Now that we have the necessary fields to operate the radar control, we need to initialize it.

Public Setup Methods

The task of initializing the radar control is divided between two different methods. The GuiRadarControl class constructor method is responsible for naming the control, creating the bitmap style, and then setting up the radar control background graphic.

```
public GuiRadarControl()
{
        Name = "GuiRadarControl";

        _bitmapStyle = new GUIBitmapStyle();
        _bitmapStyle.HasBorder = false;

        _bitmapRadar = new GUIBitmap();
        _bitmapRadar.Style = _bitmapStyle;
        _bitmapRadar.Bitmap = @"data\images\radar";
        _bitmapRadar.Visible = true;
}
```

The OnWakeUp() method is responsible for the remaining initialization once the scene has been loaded and the radar control is ready to be displayed on the screen. We begin by setting the bitmap's Folder, Size, and Position properties. Next, we find the player object by consulting the TorqueObjectDatabase. We'll use the player's position to determine the relative distances from the other objects that will appear on radar. Next, we need to locate the center of the radar control and save that for future reference. Finally, we call the AddTickCallback() to request ticks.

```
public void OnWakeUp(GUIControl control)
{
        _bitmapRadar.Folder = this.Folder;
        _bitmapRadar.SetSize( this.Size );
        _bitmapRadar.SetPosition(this.Position);

        //set the player object
```

```
_player = TorqueObjectDatabase.Instance.FindObject
    <T2DSceneObject>("player");

//get the center position of the radar scope
_radarCenter = this._bitmapRadar.Position + (this._bitmapRadar.
    Size.AsVector/2);

//request processing ticks
ProcessList.Instance.AddTickCallback(this);
}
```

By now, the radar component should be all set up with the necessary fields and set-up properties. The next step is to start updating the radar control with target positions.

Update Methods

Since this class implements the ITickObject interface, it is required to include two interface methods: ProcessTick() and InterpolateTick(). Since we won't do anything with the InterpolateTick() method, we'll just leave the method definition empty. The ProcessTick() method, however, will be a key component to this control.

Earlier, we defined a field called _interval that determines how frequently we perform a radar sweep. The ProcessTick() method is called several times per second, and that's much more frequently than we need. Performing a radar sweep per tick could really contribute to slowing down the overall game performance. Even worse, there would be no real gain for the control, since enemy units can't move that fast. Therefore, we start the ProcessTick() method with a check of the elapsed time. If the elapsed time reaches a full second, then we continue with the intensive radar sweep.

To perform the actual radar sweep, we first get the player's position as a Vector2, a two-dimensional point with an X and Y value. We also initialize the List container, which will hold all of our radar findings. Next, we use the TorqueObjectDatabase to get an object definition for the AI object type. Now, it's a simple matter of querying the scene graph for all matching scene objects, based on a distance relative to the player's position and matching the AI object type. All the discovered enemy units are stored into the List collection, ready to be rendered.

```
public void ProcessTick(Move move, float elapsed)
{
    if (_interval >= 1.0)
    {
        //get the current position of the player
        _playerPosition = _player.Position;
```

```
            //time to update the radar sweep, fill a list of all enemies
            _listEnemies = new List<ISceneContainerObject>();

            TorqueObjectType typeEnemy =
                TorqueObjectDatabase.Instance.GetObjectType("AI");

            T2DSceneGraph.Instance.FindObjects(_playerPosition, _distance,
                typeEnemy, (uint)0xFFFFFFFF, _listEnemies);
        }
        else
            _interval += elapsed;
    }

    public void InterpolateTick(float k)
    {
    }
```

The OnRender() method has the job of cycling through the list of
enemies stored in the List collection and rendering them as *blips* on the
radar console. First, the base class's OnRender() method is called. Next, we
use the RectFill() method to draw a simple blue rectangle at the center of the
radar control to represent the player. Next, we check if there are any radar
contacts in the List collection. If there are, then we iterate through the list,
using the foreach operator and again use the RectFill() method to draw their
positions within the radar control.

```
    public override void OnRender(Vector2 offset, RectangleF updateRect)
    {
        base.OnRender(offset, updateRect);

        //draw the player position
        DrawUtil.RectFill(new RectangleF(_radarCenter.X-4,
            _radarCenter.Y-4, 8, 8), Color.Blue);

        if (_listEnemies.Count > 0)
        {
            foreach (T2DSceneObject obj in _listEnemies)
            {
                Vector2 range = _playerPosition - obj.Position;
                range /= 2;
                Vector2 displayPosition = _radarCenter - range;

                DrawUtil.RectFill(new RectangleF(displayPosition.X-4,
                    displayPosition.Y-4, 8, 8), Color.Red);
```

```
        }
      }
    }
```

Remember that when you add code to the ProcessTick() method or the OnRender() method, that code is going to be called continuously, several times per second. To avoid reducing your game to a crawl, try adding a lot of exit points to the code when certain conditions are met. Also, if you do not need to perform processing on each tick or render pass, then add delays, as we have done here, to help spread out the workload.

Update the GuiPlay

Now that we have a fully functional radar control, the only task that remains is to add it to the GuiPlay screen so that it appears within the game. Add the following code to the GuiPlay class constructor.

```
GUIStyle style = new GUIStyle();
_radar = new GuiRadarControl();
_radar.Style = style;
```

Figure 16.7. Setting the AI object types in Torque X Builder.

```
_radar.Visible = true;
_radar.Folder = this;
_radar.SetSize(new SizeF(200f, 200f));
_radar.SetPosition(new Vector2(800f, 50f));

this.OnGUIWake = _radar.OnWakeUp;
```

Again, we start by defining a modest GUI style that must be applied to the control. Next, some basic properties are set for the radar control, including visibility, folder, size, and position. Finally, we send a wake-up notification to the radar control when the GuiPlay screen becomes active. This results in the radar control calling the AddTickCallback() method and starting to receive ticks.

One final task still remains: since the radar control is detecting AI units by object type, you need to open Torque X Builder, create an object type, called AI, and attach that object type to all AI units. When the game starts, the radar control should appear on screen, revealing the positions of AI units (Figure 16.7).

Summary

User interfaces represent the final polish to a game. In this chapter, we introduced the fundamental concepts of GUI as it pertains to the Torque X Framework. The GUICanvas serves as the blank sheet on which all the controls are rendered. We learned that the GUI system is described in terms of a hierarchy of controls, separated into virtual folders. Only one folder is rendered at a time with all of its visible components being displayed. We also discovered that it is easy to create new classes that inherit from GUI classes, such as GUISplash GUIBitmap, GUISceneview, and GUIControl. By piecing together our own derived classes, we can create a functional user interface.

17

Lighting, Shaders, and Materials

Lighting, Shaders, and Materials are used to add more depth and polish to a game. They are used to offer more visual enhancements to a scene than just simple textures. What makes these elements so special is that they can offer dynamic visual effects in real time. With custom lighting and normal maps, you can make a low-polygon scene object appear to have more detail by rendering detailed shadows. Shaders can be used to completely change the look of the finished scene by adding a motion blur or a warm and fuzzy bloom effect.

Working with Common Material Effects

Materials are essentially very smart textures that add much more than just displaying a simple graphic image. In many cases you might want to use a simple graphic texture for scene objects. However, you may also want to decorate scene objects with textures that can capture lighting and reveal shadows, add surface detail, or even glow. There are several material classes to help with each of these cases. While working with the material classes, be sure to include the GarageGames.Torque.Materials namespace at the top of your source code.

Staying Organized with the MaterialManager

The MaterialManager class manages all of the materials registered with the engine. Its main purpose is to map texture names to materials and handle material preloading. It also provides methods to look up materials by name and to remove them when you don't need them anymore. Although you are not required to use the MaterialManager in order to work with materials, it is a great way to keep them organized.

Drawing Textures with SimpleMaterial

The most basic material that you can work with is the SimpleMaterial which simply renders a texture or solid color. You can use the SimpleMaterial class to load a new texture into memory and apply it to any scene object, such as a T2DStaticSprite or a 3D mesh, which requires a texture. This can be accomplished in either XML or in code.

The advantage to dynamically creating a SimpleMaterial in code is that you can reduce your game's memory overhead by loading fewer textures into memory, thus improving the game's runtime performance.

```
public void CreateSimpleMaterial()
{
    //create the material
    SimpleMaterial blueMaterial = new SimpleMaterial();
    blueMaterial.TextureFilename = "data/images/blue.png";
    blueMaterial.IsTranslucent = true;
    blueMaterial.IsAdditive = false;

    //assign the material to a scene object
    T2DStaticSprite player = TorqueObjectDatabase.Instance.FindObject
        <T2DStaticSprite>("Player");
    player.Material = blueMaterial;
}
```

This method creates a new material object and points it to a local texture file, named blue.png. It is also set as translucent and enables additive color blending. This is all that's needed to create a valid material, and you do not need to register it with the object database. Next, this method assigns the new material to a sprite object. You can also set a few additional properties to the SimpleMaterial. The Opacity property takes a floating point number and makes the material translucent.

Adding Terrain Detail with DetailMaterial

The DetailMaterial is used for rendering extra detail on a scene object. It is typically overlapped on top of a single stretched texture that covers a very large scene object, such as terrain. The XTerrain class uses the DetailMaterial so that the terrain doesn't appear bland when viewed close up. At the same time, the DetailMaterial only renders out to a maximum visible distance, set by the DetailDistance property, in order to save fill rate to avoid drawing the terrain twice at far distances. Also, the detail texture can look strange if it tiles too far out.

```
public void CreateDetailMaterial()
{
    //create the material
    DetailMaterial sandDetail = new
        DetailMaterial();
    sandDetail.TextureFilename = "data/terrains/
        SandDetail01";
    sandDetail.DetailTextureRepeat = 256.0f;

    //assign the detail material to the terrain
    XTerrain terrain = TorqueObjectDatabase.
        Instance.FindObject<XTerrain>("Ground");
    terrain.Data.DetailMaterial = sandDetail;
}
```

Figure 17.1. The terrain with (left) and without (right) an overlaid detail texture.

This method creates a new DetailMaterial and sets it to a TerrainData property. As you can see from Figure 17.1, the detail material really sharpens the look of the terrain texture.

Adding Lighting Details with LightingMaterial

The LightingMaterial class is applied to textures that will receive light. This material processes light information from the scene graph based. Built-in properties indicate the maximum number of lights to be processed by the LightingMaterial as well as how each light will affect the material. Lights with greater effect will be given a higher priority.

Other material properties include opacity level, specular power, specular intensity, and specular color. When the NormalMapFilename property is set, normal mapping becomes enabled. Specular highlights are also enabled if both specular power and intensity are greater than zero and the maximum supported shader model is at least two.

Lights are usually created through the LightComponent and are automatically added to the scene graph separately. Figure 17.2 shows how a lighting material can dramatically change the look of a texture. By default, the LightingMaterial uses the LightingEffect3D effect file. For 2D materials, you need to set the public EffectFilename property to LightingEffect2D. If you're using Torque X Builder 2D, this is done automatically.

As you can see, the normal map adds a lot of detail and a sense of depth to the flat texture. When the lighting is applied, the results are stunning as simple 2D textures take on a true 3D look.

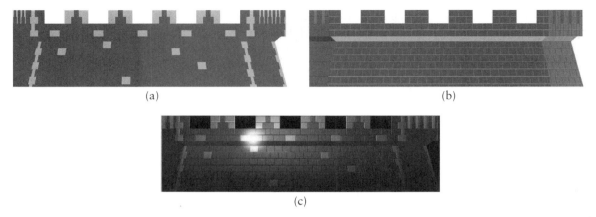

Figure 17.2. (a) A very simple diffuse map texture. (b) A matching normal map texture. (c) The resulting render with a light object created.

You can easily create normal maps using the Photoshop Normal Map Filter Plug-in from nVidia. The more common method of creating normal maps for 3D models is to create a very detailed, high-polygon version of the model, bake lighting information directly into a new normal map texture, and then apply that normal map to a lower-polygon model. In Torque X, you can create a LightingMaterial instance in code and apply it to an object as follows.

```
public void CreateLightingMaterial()
{
    //create the material
    LightingMaterial shinyMaterial = new LightingMaterial();
    shinyMaterial.Name = "ShinyMaterial";
    shinyMaterial.MaxSupportedLights = 4;
    shinyMaterial.IsTranslucent = true;
    shinyMaterial.IsAdditive = false;
    shinyMaterial.TextureFilename = "data/images/blue.png";
    shinyMaterial.NormalMapFilename = "data/images/blueNormal.
        png";
    shinyMaterial.SpecularPower = 1.5f;
    shinyMaterial.SpecularIntensity = 0.25f;
    shinyMaterial.LightingMode = LightingMode.PerPixel;
    shinyMaterial.EffectFilename = "LightingEffect2D";
    //assign the material to a scene object
    T2DStaticSprite player = TorqueObjectDatabase.Instance.FindObject
```

```
      <T2DStaticSprite>("Player");
    player.Material = shinyMaterial;
}
```

As you can see, the LightingMaterial requires more set-up than the previous materials. You can specify the number of lights that this material will process. The more lights processed, the more processing is required to render the material. Your 3D scene can have multiple lights within it, but try keeping the number of lights processed by the material to a minimum. The TextureFilename and NormalMapFilename properties specify which texture files are loaded and applied. The SpecularPower and SpecularIntensity properties specify the shininess and glossiness of the material.

This method also provides a great preview into effect files. Effect files, also known as shaders, implement specialized GPU instructions for rendering textures to the screen. There are about a dozen effect files packaged within the Torque X Framework and they have been serialized into the TorqueEngineData.dll file. In this case, the LightingEffect2D shader is being used because we are working with a 2D scene. When applying lighting to a 3D scene, use the LightingEffect3D shader instead.

Although we have a lighting material created and applied to an object, the material doesn't work until there is a light within the scene.

Adding Custom Lighting to a Scene

Lights are not individual scene objects that can be added to a scene. Instead, lights are implemented as components that are attached to a scene object. Any number of lights can be added to a scene. However, the LightingMaterial is typically set to process a maximum of eight lights. You can change the MaxSupportedLights property to reduce the number of lights that a LightingMaterial will process in order to boost runtime performance.

Lighting Types

There are two types of lighting objects that you will typically work with: point lights and directional lights. A point light casts light in all directions, emitting from a single point within the scene. Point lights can be used to represent the light sources for many scene objects, ranging from lanterns and campfires to explosion illuminations and weapon muzzle flashes.

A directional light casts light in one specific direction along a specified vector. This is useful for flashlights, hanging lights, and even sunlight. It's great for creating strong shadows within a scene. Both light types can be added to 2D and 3D scenes.

Adding Light to a 2D Scene

In a 2D game, lights must be added to scene objects as components. One benefit to this approach is that you can move around or even mount the light to an object, such as a torch. Let's add a point light to a 2D scene.

The CreatePointLightObject() method first creates a T2DSceneObject and sets a position within the scene. Next, a new PointLight object is created. Its light properties, such as attenuation and color are set. Next, a T2DLightComponent is created with its light list set to include the new point light. After the light component is attached, the scene component is registered.

```
public void CreatePointLightObject()
{
    //create a scene object to hold the light component
    T2DSceneObject lightSceneObject = new T2DSceneObject();
    lightSceneObject.Position = new Vector2(0, 0);
    lightSceneObject.Visible = true;

    //create a light object
    PointLight light = new PointLight();
    light.ConstantAttenuation = 1.0f;
    light.LinearAttenuation = 0.0f;
    light.AmbientColor = new Vector3(0.5f, 0.4f, 0.4f);
    light.DiffuseColor = new Vector3(0.75f, 0.75f, 0.75f);
    light.PositionOffset = new Vector3(0, 0, 5);

    //create the light component and add the light
    T2DLightComponent componentLight = new T2DLightComponent();
    componentLight.IsEnabled = true;
    componentLight.LightList.Add(light);
    lightSceneObject.Components.AddComponent(componentLight);

    //register the light scene object
    TorqueObjectDatabase.Instance.Register(lightSceneObject);
}
```

As the scene object is moved around the scene, the light source is moved along with it. All scene objects bearing a lighting material will be updated as the light moves aroud.

Adding Light to a 3D Scene

Adding light to a 3D scene is similar to its 2D counterpart. The lighting component is attached to a TorqueObject. In a 3D scene, lights add a lot

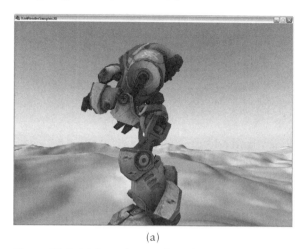
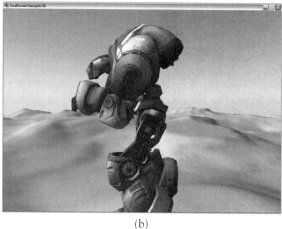

(a)   (b)

Figure 17.3. (a) Boombot mesh with SimpleMaterial and no lighting. (b) Boombot mesh with a LightingMaterial and light added.

more realism, producing softer shadows with normal maps. Figure 17.3 shows the same 3D shape without lighting (a) and with lighting (b). The lit shape looks much more realistic with soft shadows and more implied detail.

The CreateDirectionalLightObject() method creates a directional light and adds it to the 3D scene. Like any other 3D scene object, we need to first create a generic TorqueObject instance and then add the necessary rendering components. Since the light source needs a position to emit from, a scene component must also be added. Next, the DirectionalLight object is created. The light attenuation and color properties are set. Since this is a directional light, an additional property specifying direction must be added as well. Next, the directional light can be added to a T3DLightComponent, which is added to the registered TorqueObject.

```
public void CreateDirectionalLightObject()
{
    //create a scene object to hold the light component
    TorqueObject lightSceneObject = new TorqueObject();

    T3DSceneComponent componentScene = new
        T3DSceneComponent();
    componentScene.Position = _camera.Transform.Translation;
    componentScene.SceneGroup = "LightObject";
    lightSceneObject.Components.AddComponent(componentScene);
```

```
//create a light object
DirectionalLight light = new DirectionalLight();
light.ConstantAttenuation = 1.0f;
light.LinearAttenuation = 0.0f;
light.AmbientColor = new Vector3(0.5f, 0.4f, 0.4f);
light.DiffuseColor = new Vector3(0.75f, 0.75f, 0.75f);
light.Direction = Vector3.Down;

//create the light component and add the light
T3DLightComponent componentLight = new T3DLightComponent();
componentLight.SceneGroupName = "LightObject";
componentLight.IsEnabled = true;
componentLight.LightList.Add(light);
lightSceneObject.Components.AddComponent(componentLight);

//register the light object
TorqueObjectDatabase.Instance.Register(lightSceneObject);
}
```

The smooth light shading applied to the 3D shape really shows off the capabilities of shader effects. Next, we will dive deeper into shader effects and create a custom shader.

Working with Advanced Material Effects

Lighting materials are pretty basic when it comes to shaders. There are many other exciting material effects that can be produced by well-written shaders. Some of the more common examples include cube-mapping and blurring.

Figure 17.4. Applying a cube-map material to a 3D shape.

Applying a Dynamic Cube-Map Material

A cube map is a render-to-texture material effect that applies the environmental surroundings of a shape as the texture for the shape. This effect is most common for shiny or glassy objects, such as mirrors or windows.

A cube map can either be static or dynamic. A static cube map takes a picture of its surroundings and then renders the texture for the shape only once. A dynamic cube map, however, constantly renders to the texture. As you might expect, dynamic cube maps are very expensive when it comes to performance and should be used sparingly.

The cube-map material requires a couple of helper classes. The CubemapCamera class is used for rendering the dynamic cube-map faces. The Cubemap class manages the cube map by loading the static cube-map faces, managing the position of the cube map, tracking the update priority, and returning the texture for each cube-map face.

The CreateCubeMapSphere() method pulls these elements together to create a 3D sphere shape that renders a reflective cube map. A CubemapMaterial is created and set as dynamic to render the effect on each frame.

```
public void CreateCubemapSphere()
{
    TorqueObject objSphere = new TorqueObject();
    objSphere.Name = "Sphere";

    T3DSceneComponent componentScene = new
        T3DSceneComponent();
    componentScene.SceneGroup = "Sphere";
    componentScene.Position = new Vector3(1000, 1100, 300);
    objSphere.Components.AddComponent(componentScene);

    CubemapMaterial material = new CubemapMaterial();
    material.IsDynamic = true;
    material.CubemapSize = 128;
    material.Priority = 1;
    material.Cubemap.Create(true, 128, material.Camera);
```

Figure 17.5. The cube-map size is set at 32 on the left compared to 256 on the right.

```
    T3DSphere sphereComponent = new T3DSphere();
    sphereComponent.SceneGroupName = "Sphere";
    sphereComponent.Material = material;
    sphereComponent.Radius = 2.0f;
    objSphere.Components.AddComponent(sphereComponent);

    TorqueObjectDatabase.Instance.Register(objSphere);
}
```

The CubeMapSize property determines the resolution. A higher value will produce a much sharper reflection and slow down performance, whereas a lower value will produce a blurrier reflection and speed up performance. Figure 17.5 illustrates the differences in quality.

Applying a Visual Refraction Material

A visual refraction is a scene distortion that occurs when it is filtered through a distorting material. The Torque X Framework includes a RefractionMaterial to easily set up a refraction effect. The TankBuster sample game that is packaged with Torque X uses a refraction distortion to simulate a shock wave when a fuel container explodes.

The TextureFilename property specifies the texture that is being refracted or rendered to the back buffer. The NormalMapFilename property identifies a normal map texture that is assigned to the material. The RefractionAmount property indicates the amount to refract the refracted texture that is set on the material. You must also specify a normal map texture for the refraction, which will define the distortion of the refraction.

```
public void CreateRefractionSphere()
{
    TorqueObject objSphere = new TorqueObject();
    objSphere.Name = "Sphere";

    T3DSceneComponent componentScene = new
        T3DSceneComponent();
    componentScene.SceneGroup = "Sphere";
    componentScene.Position = new Vector3(1000, 1100, 300);
    objSphere.Components.AddComponent(componentScene);

    RefractionMaterial material = new RefractionMaterial();
    material.NormalMapFilename = "data/images/normalmap.jpg";
    material.RefractionAmount = 0.05f;
    material.IsRefractive = true;
```

```
    T3DSphere sphereComponent = new T3DSphere();
    sphereComponent.SceneGroupName = "Sphere";
    sphereComponent.Material = material;
    sphereComponent.Radius = 2.0f;
    objSphere.Components.AddComponent(sphereComponent);

    TorqueObjectDatabase.Instance.Register(objSphere);
}
```

Applying Full Screen Effects

Postprocess refers to the activity of modifying a rendered frame that is ready for display. Examples of postprocess effects include bloom and motion blur. The Torque X Framework provides a few key classes that help manage the implementation of postprocessing.

The PostProcessor

The PostProcessor class provides direct support for postprocessing effects. A PostProcessor object can be applied directly to the TorqueEngineComponent to produce full screen effects, affecting everything on the screen, including GUI controls. The PostProcessor can alternatively be applied only to a GuiSceneview to affect only the objects within the actual scene.

The PostProcessor class works in conjunction with a PostProcessMaterial and uses it to render the full screen quad to the back buffer. These classes can be used for simple effects like full screen blur. However, for more complex effects, such as bloom, you must create a new class that is derived from PostProcessor and override its Run() method as was done for the BloomPostProcessor. After the scene has been fully rendered, the Run() method is called to perform the postprocessing effect.

The PostProcessMaterial contains the texture that holds the completely rendered scene. This material can be used for further postprocessing effects, such as bloom and blurs.

The BloomPostProcessor

The BloomPostProcessor is a specialized postprocessor that results in a full-screen bloom effect. This is a multipass effect, so it will affect performance, especially on fill-rate-limited cards. It's a great example of how to create your own PostProcessor class. It overrides the Setup() method to set up the effect after the postprocessor is set on the GuiSceneview. Then, the Run() method is called after the scene has been rendered and is ready to perform the postprocessing effect.

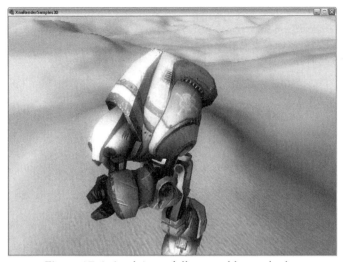

Figure 17.6. Applying a full-screen bloom shader.

You can optionally set an extract material or an instance of the BloomExtractMaterial class to pull the bright colors from the scene. This would be followed by a combine material or an instance of the BloomCombineMaterial class to merge the blurred extracted texture with the base texture. The results can be seen in Figure 17.6.

The ApplyBloomShader() method demonstrates how to create a BloomPostProcessor object. This method first creates the bloom postprocessor and then gets a local reference to the active scene graph. Next, the bloom processor sets several bloom properties relating to intensity and saturation. Finally, the bloom processor is set as the designated postprocessor for the scene view.

```
public void ApplyBloomShader()
{
    BloomPostProcessor _bloomPostProcessor = null;

    GUISceneview sceneView = TorqueObjectDatabase.
        Instance.FindObject<GUISceneview>("DefaultSceneView");

    _bloomPostProcessor = new GarageGames.Torque.Materials.
        BloomPostProcessor();
    _bloomPostProcessor.ExtractMaterial.BloomThreshold = 0.6f;
    _bloomPostProcessor.BlurMaterial.BlurAmount = 6.0f;
    _bloomPostProcessor.BlurMaterial.Size = new Vector2(1.0f, 1.0f);
```

```
_bloomPostProcessor.CombineMaterial.BaseIntensity = 1.0f;
_bloomPostProcessor.CombineMaterial.BaseSaturation = 1.0f;
_bloomPostProcessor.CombineMaterial.BloomIntensity = 1.0f;
_bloomPostProcessor.CombineMaterial.BloomSaturation = 2.0f; //
    1.0f;

sceneView.PostProcessor = _bloomPostProcessor;
}
```

Creating a Motion Blur Postprocess Effect

Another example that sets a scene view's postprocessor is a simple motion blur full-screen effect. Instead of using a BloomPostProcessor, we use another class, CopyPostProcessMaterial.

The ApplyMotionBlur() method also gets a local reference to the scene view. Next, this method creates a new instance of the PostProcessor. Next, a copy of a postprocessor material is created and assigned a BlendAmount. All that remains is to set the scene view's PostProcessor property to the motion blur's postprocessor.

Figure 17.7. Applying a full-screen bloom shader.

```
public void ApplyMotionBlur()
{
    PostProcessor _
        motionBlurPostProcessor = null;

    GUISceneview sceneView =
        TorqueObjectDatabase.Instance.
        FindObject<GUISceneview>
        ("DefaultSceneView");

    _motionBlurPostProcessor = new PostProcessor();
    CopyPostProcessMaterial material = new CopyPostProcessMaterial();
    material.BlendAmount = 0.15f;
    _motionBlurPostProcessor.Material = material;

    sceneView.PostProcessor = _motionBlurPostProcessor;

    TorqueEngineComponent.Instance.Settings.GraphicsClearSettings.
        ClearBeforeRender = false;
}
```

The bloom and motion-blur shaders both demonstrate full-screen effects using the scene view's PostProcessor property. You can also use shaders to create visual effects that only apply to a single object, instead of the entire full-screen. To do this, you need to create a new shader effect, define a new custom material, and then apply that material to an object.

Creating a Custom Material Effect

Working with a lighting material and adding lights to a scene provided our first look at working with shader effects in Torque X. In that case, we seamlessly worked with the LightingEffect2D.fx and LightingEffect.fx shader effect files that are packaged with the Torque X Framework. In this section, we'll look at how shader effects work and how to create a new shader effect from scratch.

Shader effects are coded in a specialized syntax known as the high-level shader language (HLSL). This code instructs the GPU to perform specific rendering computations very quickly. Shader effects can be coded manually or assembled with free design tools, such as ATI's Render Monkey or nVidia's FXComposer. In Torque X, the HLSL code is saved to an .fx file within the game project's data folder.

Designing a Material Shader Effect

The following shader strips the color information from a texture, turning a colored object into a grayscale object. The shader is composed of three distinct code elements: variable and structure definitions, the vertex-shader method, and the pixel-shader method.

The shader definition begins by declaring two variables to hold incoming data. The first is a world projection matrix that will be supplied by Torque X and the second is texture data that will be supplied by the material definition. Next, the shader creates two data structures that will be used to pass data into and out of the vertex-shader method.

The vertex-shader method marks the entry point for vertex processing. In this case, the vertex shader will pass all data straight to the pixel shader. A vertexshader_Input structure is provided to the vertex shader. A vertexshader_Output structure is created and all of its fields are assigned to the same values that were passed in.

For this effect, the pixel-shader method does all of the real work. It starts by sampling the color value for a specific pixel and then turns that color into a grayscale value by multiplying a color normalizing value: about 1/3 Red, 1/2 Green, and 1/8 Blue. The new normalized color replaces the sampled color and is returned out of the pixel shader, ready to be presented onscreen.

```
float4x4 worldViewProjection;
texture baseTexture;

sampler2D baseTextureSampler = sampler_state
{
        Texture = <baseTexture>;
};

struct vertexshader_Input
{
        float4 position : POSITION;
        float4 color : COLOR;
        float2 texCoord : TEXCOORD0;
};

struct vertexshader_Output
{
        float4 position : POSITION;
        float4 color : COLOR0;
        float2 texCoord : TEXCOORD0;
};

vertexshader_Output vertexshader_main(vertexshader_Input input)
{
        vertexshader_Output output;

        //pass the texture info through to the pixel shader
        output.position = mul(input.position, worldViewProjection);
        output.texCoord = input.texCoord;
        output.color = input.color;

        return output;
}

float4 pixelshader_main(vertexshader_Output input) : COLOR
{
        //get the color
        float4 color = tex2D(baseTextureSampler, input.texCoord);

        //set new color range
        float intensity = (0.299 * color.r) + (0.587 * color.g) + (0.184 *
           color.b);

        //apply the black and white color value
        color = float4(intensity.xxx,color.a);
```

```
    return color;
}

technique TexturedTechnique
{
    pass P0
    {
        VertexShader = compile vs_1_1 vertexshader_main();
        PixelShader  = compile ps_1_1 pixelshader_main();
    }
}
```

Again, this is just a simple shader that strips color from a texture. You can work with RenderMonkey and FXComposer to produce amazing and more complex shader effects. The next step is to bring the effect file into the game project.

Importing Shader Effects into Torque X

Save the new shader into your game project's folder as data\effects\MyShader.fx. Next, return to XNA Game Studio and open the Solution Explorer. Select the Project ➤ Show All Files command from the main menu. This should expose the new effects folder in the Solution Explorer. Right-click the newly exposed effects folder and select the Include in Project pop-up command. Now the shader is part of the project. You can turn off the Show All Files option to return the Solution explorer to normal.

XNA Game Studio will automatically recognize the MyShader.fx file as an effect and set its Build Action property to Compile. When you build the project, the effect file will be compiled into an .xnb file.

Applying Your Custom Material

Now that we have a new custom shader packaged within the game project, we need to apply it with a new material. The GenericMaterial object is used to create materials that are used for binding shader parameters and using shader techniques based on settings specified at runtime. This material is used for most custom shader effects. The effect file needs to be set on this material using the EffectFilename property. Other parameters that typically need to be set are listed in Table 17.1.

The generic material properties are only bound if the semantic for them is found within the effect file. Additional textures and float values can be bound using the TextureBinds and FloatBinds properties.

The technique to use can either be set directly via the Technique property or by adding entries to the technique chain. The technique that is used is

LightCount	WorldMatrixCount	ProjectionMatrix
DirectionalLightCount	WorldMatrix	TimeNow
PointLightCount	WorldInverseMatrix	TimeLast
LightColor	WorldViewMatrix	TimeElapsed
LightPosition	WorldViewProjectionMatrix	TimeFrameNumber
LightDirection	ViewMatrix	viewportScaleAndOffset
LightRange	ViewProjectionMatrix	viewportUVMinMax

Table 17.1. Common shader parameters set against the GenericMaterial object.

selected by looking for the highest entry whose profile is supported by the shader model of the current hardware.

The CreateMyShaderCube() method pulls everything together. It creates a cube shape that applies the MyShader.fx shader effect. The key to this method is that a GenericMaterial is created for the shape pointing to our new effect file. It also adds a GenericMaterialTextureBind that points to the texture file being fed into the shader. The last step is to create the visible cube shape that uses the new material and register it with the object database.

```
public void CreateMyShaderCube()
{
    TorqueObject objCube = new TorqueObject();
    objCube.Name = "Cube";

    T3DSceneComponent componentScene = new
        T3DSceneComponent();
    componentScene.SceneGroup = "Cube";
    componentScene.Position = new Vector3(1024, 1035, 286);
    objCube.Components.AddComponent(componentScene);

    GenericMaterialTextureBind textureBind = new
        GenericMaterialTextureBind();
    textureBind.BindType = BindType.Name;
    textureBind.BindAddress = "baseTexture";
    textureBind.TextureFilename = "data/images/logo.png";

    GenericMaterial material = new GenericMaterial();
    material.EffectFilename = "data/effects/MyShader.xnb";
    material.TextureBinds.Add(textureBind);

    T3DBox boxComponent = new T3DBox();
    boxComponent.SceneGroupName = "Cube";
```

```
boxComponent.Material = material;
boxComponent.Size = new Vector3(1.0f);
objCube.Components.AddComponent(boxComponent);

TorqueObjectDatabase.Instance.Register(objCube);
}
```

When this method is called, a new cube object is created. The GenericMaterial uses our new custom shader to take the incoming texture data and strip out the color, producing a grayscale version of the texture. In this example, the material definition was created along with the shape creation. If you plan to use a custom material for multiple objects in the scene, be sure to create the material once. Then, set that material reference to each object that should have it.

Summary

This chapter explored the basics of lighting, shaders, and materials. We started with an overview of what materials are and how we create them. Since lighting materials require light objects within the scene, we took a closer look at what is involved in creating different types of lights, including point and directional lights. Since lighting really just makes use of built-in shader effects, we looked at a couple of other built-in effects, such as bloom and motion blur. Lastly, we pushed on to create our own custom shader effect and applied it as a material for a simple 3D shape. In the next chapter, we will look at the final steps of creating a Torque X game: deployment and distribution.

Torque X Game Distribution   18

Throughout the last seventeen chapters, this book has explained the foundations of the Torque X 2D and 3D Frameworks and what it takes to create a new game. In this concluding chapter, we focus on what's involved with moving your game over to the Xbox 360 game console and packaging it for general release. First, we focus on what it really takes to create a game for the console and television. There are several important considerations that don't exist when creating a game for personal computers. Lastly, we'll describe the specific steps involved in moving your game code from your Windows computer to your Xbox 360.

Game Console Considerations

The most important consideration when programming for the Xbox 360 console is the wide variety of televisions to which it can be connected. The Xbox 360 supports both high-definition and standard-definition television sets at multiple resolutions, such as 480p, 720p, 1080i, and 1080p, as well as multiple aspect ratios, such as 4:3, 16:9, and 16:10. The console will automatically scale the output of a game to the resolution of the television display. If the game is using a widescreen-aspect ratio, the Xbox 360 will automatically add letterboxing black bars if the television is not widescreen.

Television Resolution

One of the greatest considerations you should bear in mind is display resolution. Common household televisions use cathode-ray tube (CRT) technology. These televisions are wildly inaccurate when it comes to rendering a digital signal. This is because a high-resolution digital image needs to be downscaled to a lower resolution and then projected to the television screen at a regular frequency.

Pixel resolution is the amount of individual points known as pixels on a given screen. A typical HDTV resolution of 720 × 480 means that the television display has 720 pixels across and 480 pixels on the vertical axis. The higher the resolution on a specified display the sharper the image.

Title-Safe Render Areas

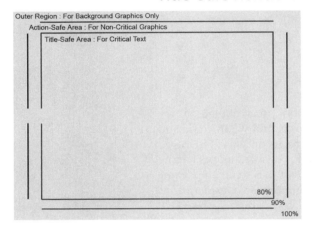

Figure 18.1. Identifying the title-safe area.

On standard tube televisions, the display area of the television is normally not a perfect rectangle. In fact, a significant amount of the display may not be visible on a CRT tube. In television, the inner 80–90% of the picture is considered the "title-safe" region. Any graphics displayed outside of this region on a standard television may be obscured or distorted.

You should ensure that any critical information, such as score, number of lives, ammo, etc., is displayed within the title-safe region while drawing the background or a 3D scene across the entire display. Critical text should be displayed within the inner 80 percent of the screen.

Limited Color Palettes

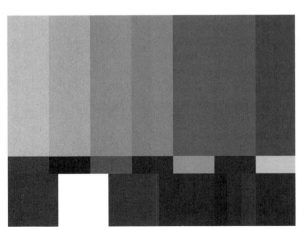

Figure 18.2. A traditional color television test pattern.

When creating games for a game console, the ultimate goal is to make the game look as best as it can on all possible televisions. Again, this is a challenge when you target both a high-definition plasma television and a standard-definition CRT television. In addition to resolution, you must also deal with differences in color palettes. High-definition televisions can support millions of colors, whereas CRT televisions support thousands. Even worse, in many cases CRT televisions suffer from bleeding issues. For example, the color red tends to dominate the color palette whereas the color cyan tends to fade out.

Try experimenting with different colors in a test screen and compare the color clarity

0123456789

Figure 18.3. Stroking light color text keeps it readable.

between a computer display and a television display. You will quickly find out which colors hold their intensity and which colors fade away. This doesn't necessarily mean you need to change your game's art style. However, you can make some small changes that will help. For example, try avoiding on-screen text that is cyan color. If you absolutely must have cyan-colored text, try outlining (or stroking) the text with a darker color so that the text is still readable on televisions with fading color.

Larger Fonts and Sizes

When creating game screens that will appear on televisions, keep in mind that font sizes need to be large enough to read from a distance. Computer games can get away with smaller fonts since a player tends to sit between one or two feet from the display. However, with console games, a player will typically be sitting on a sofa about ten feet away. Although the display screen might be larger, it will still be difficult to read small fonts from a distance.

For fun, try taking an eye-chart image and use it for the background of a sample game set-up screen. Run the game on your computer and determine how far down the chart you can read. Then, take the same project and run it on the Xbox360 and repeat the exercise using your television. You will also find a tremendous difference in how far down you can go when testing on a 44-inch plasma television versus a 28-inch CRT television.

Determining the right font size for your game is a lot like our eye-chart example. Typically, the size of the graphic is proportional to the importance of the text. For example, dialogue subtitles are considered important since they may reveal game-solving clues. The font size should be fairly large, similar to closed-captioned text. However, the ammo label over a box indicating how much ammunition is left is fairly constant and self-explanatory and can be a much smaller font as long as the actual number that indicates the number of ammunition rounds left is large enough to read.

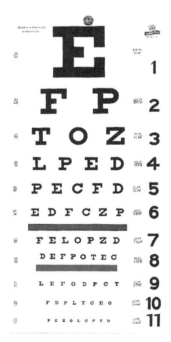

Figure 18.4. Testing different font sizes.

You will probably need to start with some educated guesses about font sizes for different screen elements. Later, when you test your game, you will get more feedback about the text size and can rescale the text as needed.

Different Aspect Ratios

Another issue to be aware of for console games is the screen aspect ratio. For years, televisions have been manufactured in the 4:3 aspect ratio. In other words, screen proportions were four units wide by three units high. This translates to a resolution of 320 × 240.

The 4:3 ratio for standard television has been in use since television's origins and most computer monitors use the same aspect ratio. The aspect ratio 4:3 was defined by the Academy of Motion Picture Arts and Sciences as a standard after the advent of optical sound-on-film. By having TV match this aspect ratio, films previously photographed on film could be satisfactorily viewed on TV in the early days of television around the 1940s and 1950s. When cinema attendance dropped, Hollywood created widescreen-aspect ratios (to differentiate their industry from the TV industry). The international standard format of HDTV has since evolved to become 16:9.

The Xbox 360 does a great job of adapting to the resolution of a game. If the aspect ratio of the back buffer is widescreen and the aspect ratio of the television display is not, the Xbox 360 will automatically add black bars at the top of the display so that the entire back buffer is onscreen.

To avoid letterboxing completely, you must create your game with both standard and widescreen aspect ratios, and adjust the display to the default aspect ratio offered by the Xbox 360.

If you want to optimize one GUI for HDTV, it seems like you should be able to create your game GUI screens for a 16 × 9 format, such as 1280 × 720. Then, in your GUI screen's GuiStyle, set the PreserveAspectRatio property to true. This means you would create two different GuiScreens, one for each aspect ratio, and present the appropriate screen at runtime based on the detected screen dimensions. The code would look something like this.

```
if (GarageGames.Torque.GFX.GFXDevice.IsWideScreen(
    Game.Instance.Window.ClientBounds.Width,
    Game.Instance.Window.ClientBounds.Height))
{
    //show HDTV GuiScreen with a 1280 × 720 Bitmap
    GUICanvas.Instance.SetContentControl("MenuScreenHD");
}
else
{
    //show Standard GuiScreen with a 1024 × 768 Bitmap
```

```
      GUICanvas.Instance.SetContentControl("MenuScreen");
}
```

Now all that you need to do is to create two versions for every screen within the game. Clearly, it's a fair bit of work to produce two different sets of GUI just to avoid letterboxing. It might be important for some games, but you should consider the extra cost of time to create it.

Creating an Xbox 360 Project

When your game compiles without errors and runs smoothly on Windows, you can start testing your game on the Xbox 360. There are a few steps involved in preparing your game project for transfer and preparing your Xbox 360 for receiving. In short, the steps include creating an Xbox version of your game project, setting up XNA Connect on your Xbox 360, and then transferring your compiled project.

Preparing Your Game Project

When you first created your game project with the Starter Game 2D/3D template, the game project file was automatically created for you with Windows set as the target platform. This platform configuration tells the Visual Studio to compile the game code and art assets into a format specific to the Windows operating system. Now that you want to run your game on the Xbox 360, a new project needs to be created. Fortunately, XNA Game Studio makes this very easy.

XNA Game Studio comes packaged with a game project converter. To convert your game project, select it within the Solution Explorer and then right-click the mouse. In the pop-up menu, select Create Copy of Project for Xbox 360..., as shown in Figure 18.5. Torque X Pro licensees should only perform this task on the Game project. The engine project will automatically be detected as a dependency and be properly converted.

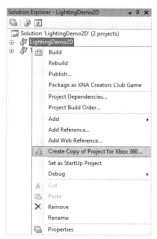

A notification message will appear, informing you that your game's source code will be shared between the two projects. This is an important reminder and a great feature. Although it will appear that your game's source code has been copied to the new Xbox 360 project, they are really the same exact files. So, edits to the file

Figure 18.5. Creating an Xbox 360 project.

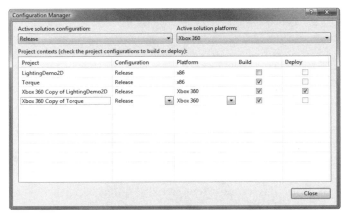

Figure 18.6. Setting the build configurations.

in one project are reflected in the other project, which is a great time-saver.

Now that you have a new project that targets the Xbox 360 platform, there's just one more step, setting the build configuration. Open the build configuration manager by selecting the Build ➤ Configuration Manager... command from the main menu. The Configuration Manager is opened as shown in Figure 18.6. Make sure that the build platforms are properly set so that the Xbox 360 projects have the Xbox 360 target platform and the Windows projects have the x86 target platform set.

Now that the build configurations look good, you can rebuild the entire solution. The Windows and Xbox 360 versions of the game will be written out to separate folders. The next step is to configure your Xbox 360 with XNA Connect.

Transferring the Game to the Xbox 360

After you have a game project running successfully on your Windows computer, you can try deploying it to the Xbox 360. The deployment process comes with a few requirements and steps. Your Xbox 360 has a hard drive and is connected to the internet. You must be signed into an Xbox LIVE Silver or Gold membership and have an XNA Creator's Club membership.

Downloading XNA Game Studio Connect

First, XNA Game Studio Connect must be downloaded from Xbox LIVE Marketplace and installed on your Xbox 360 console. You can find it on the Xbox LIVE Marketplace by selecting Game Store ➤ More... ➤ Genres ➤ Other.

Configuring the Network

Your compiled Torque X game will be transferred from your Windows computer to your Xbox 360 over a network connection, so both need to be connected on the same networking subnet. Most home networks support this configuration, especially if your computer and Xbox 360 share a router or hub.

Generating a Connection Key

In order to ensure a secure connection between your Windows computer and your Xbox 360, you must enter a connection key into your computer. To view the random key, you need to run XNA Game Studio Connect. From the Xbox 360 Dashboard, switch to the Games blade. Next, select Games Library ➤ My Games ➤ XNA Game Studio Connect ➤ Launch. If this is the first time running XNA Game Studio Connect, it will display a connection key as shown in Figure 18.7. If the connection key is not displayed and you need a new one generated, press the X controller button.

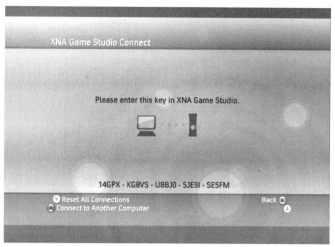

Figure 18.7. Example of a key generation screen.

Entering the Connection Key

The connection key generated by the Xbox 360 needs to be entered into your Windows computer. Open the XNA Game Studio Device Center by going to the Windows Desktop and clicking Start ➤ Programs ➤ Microsoft XNA Game Studio 2.0 ➤ XNA Game Studio Device Center. Next, click the Add Device button. Next, enter a reference name for your Xbox 360 console, as shown in Figure 18.8(a).

Next, enter the connection key provided by XNA Game Studio Connect (Figure 18.8(b)). The connection key can be hard to read on a standard television. Microsoft offers the following guidelines when reading the displayed connection key. If the connection key is still too difficult to read, press the X controller button to generate a new one.

- Number "1" has a small tick at its top left, whereas the letter "I" does not.

- Number "8" does not have a straight side at the left, whereas the letter "B" does.

- Number "3" has no straight side at the left, whereas the letter "B" does.

- Number "0" and the letter "O" are so similar, that both are interchangeable.

After you have entered the correct connection key, click the Next button on the XNA Game Studio Devices dialog box. XNA Game Studio Device Center will test the connection with the Xbox 360 console.

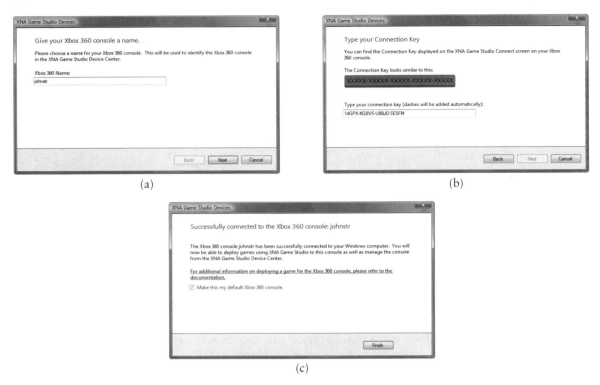

(a)

(b)

(c)

Figure 18.8. Connecting your computer to an Xbox 360: (a) reference name screen, (b) connection key screen, (c) confirmation screen.

If the connection is successful, the XNA Game Studio Device Center on the Windows-based computer will display: "Successfully connected to the Xbox 360 console" (Figure 18.8(c)). XNA Game Studio Connect on the Xbox 360 console will display: "Waiting for computer connection" followed by the name you have chosen for your Xbox 360 console in the XNA Game Studio Device Center.

If the XNA Game Studio Device Center fails to connect to the Xbox 360 console, click Try again to edit the connection key and try again. If the connection continues to fail, make a careful note of the error message displayed at the bottom of the XNA Game Studio Devices dialog box.

Click Finish. The name you gave to your Xbox 360 console will be listed in the XNA Game Studio Device Center. From now on, your computer and your console can connect to each other easily.

Deploying to the Xbox 360

Now that the Xbox 360 has XNA Connect set-up and your Windows computer has a trusted connection to it, you can begin transferring your Torque X game. Begin by opening XNA Game Studio Connect. From the Xbox Dashboard, select the Games blade. Next, select Games Library ➢ My Games ➢ XNA Game Studio Connect. XNA Game Studio Connect displays a waiting screen as shown in Figure 18.9.

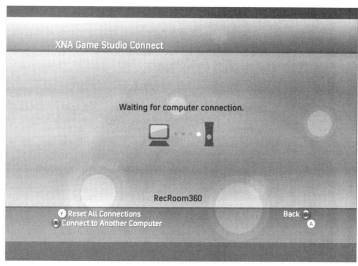

Next, return to XNA Game Studio and select the Xbox 360 version of your game project. Press the F5 button or select Debug ➢ Start Debugging from the main menu. After XNA Game Studio compiles your game code and assets, it will begin to transfer the files to your Xbox 360. The XNA Game Studio Connect waiting screen will begin listing the files that are copied over. After all of the game files have been copied, your Torque X game will begin running on the console.

Figure 18.9. XNA Game Studio Connect waiting for a computer connection.

To stop the game and return to the main screen of XNA Game Studio Connect, either press the BACK button on your Xbox 360 gamepad, or stop debugging on your computer by pressing SHIFT+F5.

Now that your game has been deployed to the Xbox 360, you can play it anytime by choosing it from the My Games library.

Sharing Your Game with Other Players

Sharing your game with others is the most rewarding experience for game creators and the XNA team has been working hard to perfect this final leg of the game-creation process. Currently there are a few different ways to share your game.

Torque X Games for Windows

Games for Windows can be compiled and bundled into a common installer and shared just as any traditional game. Just as existing game installers check for the presence of DirectX, a Torque X game installer must additionally check for the presence of the .NET Framework and the XNA Framework. The XNA and DirectX redistributable files are already located on your computer. The XNA Game Studio installer copies these files to the following default location.

C:\Program Files\Microsoft XNA\XNA Game Studio\v2.0\Redist\DX Redist

C:\Program Files\Microsoft XNA\XNA Game Studio\v2.0\Redist\XNA FX Redist

Your game installer should check for the presence of these frameworks and install them if they are not present. The remaining game project files resulting from your build process can be installed, just as any other .NET program.

Compiling Your Xbox Game for Distribution

Sharing your game while protecting your code and assets is made easier with the XNA Game Studio Package Utility. It compresses your game's compiled executable and assets into a special format that other XNA Game Studio users can open and play. You can only package XNA Game Studio projects since the tool doesn't support library projects.

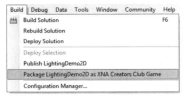

Figure 18.10. Packaging a game to share.

You can package your game using the XNA Game Studio Package Utility straight from within XNA Game Studio. Simply select your Torque X game project within the Solution Explorer and right-click to open the pop-up menu. Select Package Game as Creators Club Game, as shown in Figure 18.10.

The Output window indicates the status of the packing operation. If the packing operation is successful, the package file is created with a .ccgame extension and placed in the project's output folder. You can share this .ccgame file with other XNA Game Studio users. Since it's a compressed version of your project that contains no source code or source assets, other users can play it, but they will not be able to view or modify your source files.

When you receive a .ccgame file from another XNA Game Studio user, you can unpack it using the graphical unpacking utility. Windows games must have the same version of the XNA Framework installed that created the .ccgame file. Xbox 360 games must already have an Xbox 360 console specified in XNA Game Studio Device Center, a valid XNA Creators Club membership, and XNA Game Studio Connect must be running on the Xbox 360 console to which the game is being deployed.

To unpack the packaged game, find the .ccgame file using Windows Explorer and double-click it. When the utility starts, click the Unpack button to begin the unpacking process. When a Windows game finishes unpacking, a folder containing the game executable opens in Windows Explorer and you can run the game by double-clicking the executable. When an Xbox 360 game finishes unpacking, you can run the game from the My Games screen located off the Xbox 360 dashboard. In both cases, your game's source code and original art assets remain protected.

Summary

This chapter concentrated on the final stages of game creation. After pouring months of hard work into developing a game, it's natural to want to quickly rush through the final stages of packaging to get it out the door. It's important, however, to remember that your last step of development is the game player's first encounter with it. It's important to ensure a smooth and easy game set-up so that players can mentally prepare themselves for a fun game experience.

This chapter covered some important topics relating to console-game creation that are not usually applicable to making games for the PC. Attention to user-interface onscreen positioning, colors, and font sizes need to be considered for game players sitting in the middle of a living room. We also walked through the steps of bringing your Torque X Game to the Xbox 360 by preparing your project and preparing your console. Finally, we looked at some different methods of Windows and Xbox 360 game delivery, so that friends can play your game.

Torque X is an amazing technology. It takes Microsoft's XNA Framework to a whole new level of productivity to help you quickly turn your ideas into games that others can play. The rich Torque X 2D and 3D Frameworks are flexible and easy to master. Once you grasp the core concepts of the TorqueObject, the TorqueObjectDatabase, and using TorqueComponents, you can unleash your imagination to create just about anything. Now, it's your turn. Start making the games you've always wanted to make.

Index

A

AddTickCallback(), 150
AngleFromInput(), 199
AngleFromTarget(), 199, 212
AngleFromVector(), 199
Animated Sprite, 28
animations
    multistate, 158
    single-state, 155
animation threads, 233
animation triggers, 235
array, 91
aspect ratio, 367
    PreserveAspectRatio, 370
Asset Browser, 70
Audacity, 313
axis gizmos, 68

B

BindCommand(), 294
BindMove(), 257
BloomPostProcessor, 359
build configurations, 372

C

C#, 79
    program, 80

camera
    2D custom, 165
    3D, 264
    mounting, 168
Camera
    2D, 26
.ccgame, 376
class, 81
code aggregation, 110
collection, 91
CollidesWith, 109
collision
    delegate, 192
collision polygon, 23
CollisionXTerrainShape, 274
color palettes, 368
Component Editor
    3D, 73
Components
    2D Builder, 31
coordinates
    3D, 222
    object, 222
    world, 222
CopyTo(), 117
CreateFromYawPitchRoll(), 257
CreatePlayer(), 240
Creators Club distribution, 376

cube map, 356
CubemapCamera, 357
cue, 318

D

Debug Rendering, 28
delegate, 97
    calling, 119
    collision, 183
DestructibleComponent, 175
DetailMaterial, 350
do-while, 90
DTS, 230
    animations, 233
    collision meshes, 232
    level of detail, 232
    mesh groups, 231
    object hierarchy, 231
    texture mapping, 232

E

event, 100

F

fields, 82
FindObject, 108
fog, 272
fog material, 272
foreach, 89, 91

G

game state, 194
GameState, 195
GeneratedTerrainData, 277
GenericMaterial, 364
GUI, 325
GUIBitmapStyle, 336
GUICanvas, 326
GUIControls, 327
GUISceneView, 241
GuiSplash, 334
GUIStyle, 330
GUITextStyle, 341

H

HUD, 326

I

if-else, 87
IGUIScreen, 333
IncreaseHealth(), 177
input
    BindMove(), 147
    device, 145
    InputMap, 146
    manager, 146
    MoveManager, 148
    PlayerManager, 152
InputManager, 329
InputMap, 134
    3D, 255
interface, 96
InterpolateTick(), 119
InventoryItemComponent, 186
InventoryManagerComponent, 188

K

keywords, 83

L

Layer Management, 27
LightComponent, 351
LightingMaterial, 351
LightRegisterComponent, 33
link points, 24

M

MarkForDelete, 293
Material Builder, 19
Material Editor
    3D, 74
MaterialManager, 349
MatrixUtil, 257
mesh, 221
method, 82

mount
  2D, 25
  3D, 294
MovementComponent, 33
MovementComponent3D, 252

N

namespaces, 80

O

object position markers, 69
object type, 38
Object Type Editor, 74
OnGUIWake, 336
_OnRegister(), 115
OnRender(), 345
OnSplashFinished(), 334
_OnUnregister(), 116
operators, 84

P

particle effect
  2D Builder, 50
  emitter graph, 52
  keyframes, 52
  properties, 50
Particle Effect
  2D Component, 29
particle effects
  3D, 230
polygons, 221
pooling, 106
PostProcessor, 359
  motion blur, 361
ProcessTick(), 118
projectile
  2D, 179
  3D, 291
Project Template
  2D Game, 14
  3D Game, 65
properties, 82

Properties, 73
PushDialogControl(), 328

Q

quaternion, 257

R

RAWTerrainData, 276
ReduceHealth(), 177
reference, 86, 94
RefractionMaterial, 358
_RegisterInterfaces(), 116
RigidCollisionManager, 249
rotation, 225

S

safe region, 368
scale, 224
Scene Data, 26
Scene Explorer, 72, 73
SceneGroupName, 247
Screen Capture, 69
Scripting, 30
Scroller, 29
SetContentControl(), 327, 337
SimpleMaterial, 350
Sky, 229
sky box, 269
sort point, 24
sound bank, 317
sounds, 318
Static Sprite, 28
Sun, 230, 271
switch, 88

T

T2DCollisionComponent, 34
T2DComponent, 114
T2DForceComponent, 36
T2DLightComponent, 354
T2DPhysicsComponent, 33, 180
T2DTileLayer, 127

T2DTileObject, 128
T2DTileType, 129
T2DVectorUtil, 197
T2DWorldLimitComponent, 35
T3DAnimationComponent, 251
T3DBlobShadowCaster
       Component, 267
T3DBox, 280
T3DCameraComponent, 227, 246
T3DInputComponent, 228
T3DLightComponent, 355
T3DParticleEffectComponent, 278
T3DPlane, 283
T3DRigidComponent, 228
T3DRigidConstraintComponent,
       228
T3DSceneComponent, 227, 247
T3DSceneGraph, 227
T3DSphere, 282
T3DStaticTSRenderComponent,
       228, 283
T3DTriggerComponent, 229, 285
T3DTSRenderComponent, 227
template
       cloning, 105
Template
       2D Builder, 32
       creating, 104
TerrainData, 274
TGETerrainData, 275
Tilemap
       brush, 48
       collisions, 49
       creating in code, 125
       designing, 45
       layers, 49
       painting, 47
       properties, 29
       size, 46
       saving and loading, 46
TorqueComponent
       anatomy, 111
TorqueComponents, 109

TorqueEvent, 183
TorqueGame, 101
TorqueObject, 103
TorqueObjectDatabase, 103, 298
TorqueObjectType, 106
       GetObjectType, 107
Torque X, 3
Torque X Builder 2D, 15
TorqueXmlSchemaField, 189
transformation, 224
translation, 225
TSAnimation, 227

U

_UpdateInput(), 256, 260

V

ValueInPlaceInterface, 120
ValueInterface, 121
variables, 85
vector
       defined, 224
Vector2, 197
VectorFromAngle, 199
vector mathematics, 197
VelocityFromInput, 199
VelocityFromTarget, 199
voice, 314

W

wave banks, 315
WeaponComponent, 180
while, 90
Windows deployment, 376
world limits, 25

X

XACT, 315
Xbox 360
       connection key, 373
       convert project, 371
       deploy, 375
       networking, 373

XNA Game Studio Connect, 372
XNA, 1

XnaTetris, 130
XTerrain, 229, 273